Crafting
the
Soul

For Alice,
All the best in life,

Bryan

Crafting
the
Soul

CREATING YOUR
LIFE AS A
WORK OF ART

RABBI BYRON L. SHERWIN, Ph.D.

Park Street Press
Rochester, Vermont

Park Street Press
One Park Street
Rochester, Vermont 05767
www.gotoit.com

Library of Congress Cataloging-in-Publication Data

Sherwin, Byron L.
        Crafting the soul : creating your life as a work of art / Byron L.
Sherwin.
                p.   cm.
        Includes bibliographical references.
        ISBN 0-89281-704-6 (pbk. : alk. paper)
        1. Self-actualization (Psychology)   I. Title.
BF637.S4S525   1998   97-52982
291.4'4—dc21   CIP

Printed and bound in Canada

10 9 8 7 6 5 4 3 2 1

Text design and layout by Kristin Camp
This book was typeset in Garamond with Florens as the display typeface

Park Street Press is a division of Inner Traditions International

Distributed to the book trade in Canada by Publishers Group West (PGW),
    Toronto
Distributed to the book trade in the United Kingdom by Deep Books,
    London
Distributed to the book trade in Australia by Gemcraft Books, Burwood
Distributed to the book trade in New Zealand by Tandem Press, Auckland
Distributed to the book trade in South Africa by Alternative Books, Ferndale

For my son, Jason:
*Thank you for
the inestimable joy
your life bestows
upon my life.*

Contents

In the eyes of the world, I am average. But in my own heart I am of great moment. The challenge I face is how to actualize, how to concretize, the quiet eminence of my being.

Abraham Joshua Heschel

chapter one

What Do You Mean?

It is told that when Rabbi Zusya of Anipol was on his deathbed, he began to cry. His disciples asked, "Master, why do you cry? Is it because you are afraid that in the next world they will ask you: 'Zusya, why were you not like Moses?'"

"No," he said. "I am afraid that they will ask me: 'Zusya, why were you not Zusya?' If I am asked this question, what shall I answer?"

*E*ither the third millennium will be a spiritual age or there will be no third millennium," wrote the French novelist André Malraux. In a similar vein, the inscription over President Woodrow Wilson's tomb in the National Cathedral in Washington, D.C., reads: "The sum of the whole matter is this, that our civilization cannot survive materially unless it be redeemed spiritually."

The spiritual quest is a forthright confrontation with the fundamental questions of human existence: Who am I? Where am I? What am I doing here? What should I be doing here? What is the meaning of my life? The Hasidic master Rabbi Israel of Rhyzen once prayed, "Dear God, I do not ask you to explain to me why the world has been created, or why the good suffer and the evil prosper. Only, please, tell me: What am I doing in this world of yours?"[1] Whether or not a person is aware of it, the spiritual is at the core of his or her existence. As the New Testament puts it, "What does it benefit a person if he gains the entire world, but loses his own soul?"[2]

The question of human existence was expressed by the seventeenth-century French philosopher Blaise Pascal with a sharpness and poignancy never since equaled. He wrote:

> When I consider the short duration of my life, swallowed up in the eternity before and after, the little space which I fill, and even can see, engulfed in the infinite immensity of spaces of which I am ignorant and which know me not, I am frightened and I am astonished at being here rather than there; for there is no reason why here rather than there, why now rather than then. Who has put me here? By whose order and direction have this place and time been allotted to me? The eternal silence of those infinite spaces frightens me.[3]

When asked why he composed music, Mozart is alleged to have responded, "Because I have to." Similarly, embarking upon the spiritual quest, locating foci for life's meaning and purpose, are tasks that must be undertaken by each person—because we have to. The alternative is a listless life, a meaningless existence. Sooner or later everyone becomes a pilgrim in search of the meaning of his or her own existence. As the Nobel Prize-winning German novelist Hermann Hesse wrote, "Even a superficial person disinclined to thought feels the age-old need of finding meaning in his life. When he ceases to find one, private life falls prey to frenzied self-seeking and deadly fear."[4] In his book *When All You've Ever Wanted Isn't Enough* Rabbi Harold Kushner, author of *When Bad Things Happen to Good People*, writes:

> If a tree falls in the forest and there is no ear to hear it, does it make a sound? If a person lives and dies and no one notices, if the world continues as it was, was that person ever really alive? I am convinced that it is not the fear of death, of our lives ending, that haunts

our sleep so much as the fear that our lives will not have mattered, that as far as the world is concerned, we might as well never have lived. What we miss in our lives, no matter how much we have, is that sense of meaning.[5]

Ask most people if they would prefer a meaningless or a meaningful life, and they will tell you that a meaningless life horrifies them. But if you then ask most people why their lives are meaningful, they tend to fumble for an answer. Often people remain too distracted by transient concerns to focus on the deeper problems of human existence, such as the meaning of life. Many operate on the assumption that if their needs are fulfilled, if their physical ailments are cured, if their "inner child" is healed, if their professional and financial goals are met, then their lives will be replete with happiness, meaning, and fulfillment. But experience seems to indicate something else. Without first establishing a basis of meaning, addressing these other concerns is like furnishing a home that has no foundation upon which to rest. It is like providing an answer when we have not yet heard the question. It's putting the cart before the horse—the "how to" before the "why to." As the German philosopher Nietzsche reminds us, "A person who has a 'why' can contend with almost any 'how.'"[6] We all want to live, *but what for?*

As University of Chicago psychology professor Mihaly Csikszentmihalyi indicates in his groundbreaking book *Flow:*

The fact that one is not slim, rich or powerful no longer matters. . . . It is not just a matter of losing a few pounds. It is a matter of losing the chance to have a life worth living. . . . Sooner or later we wake sensing that there is no way this affluent, scientific, and sophisticated world is going to provide us with happiness. . . . Despite the fact that we are now healthier and grow to be older, despite the fact that even the least affluent among us are surrounded by material luxuries undreamed of even a few decades ago. . . and regardless of all the stupendous scientific knowledge we can summon at will, people often end up feeling that their lives have been wasted, that instead of being filled with happiness their years were spent in anxiety and boredom."[7]

Let us imagine that there is a device that can diagnose our state of spiritual health, that can determine our spiritual standard of living. What would it reveal? Already in the 1930s, the eminent psychotherapist Carl Jung offered his diagnosis. He wrote, "About a third of my cases are suffering from no clinically definable neurosis, but from the senselessness and emptiness of their lives. This can be described as the general neurosis of our time."[8]

Both medical science and psychotherapy are beginning to realize that a spiritual crisis often lies at the root of a psychological or physical malady. For example, in his 1993 study *Hope and Dread in Psychoanalysis,* psychoanalyst Stephen Mitchell writes, "On the level of clinical theory, there has been a marked shift in emphasis from the clarification and renunciation of infantile fantasies to the revitalization and elaboration of a patient's sense of personal meaning."[9] People with little meaning in their lives or in their work are primary candidates for "premature death" from a variety of diseases. For example, a recent study of people who died from a first heart attack found that at least half had not been at risk because of the usual factors such as a family history of cardiovascular disease, high cholesterol, smoking, or obesity. Rather, the one variable that they shared was a strong abhorrence of their job and difficulty with finding meaning and fulfillment in their lives. The relationship between work dissatisfaction and fatal heart attacks was further corroborated by the fact that the most likely time for a heart attack to occur is Monday morning, when one has to face a new work week.[10]

Dealing with the problem of life's meaning can be a matter of life and death. It is not an abstract philosophical exercise, but the most deeply personal problem with which a human being can deal. The real question is not: Does life have meaning? Rather, the real problem is: Does *my* particular life have meaning? The single issue in the life of each individual that both encompasses and supersedes all others is: *What am I here for?*

The problem of meaning confronts each of us at various junctures of our lives. Events—often tragic or traumatic ones—act as an alarm clock to stimulate an encounter with the problem of meaning. Such an event can be the death of a relative or a friend, particularly a parent, a child, or a contemporary. It can be the diagnosis of a disease, the loss of a job, or surviving a natural disaster. It can be a turning point in life, such as retirement, the marriage of a child, or a child going off to school. It can be "midlife crisis" or simply life crisis. Like a genetic time bomb waiting to be detonated, the necessity of working through the meaning of one's life inevitably appears sooner or later. Perhaps it comes as no surprise to a person contending with illness, tragedy, trauma, or loss. But even if a person is spared trauma, the problem of meaning can suddenly become an unwelcome guest at the acme of one's success, at the peak of one's achievements, at the height of one's prowess. Most often it sneaks up on us as we accelerate, all too rapidly, through our forties, quickly approaching our fiftieth year.

This is precisely what happened to the great Russian novelist Tolstoy. Suddenly and unexpectedly, as Tolstoy navigated through his late forties, he began to feel as if his life abruptly had "come to a stop." He felt lost, off-balance, stuck, as if he were being suffocated by some unknown force. As he put it, "The time had come when I had ceased to grow, and I felt I was not developing but drying up."

In a remarkable literary and psychological document about this experience called "A Confession," Tolstoy drew a sharp contrast between his enviable life and his increasing difficulties in coping with the state of his life. He wrote:

> All this befell me at a time when all around me I had what is considered complete good fortune. I was not yet fifty. I had a good wife who loved me and whom I loved, good children, a large estate which without much effort on my part improved and increased. I was respected by my relations and acquaintances more than at any previous time. I was praised by others and without much deception could consider that my name was famous. And far from being insane or mentally diseased, I enjoyed on the contrary a strength of

mind and body such as I have seldom met with among men of my kind. . . . And in this situation I came to this—that I could not live, and fearing death, had to employ cunning with myself to avoid taking my own life.[11]

Since the dawn of civilization, contending with the certainty of death and with the challenge of discovering meaning in life has been an ongoing human preoccupation. As we age, we tend to reflect back upon the meaning of our life. According to psychoanalyst Erik Erikson, "life review" is a normal characteristic of the aging individual. Often beginning in middle age, it is natural to look back at the life lived to that point. In so doing one recalls not only the successes achieved, the goals met, and the joys celebrated, but also the expectations never met, the dreams left unfulfilled, the difficulties persevered, the disappointments experienced. In Tolstoy's story "The Death of Ivan Illich," the protagonist reflects back upon his life, and he says:

> What does it mean? Why? It can't be that life is so senseless and horrible. . . . Maybe I did not live as I ought to have done. . . . But how could that be, when I did everything properly? . . . It is as if I had been going downhill while I imagined I was going up.[12]

As a person moves closer to the end of life than to its beginning, one tends to evaluate what already has transpired, and what may yet happen. As an individual confronts the challenge of life review, one seeks a source of cohesion, a plot, to give life meaning and continuity. The individual seeks validation, justification, to ensure that the life already lived has not been wasted, that life has not been a meaningless game of Trivial Pursuit. Looking back at one's own life, each person is in danger of having to admit: "My life went on without me." Or, as John Lennon said, "Life is what happens when you are making other plans."[13]

Ironically, such a person may be startled at his or her achievements while wondering whether life's earlier goals still have purpose. One may exude self-confidence while being profoundly unsure about what one most deeply believes. Such an individual may effectively manage a home or may manage considerable fiscal and human resources while being inexplicably unable to manage feelings of boredom, emptiness, meaninglessness, depression, and of "being stuck." Such a person may be fiscally secure, yet plagued by insecurities about the task of being a spouse, a parent, a child, or a friend.

The quest for meaning is not a symptom of mental illness but a natural outcome of the process of living. It is a uniquely human enterprise that distinguishes the human species from the rest of the creatures of the world. It is more likely to be encountered among the educated and the "successful" who, like Tolstoy, find themselves at an impasse in life. It is a symptom, not of a neurosis, but of the normal spiritual anxiety characteristic of our times. As philosopher Irving Singer has pointed out, the condition described by Tolstoy somewhat resembles that of aging baby boomers in contemporary America.[14]

In the Talmud it is written, "If I am not for myself, who will be for me? If I am only for myself, what am I? And, if not now, when?"[15] The great medieval Jewish philosopher Moses Maimonides interpreted, "If I am not for myself, who will be for me?" to mean that no one but one's own self can create the work of art that is one's own self.[16] In a similar vein, the Danish philosopher Soren Kierkegaard translated Socrates' admonition "Know Thyself" as "Choose Thyself,"[17] that is, choose the person that you want to become, and can become. Choosing the self one wishes to become begins with the awareness of the spiritual dimension of life. It begins by discerning that the soul is a seed implanted within each of us. Each person is like a tree that may choose whether to bring forth its own fruit. At life's end, each person may return a diminished form of what was received, or more than was received at life's beginning. Each person has the choice to corrode or to cultivate what initially has been granted. Meaning cannot be acquired by proxy. No pill can induce it. No fee can purchase it.

The spiritual dimension deals with the most visceral issues of human existence. As such, it offers a focal point for a true "needs assessment" for our lives. A spiritual perspective helps us to establish criteria, to identify values, to discern convictions by which to distinguish between authentic needs and passing impulses, real needs and ephemeral fads. It offers us a way to audit the deficits of our deepest needs. It provides us with a mission statement for each of our lives.

The ideal reader of this book is someone who is curious about the meaning of life, who is suspect of simplistic and doctrinaire claims to have found it, who is prepared to set out on an intellectual and spiritual adventure to locate it, and who is willing to enact an action plan to express it. The goal of this book is twofold. First, to critique certain popular contemporary approaches that, in effect, stifle the quest for life's meaning, and that sabotage our efforts to craft our existence in a meaningful way. Second, to offer a path toward implementing meaning in life by means of the art of soulcrafting. The purpose of this first chapter is to pose some of the problems that this book addresses, foremost the problem of meaning. But, as will soon be apparent, the task here is not only to try to answer certain questions, but to question certain answers that are readily assumed by our society and our culture.

A disciple once asked his master, "Why do human beings have two eyes, rather than one or four?" The master replied, "A person needs one eye for looking outward at the world and a second eye for peering inward at the self." The spiritual quest entails an intensive look outward—at our world, at our place in history, at the ideas of others, at how past and present maestros of the mind and spirit have discovered meaning beyond absurdity, meaning within mystery. And the spiritual quest also requires a deep, peering glance at our innermost selves. However, before intensely embarking on this pilgrimage, one must first locate the self within coordinates of space and time. Indeed, our very notions of self do not begin with a blank slate. They are highly influenced by the cultural assumptions of where and when we live. To understand the problems affecting ourselves, to appreciate the assumptions we readily take for granted, we must better apprehend the views and attitudes that characterize our particular, and often peculiar, juncture on the continuum of history and geography. Put another way, before one reflects on the meaning of one's own particular life, one must first know clearly where, when, and who one is. But people often embark on their spiritual journey without first having established their moorings, without adequate knowledge of the currents that flow throughout the sea in which they find themselves adrift, without the benefit of the knowledge and experience of others who have managed successfully to navigate their paths through similar shoals.

The great historian of ideas, Arthur Lovejoy, pointed out that each society rests upon certain unconscious "mental habits" so fundamental to its cultural and social life that people in that society tacitly assume them to be true without questioning, and often without even being consciously aware that their view of reality is based upon them.[18] However, when change begins to occur, when things no longer "work" the way they used to, these implicit cultural assumptions become explicit. What once had been readily presumed to be true and valid is suddenly open to question. Once challenged, these assumptions may be replaced by a new way of looking at the world and at the self. Just as certain animals can sense the coming of earthquakes, certain individuals in a society sense these coming changes before others. Often such individuals are vilified and ostracized by the "establishment" of their times, only to be heralded as visionaries later on.

One does not have to be a visionary to perceive that our society is undergoing a transition of its cultural and social assumptions. The shifting ground upon which we stand casts us off-balance, stimulating us to ask certain fundamental questions about life, meaning, values, and goals that not so long ago seemed resolved.

We find ourselves living through an earthquake with its epicenter in the self. We suddenly realize that the emperor has no clothes, and that the clothes have no emperor. Many of the cultural, social, political, and economic conditions that we readily assumed to be lasting have been jarred off their moorings. Many of the values, ideas, and institutions that seemed firmly in place not so long ago have been shaken to their core. Foci of meaning and purpose, traditionally characteristic of our national and individual identities, have become vague and amorphous rather than clear and reliable. In the words of the poet Matthew Arnold, we are "wandering between two worlds, one dead and the other powerless to be born."[19] The shocks and aftershocks that have convulsed the topography of our daily life inevitably register on the seismograph of our souls, our innermost selves. What is happening all around us is also happening within us. The various upheavals and crises that we witness daily are a macrocosm of the spiritual malaise that many individuals are increasingly experiencing. At the roots of our collective anxiety there is a spiritual crisis. The gyroscope of our civilization is broken, and no one seems to know how to fix it. From our moorings in a safe harbor, we now feel cast adrift on a sea of uncertainty.

The malaise that so many feel is a symptom of the *spiritual* homelessness many now experience. The spiritually homeless individual is a person preoccupied with why flashes of depression regularly make their unwelcome appearance, with why "success" has not brought anticipated self-fulfillment, with why a full schedule of daily activities seems undermined by feelings of emptiness, with why relationships have not dispelled loneliness, with why seasoned experience has not induced certainty about one's convictions and values, with why the future is suddenly so foreboding, with why the contemplation of death has become increasingly frequent and terrifying.

What we see when we look outward is often but a reflection of what we see when we look inward, and vice versa. The microcosm and the macrocosm are often two sides of the same coin, two mirrors reflecting complementary dimensions of an identical reality. It would be myopic to disregard either dimension, or to consider each as independent of the other. For example, the origins of the spiritual malaise afflicting growing numbers of people today who, in Thoreau's words, "live lives of quiet desperation,"[20] are deeply embedded in our culture. The various social upheavals and crises that we witness daily are symptoms of the same underlying conditions that currently afflict individuals physically and spiritually. The person in spiritual stress is a microcosm of a society in the throes of spiritual anxiety. Society, in turn, is a macrocosm of the collective anxiety of the individuals who comprise it. Political instabilities, wars, economic oscillations, and social transitions are the expression of the collective anxieties of individuals on a panoramic scale. To understand the problems affecting ourselves, we must better understand the peculiar nature of our times and how things got to be the way they are.

We do not have to review the entire course of history to identify the cultural assumptions that characterize our time and place. What we need to do is something more precise. We need to offer a composite portrait of some of the key presuppositions that together comprise the worldview that drives our society, that informs our thinking, and that influences both our behavior and our self-understanding. Once this has been done we will be in a better position to evaluate how those presuppositions may prove helpful or harmful, useful or dispensable, as we commence the inward journey.

For example, one of the main presuppositions of our society (discussed in greater detail below) is that any problem can be solved through the proper employment of the relevant technique. Psychotherapist Rollo May called this approach "salvation through technique"; philosopher William Barrett called it "the illusion of technique."[21] One of the many problems with this technological approach is that it is not pertinent to the deepest of human problems, such as the quest for meaning. The most fundamental human problems are "why to" problems, not "how to" problems. Unless a person has clarified the why-to problems, particularly the problem of the meaning of one's existence, all of the available techniques will prove to no avail. Without meaning, method is meaningless.

A review of many how-to books reveals that they offer methods and techniques that promise to alleviate our problems and disorders, and to replace them with various components of assured happiness and fulfillment, that is, health, slimness, wealth, and social acceptance. Commenting on the how-to literature, Csikszentmihalyi writes:

Like cookbooks, they tell you how to accomplish a specific limited goal on which few people actually follow through. Yet even if their advice were to work, what would be the result afterward in the unlikely event that one did turn into a slim, well-loved, powerful millionaire? Usually what happens is that the person finds himself back at square one, with a new list of wishes, just as dissatisfied as before.[22]

It is no wonder that many people who have assiduously mastered the techniques prescribed in how-to manuals and seminars still feel unfulfilled. Having found est, gestalt, bioenergetics, acupuncture, rolfing, tai chi, and the entire polyglot menu of methods to clean up one's life, many ask why their spiritual lives continue to be such a mess. Having conscientiously attended workshops in personal growth, many still find themselves spiritually stunted. After hours spent in motivational seminars, many still find themselves unmotivated to get out of bed in the morning. Having partaken of the smorgasbord of exotic delights offered by the helping professions, many find their innermost selves continuing to cry out for help and for meaning. Having undergone extensive psychotherapy, having achieved social adjustment and needs satisfaction, many still feel the need to be needed, the need to discover a nexus of meaning for their lives. Having labored to get in touch with their feelings, many inquire why passion remains so elusive. Having climbed the twelve steps toward recovery and health, many continue to seek to overcome the onset of anxiety and malaise, to wonder whether their lives consist of only moving away from addiction and illness or whether life means moving toward something more. Having healed their "inner child," many still face the task of creating a life of truth, meaning, and beauty for their inner adult. And, even if a person manages to find their "true self," the question remains: What do you do with it once you find it?

The doctrine of salvation through technique is based upon another popular belief of our culture—that a human being is like a machine, and that when there is a malfunction, the application of the proper method and technique can be employed to correct it. To feed the growing industry of the helping professions, an increasing supply of dysfunctional people had to become available. This was accomplished by the conversion of American society from a group of self-reliant "rugged individualists" to a "therapeutic society," where virtually everyone could be characterized as having one or more of a plethora of diseases, disorders, or dysfunctions for which a wide variety of therapies, remedies, procedures, and cures are required. Put another way, this approach maintains that we are sick, and therefore that we are victims, bereft of responsibility, stripped of initiative, requiring the intercession of practitioners of an exploding number of helping professions to restore us to health. In my view, the intrusion of the dogmas and the rituals of the therapeutic society have proven, in the long run, to be harmful rather than helpful in the development of the spiritual dimension of our lives. It is ironic that, in a society that traditionally has cherished individualism and self-initiative, the therapeutic approach largely has succeeded in disenfranchising us of independence and self-initiative in order to make us dependent upon the "helping professionals" for virtually every aspect of our daily existence. This prevents us from initiating our own individual spiritual journey because it makes us dependent upon others with regard to tasks that each of us must undertake on our own. The therapeutic approach casts us in the role of participants in a show that could be entitled "Name Your Wound." It encourages us to organize our lives around our wounds, maladies, and syndromes rather than around our life's meaning, our spiritual development, and our ability to create our lives as works of art. Spiritual development is often mistakenly equated with healing. But they are not identical. Healing is restorative, therapeutic. Spiritual development is creative, dynamic.

The crafting of life as a work of art challenges us with becoming practitioners of evolution rather than victims of evolution and environment. The doctrine of salvation through technique, as employed by our therapeutic society, begins with the assumption that you are sick, broken, and flawed. However, the starting point here is altogether different. Here the assumption is that your life is potentially a work of art, and that you are the artist who can bring it from potentiality to actuality. Rather than beginning with identifying what is wrong with you and how to treat it—with what may be a never-ending process that avoids the core issues of human existence—the present point of departure is with the fundamental issues, that is, the why-to problems. The present point of departure asks you to focus first not on your flaws and blemishes but on your potentials and your possibilities. The place to begin the task of composing the remaining chapters of the novel that is your life is by formulating its plot. Put another way, the place to begin is with that which offers coherence to the story-line— and that brings us back again to the quest for meaning and purpose. The remedy for spiritual anorexia is spiritual resurrection—self-discovery rather than self-recovery. The challenge is not to despair of life, but to inject and to revitalize it with a potent dose of meaning and purpose.

Once a person has moved from healing one's inner child, from recovering from physical and psychological addictions, it is about time to pay attention to one's soul, to crafting life as an art form by letting go of dependencies upon parents, lovers, gurus, therapists, helping professionals and techniques. Otherwise one has simply dispensed with some dependencies only to hold more tightly onto those that remain; otherwise one has merely exchanged one dependency for another. For years, psychological theories of motivation were grounded in the view that the avoidance of discomfort and the introduction of comfort were the primary motivating factors for human behavior, that the promise of a future reward and the elimination of a past or present pain were what motivates us. However, more recent studies recommend another view altogether, that is, that our major motivation comes from being involved in activities that we find *intrinsically* meaningful, enjoyable, and rewarding.

If we cannot find happiness, fulfillment, and spiritual augmentation in the remedies of the therapeutic society or the demands of socialization, then where are we to look? If we have been looking in the wrong places, then where is the right place to look to create life as an art form? Fortunately, in recent years a new trend of thought may be discerned. Rather than focusing on the pathology of normalcy and the normalcy of pathology, it focuses on the possibilities of spiritual development and personal fulfillment. Rather than defining our strengths as weaknesses, our virtues as vices, our commitments as expressions of rigidity, it attends to the challenge of channeling our abilities and our potentialities into building-blocks for the creation of life as an art form. Rather than focusing upon physical comfort, it focuses on the care of the soul. Rather than utilizing studies of the physiologically and psychologically afflicted as paradigms to be imposed upon us, this approach attempts to utilize paradigms of creativity—"peak experiences" (Abraham Maslow), "flow" (Mihaly Csikszentmihalyi), "care of the soul" (Thomas Moore), "peace, love, and healing" (Bernie Siegel), and "pathfinders" (Gail Sheehy)—as a foundation for a proactive, creative, and effective implementation of the quest for fulfillment. The old question was: How do I overcome the maladies, syndromes, and disabilities that have victimized me? The new questions are: What are the minimum daily requirements for spiritual sustenance, and where and how do we locate them? How can I create my life as a work of art?

To a person grounded in the teachings of the great religious and philosophical traditions of the past, most of the teachings of this recent trend are remarkably familiar. They are not new at all. Rather, they seem merely to translate into a contemporary idiom observations and teachings known and cultivated for many generations. The recent "discovery" of the soul, of the spiritual, is really a rediscovery of problems and responses to problems that have preoccupied past cartographers of the spiritual quest for thousands of years. In the pages that follow we shall consult with many of these maestros of the human spirit, these erstwhile physicians of the human soul.

For years we have disregarded the spiritual resources bequeathed to us from the past. For years our modern hubris has disenfranchised us from utilizing the hard-won cumulative wisdom and experience readily available from a much needed and readily accessible spiritual heritage. Yet these easily accessible resources provide us with ways of repairing and resurrecting our souls, and of recovering the seemingly lost art of soulcrafting. In our insatiable desire for the innovative and the new, we have too flippantly jettisoned the classical sources of wisdom, the traditional sources of guidance that offer a home for the soul. Startled by the miracles of technology, we have bartered fulfillment for convenience, loyalty for success, relationships for networking, wisdom for data, and tradition for fashion.

"Instead of charting the stars, concentrate on discovering the paradoxes of your own existence." So advises the semi-divine character called "Q" in the last television episode of *Star Trek: The Next Generation.* A crucial component in the spiritual development of each human being, self-discovery and self-actualization may very well constitute the primary mission of the human species. Despite our remarkable scientific discoveries and technological advances, our spiritual homeland largely remains an underdeveloped country. In this regard, the scientist and inventor Charles Steinmetz said, "The greatest discovery will be made along spiritual lines. The spiritual forces have as yet hardly been scratched. When this day comes, the world will see more advancement in one generation than it has seen in the past four."[23]

To engage in the lifelong process of crafting the soul, it is necessary to think through a number of issues. The pages that follow are aimed at stimulating you to do just that. One such issue is: Where are we?, that is, what characterizes our specific place on the space-time continuum? Our spiritual journey, as was noted above, must begin at the particular place in time and space, in history and geography, that we inhabit. In seeing where we are, we inevitably become increasingly aware not only of the meaning of the history we are living through, but we also gain an understanding of the mental habits, of the cultural assumptions that have informed our view of reality, our view of ourselves. But it is not enough to review the assumptions that have come to characterize modern thought, experience, and behavior. It is also necessary to think about them—to subject them to critical analysis in order to determine whether they are helpful or harmful in one's own spiritual quest. To begin this task is the purpose of the chapter that now follows.

chapter two

Anchors Away

It is told that a certain Rabbi Joseph, who lived almost two thousand years ago, became critically ill and slipped into a coma. His father, Rabbi Joshua, remained by his bedside praying for his recovery.

Fortunately, Rabbi Joseph recovered. When he awoke from his coma, his father asked, "What did you see as you hovered between this world and the next world?"

Said Rabbi Joseph: "I saw a world turned upside down. I saw a topsy-turvy world."

Rabbi Joshua listened, thought for a while, and said, "You saw a clear vision of how things really are. You saw the world clearly."

*F*ranz Kafka once said that life requires three essential ingredients: beauty, stability, and meaning. But we often find that these spiritual nutrients elude us precisely when they seem readily within our grasp. A characteristic of life in our century has been the casting away of many of the anchors upon which people once used to tether their lives.

As we compare the expectations of the late nineteenth century with the events of the early twentieth century, as we contrast the American

experience in the immediate post-World War II period to the decades
at the twilight of the twentieth century, we can discern a pattern. Tem-
pered by historical events, naive optimism has given way to anxiety.
For example, in 1893 representatives of the religions of the world met
in Chicago at the first Parliament of the World's Religions. The pro-
ceedings opened with a prayer that began, "Let us rejoice that we have
lived to see this glorious day." A century later in Chicago, the Parliament reconvened. By its conclusion on Labor Day 1993, representatives of the world's religions had signed a Declaration of a Global Ethic
that proclaimed, "The world is in agony. . . . Peace eludes us. . . . The
planet is being destroyed. . . . Neighbors live in fear. . . . Men and
women are estranged from each other. . . . Children die!"[1] During a
century the mood had changed radically. The perspective had shifted
from Pollyannaism to pessimism, from buoyancy to anxiety, from hope
to horror.

As we and our contemporaries have anticipated the dawning of the
twenty-first century, so those who lived at the end of the nineteenth
century tried to anticipate what the new twentieth century would be
like. As we shall see, the collision between expectation and reality, hope
and dismay, is a feature not only of our own life experience but also of
recent history.

In the twilight years of the nineteenth century, a British debat-
ing club met to discuss an urgent issue: What will we discuss once
we know everything? At Harvard in the 1880s the chairman of the
physics department, John Throwbridge, told his students not to
pursue careers in physics because every important discovery in the
field already had been made. Similarly, in 1902 Albert Michelson,
America's first Nobel Prize winner, said, "The most important fundamental laws and facts of physical science have all been discovered and these are now so firmly established that the possibility of
their ever being supplanted in consequence of new discoveries is
remote."[2] The irony is that one of Michelson's own experiments
was to belie this very prediction. This attitude, which saw Utopia
right around the corner, which believed all knowledge to be readily

within our grasp, was prevalent in the late nineteenth and early twentieth centuries in Western Europe and in America.

Though it seems incredibly naive to us today, a century ago people believed that the march of inevitable and unstoppable "progress" and "evolution" would sweep away all human problems in their path. Science, it was believed, would reveal all available truth, and its application as technology would eradicate disease and would turn earth into a heaven through the human control of the forces of nature. The great mysteries of existence would be solved, and human omniscience and omnipotence would be achieved. From advances in science, economic abundance for all would ensue. Poverty and its attendant suffering would be eradicated. Hunger would disappear. What once had been the inheritance of the wealthy few would become the daily fare of the average person. With an end of poverty, an end would come to social strife. Political stability would result from economic abundance. Health and happiness would reign supreme. War would become unnecessary and hence obsolete. The world would be "made safe for democracy."[3] Universal education would free people from ignorance and moral vice. Since "knowledge is virtue," an educated populace would create an unprecedented world order of morality and virtue. Peoples of the world would pool their knowledge for the advancement of the common good. Reason would rule. Utopia would become real.

One by one these certainties were unmasked as delusions by the unfolding of historical events. Instead of solving all problems, science realized that the more we know, the more we have yet to know; that scientific knowledge is provisional and statistical rather than final and certain. As Jacob Bronowski wrote in his now classical work, *The Ascent of Man,* "There is no absolute knowledge. And those who claim it, whether they are scientists or dogmatists, open the door to tragedy. All information is imperfect. We have to treat it with humility."[4]

Discoveries in mathematics (such as Godel's theorem) and in physics (such as Heisenberg's indeterminacy theory) demonstrated that there are unknowable, unpredictable, and random elements of reality. Einstein showed how scientific truth is not absolute or objective, but relative. The second law of thermodynamics offered a view of the universe not as an evolving entity, but as a slow and steady march toward chaos. Technology introduced wondrous conveniences, but also ways of bringing mass death and destruction on a previously inconceivable scale. Some diseases were conquered, only to have new and more virulent ones replace them. "Wonder drugs" were discovered, but viruses mutated faster than new drugs could be developed. Hopes for economic abundance were dashed in the 1930s by the onset of a worldwide economic depression. Dreams of peace dissolved into the nightmares of two devastating world wars. Democracies gave way to oppressive dictatorships. Cultural securities were shattered as Germany, the most cultured and educated nation in Europe, murdered millions as part of a "scientifically" affirmed and academically endorsed theory of racial genocide.

Already in late nineteenth-century England, the poet Matthew Arnold previsaged conditions characteristic of the century yet to dawn. He wrote:

Ah, love, let us be true
To one another! for the world which seems
To lie before us like a land of dreams,
So various, so beautiful, so new,
Hath really neither joy, nor love, nor light,
Nor certitude, nor peace, nor help for pain;
And we are here as on a darkling plain
Swept with confused alarms of struggle and flight,
Where ignorant armies clash by night.[5]

In the post-World War II era, Western European philosophers and artists became preoccupied with anxiety, despair, and absurdity. Europe had been devastated by war, and art and philosophy reflected the contemporary conditions. Eastern Europe fell under Stalin's fist, and free expression was squelched. But in America things were radically different. As the only major country intact after the war, the United

States was poised for the greatest economic boom in world history. Dominating world economic markets, America soon became the world's largest creditor nation. Cheap money, high wages, and a soaring rise in the standard of living made Americans flourish and prosper as never before. Everything seemed for the asking or the taking. With all its wars won, with unparalleled military might at its command, with seemingly limitless economic expansion a perpetual feature of life, with technology in high gear to bring miraculous conveniences to each home, with staggering affluence and prosperity, the realization of the American dream appeared even better than had ever been expected. The promise of "a chicken in every pot and a car in every garage" seemed to have been far exceeded. As the 1960s began America entered a new frontier with a new, young, vibrant, and handsome president. In his inaugural address President Kennedy caught the tenor of the times. There were now no problems that could not be solved, no expectations that could not be realized, no legitimate need that could not be met. Kennedy said, "Let us explore the stars, conquer the deserts, eradicate disease, tap the ocean depths. . . ." Humans had now achieved an almost divine omnipotence. In Kennedy's words, "Man holds in his mortal hands the power to abolish all forms of human poverty and all forms of human life."[6]

Once again, a naive utopianism reigned. As its predecessor, this one too was short-lived. Soon the disappointments of high hopes engendered despair and a deep spiritual malaise.

The utopian hopes of the post-war period began to fade with the Kennedy assassination in November 1963. Despite President Johnson's offer of almost messianic assurances of a Great Society, where peace, prosperity, and racial harmony would prevail, American life already was in disarray. What Americans had failed to realize was not only that they had been naive, but that they had mistakenly identified an historical aberration with a national birthright. The post-World War II situation was a unique and unprecedented one that could not be sustained for long. Instead, it had been incorrectly taken by many as a perpetual feature of American life.

The year 1968 had seen the assassinations of Robert Kennedy and Martin Luther King Jr. Riots erupted in American cities and on college campuses. America was on the verge of losing its first war—Vietnam, a war Americans seemed not to know why they were fighting. Inflation, coupled with increasingly frequent recessions, began to burst the bubble of American affluence and of a progressively rising standard of living. Racial strife increased. The nuclear family imploded. American cities began to deteriorate. Educational quality began to decline. Soon there was Watergate, Iran-gate, and the savings and loan scandals. The national debt climbed dramatically. A generation of Americans came of age convinced they would not be better off than their parents—a first in American history.

For almost three decades the American economy was marked by dynamic, rapid growth and expanding opportunities. Year after year people improved their lot; their standard of living was progressively upwardly mobile. Americans came to take for granted ever-increasing levels of material well-being. Between 1950 and 1973 the average American family income doubled in constant dollars. But when the OPEC oil crisis hit in 1973, Americans found themselves traumatized. Used to the unlimited availability of commodities, they suddenly had to adjust to the reality of limited resources. Used to domineering the world economy, they found themselves at the mercy of foreign economies. Used to military domination, they had to contend with the quagmire of Vietnam. Used to domestic tranquillity, they found themselves having to live with riots in their cities. When the bills for the butter and guns expenses of the Great Society and the Vietnam war came due, they found the U.S. dollar had lost much of its value, that Americans no longer enjoyed the world's highest standard of living, that the future was not as bright as it always had seemed to be.

Once the policemen of the world, Americans gradually discovered that they had difficulty policing their own cities. Seemingly endless economic expansion gave way to economic uncertainty and to the ever-threatening fear of downsizing. Once the largest creditor nation, America became the largest debtor nation. Its standard of living fell below that of many western European nations, as did the life expectancy of its citizens—despite unprecedented expenditures for health care. The educational achievements of American students fell below those of many impoverished nations of the former Communist bloc in Eastern Europe. "America the beautiful" became America the polluted. A generation earlier, Americans hoped to explore the stars; more recently the concern has become how much longer can we continue to inhabit the earth.

Our roads and bridges are rapidly deteriorating. Once the American frontier seemed limitless; now we are even running out of space to put our garbage. With the end of the Cold War we thought that peace would reign, that the nuclear threat would dissipate. Instead we witness ethnic wars, racial conflicts both at home and abroad. The threat of nuclear terrorism haunts us. Concentration camps and genocide have reappeared. The "big stick" we carry has become limp. In 1957, when Sputnik went up, we tried to improve American education as a matter of national defense. But in 1984 a study of our educational system, *A Nation at Risk,* reported that "if a foreign power had attempted to impose on America the mediocre educational performance that exists today, we might well have viewed it as an act of war. . . We have committed unilateral educational disarmament."[7] The disaster of our schools severely threatens to stifle our attempts to be competitive in world markets. For the first time in American history our basic social securities seem uncertain. Once convinced that "we shall overcome," we feel instead overwhelmed.

No longer content to "leave it to Beaver," no longer convinced that "father knows best," Americans since the 1960s have witnessed the progressive demise of many of their most cherished certainties. The cultural, economic, and geopolitical anchors that offered beauty, balance, stability, and meaning to American existence seem to suffer from systemic corrosion. The American dream has been replaced with new fears, uncertainties, and instabilities. The light at the end of the tunnel may simply be that of another train hurtling toward us, inviting catastrophe.

Jeffrey Hart summarized American life in the fifties by entitling his book on that subject *When the Going Was Good*. Expressing expectations for the new decade of the 1960s, *Look* magazine in January 1960 reported that Americans polled agreed that they "naturally expect to go on enjoying their peaceful, plentiful existence—right through the 1960s and maybe forever." But in the views of most Americans today, particularly those of the baby-boom generation, the optimism that characterized the beginning of the seventh decade of the twentieth century is a bubble that has burst. As a tearful Daniel Patrick Moynihan said after the Kennedy assassination, "When you're Irish, one of the first things you learn is that sooner or later this world will break your heart."[8]

Suddenly, in the 1960s and 1970s, middle-class America discovered that alongside prosperity there was gnawing poverty. Together with freedom and opportunity there was racism and discrimination. Movies like *Advise and Consent* reflected corruption in government; *The Godfather* revealed the pervasive influence of organized crime in our nation; *The Andromeda Strain* demonstrated that science was as much a threat as a panacea; *Fail-Safe* and *On the Beach* illustrated how a nuclear accident could readily lead to the sudden annihilation of the human species. America, the most powerful nation on earth, was suddenly seen to be the most vulnerable. America might be secure, but Americans were not. In peaceful suburbs children played with their hula hoops next to their family fallout shelters. The superficiality of the period, the facade equated with reality, was symbolized by one word in the movie *The Graduate*—that word was *plastics*. Evils and problems that seemed relegated only to nations abroad were catapulted into the center of the American consciousness. As the cartoon character Pogo put it, "We have met the enemy, and they are us."

The fear of loss and of frustrated expectations, characteristic of the generation raised during the Great Depression, has become the reality of the baby-boom generation. The late 1980s and early 1990s have seen an explosion of studies by social scientists reflecting the pessimistic and even fatalistic tenor of the times. For example, Columbia

University anthropologist Katherine Newman writes about *Declining Fortunes: The Withering of the American Dream,* and *Falling from Grace: The Experience of Downward Mobility in the American Middle-Class.* Kathryn Dudley analyzes the deindustrialization of America in *End of the Line.* Bennett Harrison and Barry Bluestone portray *The Great U-Turn: Corporate Restructuring and the Polarizing of America,* and *The Deindustrializing of America: Plant Closings, Community Abandonment and the Dismantling of Basic Industry.* Arlene Skolnick describes *Embattled Paradise: The American Family in an Age of Uncertainty.* The Brookings Institute publishes studies about *A Future of Lousy Jobs: The Changing Structure of U.S. Wages.* Even terrorism has become a feature of American life.

A generation of Americans that grew up with the assumption that prosperity was their birthright, that each generation would exceed the standard of living the previous generation had struggled to achieve, now finds itself unable on two incomes to support a lifestyle equivalent to that provided a generation earlier by a single income. Better educated, better credentialed, and often with jobs of higher prestige than their parents, most baby boomers now find the home in which they grew up to be beyond their fiscal capacity to acquire. What their parents took for granted they often find out of reach. Children have become a luxury that few really can afford, even with two incomes. The delay in starting families because of occupational considerations has resulted in high rates of infertility. A generation that worried about unwanted high school pregnancies now finds beginning a family often requires medical intervention. Job security and adequate retirement pensions largely have gone by the wayside. Social Security may prove, upon retirement, to offer little security, to be a well run dry. Good public education has become a rare commodity. Not only do parents expect less for themselves, but they must contend with the reality of not being able to provide as well for their children as their parents provided for them. They had assumed that working hard to procure a good education and appropriate professional credentials, along with sustained occupational achievement and commitment, would guarantee for them the good life as it had done for the preceding generation. But the magic formula for achieving one's goals no longer seems to work. Just when the carrot at the end of the stick came within reach, it suddenly began to wither.

There is no aspect of daily life that has not been left unaffected by the disappointment, the anger, the feeling of being stuck, the insecurity, and the apprehension that many baby boomers—the largest segment of the American population—are now feeling. While their parents found an expanding job market with an inexhaustible thirst for their talents, the baby boomers have found a crowded, competitive market that often deems them expendable. Brought up to believe they were special, many now have discovered themselves superfluous. Flatter job pyramids are leveling off at distressingly early ages. The "glass ceiling" is getting progressively lower. Women seeking to enter the job market at a time of decreasing opportunities are finding a new form of restricted options precisely at a time when the opportunities granted by women's liberation seemed more readily available. After two or three decades of hard work aimed at increased leisure, the number of work hours has increased and the number of hours available for leisure has substantially decreased. Parents, who vowed when they were children not to be absentee fathers, now find their occupational obligations making them into both absentee fathers and mothers.

A generation of Americans is being challenged by the experiences of the present and of the recent past to rethink their most cherished assumptions and to reevaluate their most fervently accepted expectations. The certainties that once characterized American life are now being replaced by instabilities and disarray. The conviction that new challenges can readily be met is being replaced by the observation that the problems of the past—that is, poverty, race relations, recession—have not yet been resolved, and that new problems, such as dire environmental conditions, may be beyond our capacity and those of our resources to solve.

Writing in 1871 of the expected glorious twentieth century soon to dawn, poet Charles Swinburne wrote:

Glory to man in the highest
The maker and master of things.[9]

Less than a century later Jean-Paul Sartre reflected on the progress of the early twentieth century in his 1960 play, *The Condemned of Altona:*

My century was a rummage sale in which the liquidation of the human species was decided upon in high places. . . . The century might have been a good one had not men been watched from time immemorial by the cruel enemy who has sworn to destroy him, that hairless, evil, flesh-eating beast—man himself.[10]

As Marc Connelly wrote in his famous play, *The Green Pastures,* "Everything dat's fastened down is comin' loose."[11] But one thing is for sure: "The future is not what it used to be."[12]

The spiritual malaise that many currently apprehend is a condition of our modern age. The symptoms that many people manifest today are the explosion of mines buried in our cultural topography hundreds of years ago. The historical events and personal traumas of our times merely have triggered what had been buried in the minefields of Western civilization, awaiting their inevitable detonation. To better understand where we are, we must appreciate how we arrived at our current condition. To do so is the purpose of the chapter that now follows.

chapter three

Lost in the World

Once a man wandered into an enchanted forest. Over-
whelmed by its beauties and its delights, he continued to
wander until suddenly he found himself in the midst of a
dark thicket. The sun was setting and he was frightened lest
he be lost in the darkness of the night. Path after path that he
chose only led him deeper and deeper into the labyrinth of
the forest. Finally, he saw another man in the thicket. He ran
to him thinking, "This man can help me find my way out of
the forest and into the meadow."

He approached the man and begged for his help. The man
sighed and said, "Alas, I too am lost in the forest."

The first man tore at his hair in despair and said, "We
are lost. We are truly lost."

"Perhaps not," said the second man. "I have tried many
paths to find my way out of the forest. So, I assume, have
you. What we know is which paths lead nowhere. So, let us
pool our knowledge and perhaps together we can learn from
our experiences, and together find our way out of the forest
and into the light."

*D*ante opens his great work *The Divine Comedy* with the words:

> *Midway in my life,*
> *I found myself in a dark wood,*
> *where I had lost the way.*[1]

Like Dante, many people today feel lost in the wood, homeless in the world we call home. Identifying the minefields to meaning embedded in our culture and society is the first step to finding a way out of the thicket in which we have become enmeshed.

That loneliness, anxiety, boredom, and a general feeling of emptiness—of feeling lost in the world—have become pervasive attitudes since the inception of modern times has been confirmed by psychologists, philosophers, historians, novelists, artists, sociologists, and theologians. For example, writing in the 1950s, the American psychotherapist Rollo May stated that "the chief problem of people in the middle decade of the twentieth century is emptiness."[2] Writing in 1986 of the modern *Death of the Soul*, philosopher William Barrett comments that "our [modern] culture itself presents no theory of a stable self; when, in fact, it advances theories to promote the opposite persuasion; namely, that this poor human self of ours is itself only a fugitive and fragmented phantom."[3] Summarizing prevalent themes in modern literature, Professor Nathan Scott notes that "much of the literature of the modern period might be said to be a literature of metaphysical isolation, for the modern artist—and this is perhaps the fundamental truth about him—has experienced a great loneliness, the kind of loneliness known by the soul when, unaided by ministries either of Church or of culture, it undertakes the adventure of discovering the fundamental principles of meaning."[4]

The feeling of being lost and alone in the world is a feature characteristic of modern life. In the premodern period, however, individuals usually did not experience such an identity crisis. This is because the idea of an individual identity did not really develop into its present form until after the Middle Ages. Until then, identity was vested in a group, a class, a caste. In the premodern period, the identity of most individuals was provided at birth—if not before. Who a person was, who a person could become, was defined in advance of any given person's birth by the traditions of the group into which he or she was born. An example of this mentality is reflected in the popular song "Tradition" from *Fiddler on the Roof.* The role of men, women, children, clergy, milkmen are all defined by tradition. One's options in life, roles in life, place in society, behavior at any given occasion are all defined by tradition. In such a society, individual identity is conferred by tradition; there is neither need nor opportunity for an identity crisis. But with the beginning of the breakdown of tradition, things radically changed. Without tradition, without imposed preconceived identities, the individual became challenged to determine who he is, and who he wants to become.

The French philosopher Jean-Paul Sartre distinguished between medieval and modern thought by stating that, for the medievals, essence preceded existence, whereas for moderns, existence precedes essence. What this means is that, for premoderns, who one is is determined even before one is born, before one exists; in the modern period, however, once a person is born, once a person exists, the individual must determine his essence, that is, who he is and desires to become. The medieval person was like an actor, playing out in life a script already written. The modern person is like a playwright who acts out the script he writes for his own life. The medieval person inherited a secure identity but often lacked the freedom to alter this inherited identity, this inherited script. The modern person, in Sartre's words, is "condemned to freedom."[5] The modern person has no choice but to choose to become a product of the exercising of his or her own choice.

Premoderns sought wisdom with which to address contemporary problems from inherited traditions. In contrast, the view that has dominated modern times is that the past represents obsolescence rather than wisdom. In confronting the future, premoderns looked to the wisdom and the cumulated experience of the past for guidance. Moderns tend only to look forward, without a backward glance. This is especially true in America, where Henry Ford's statement "History is bunk"[6] characterizes a pervasive attitude toward the past.

From the Renaissance onward, novelty and newness became equated with that which is desirable and good. The improvements in daily life brought by science and technology helped to ingrain in the modern psyche the conviction that new is better. The modern obsession with newness became much more influential in America than it did in the Old World, that is, in Europe. The New World became an arena for the creation of a new man. Here one could find a new life, a new lifestyle. Here one could create one's own new self. In 1832 the American statesman Henry Clay coined the term "self-made man." But as that most American of authors, Mark Twain, observed: "A self-made man is about as likely as a self-laid egg."

It is not surprising that in the United States, cities and states have appropriated the word "new" as part of their names—New York, New Haven, New Mexico. Already in the nineteenth century, Tocqueville understood that newness and change had become vital American values. He wrote, "The American has not tied himself to anything, he grows accustomed only to change, and ends by regarding it as the natural state of man."[7] Yet, it was Mark Twain again who raised the question of whether change for the sake of change is good in itself, whether change necessarily offers improvement in the quality of life. In Twain's words, "A person must never confuse change with progress."

Sociologist Philip Slater reminds us that "one of the better-kept secrets of medical science is that the major cause of disease is change. People who live in stable environments with adequate nutrition have generally good health, while those who, like ourselves, are subject to constantly shifting living contexts tend to be more sickly."[8] Furthermore, as Alvin Toffler notes, "there is a direct correlation between the number of major changes (residence, spouse, job, etc.) experienced by a person in a given period and the likelihood of his falling ill. Most important of all, this effect holds true even if the changes were desired. Change, in other words, has been found dangerous to your health."

The American preoccupation with change and newness has created a cult of growth. Not surprisingly, the greatest American philosopher, John Dewey, identified growth as the greatest moral value. What seems to have slipped Dewey's mind is that cancers also grow. Moreover, personal growth can neither stifle nor camouflage the fears either of aging or dying.

The horror of old age is predictable in a society that worships the new. If the wisdom that comes of the cumulative experiences of the ages is designated as being obsolete, then how much more so the experiences of the aged. If all knowledge has a built-in factor of obsolescence, then education—which is the transmission of the wisdom of the past to the future through the present—loses its raison d'être.

Planned obsolescence is a built-in feature of our technological age. The trivialization and devaluation of the past leaves the person in the present disenfranchised from the spiritual treasury that the accumulated wisdom of the past represents. Rather than perceive the past as a storehouse of experience and wisdom that can contribute to enriching life in the present, moderns tend to see the past only as an example of foolishness and naivete. Many see the past merely as a repository of oppressive rules and obsolete theories rather than as a treasure trove of wisdom verified through experience.

Modern thought is predicated on the view that the new represents an improvement over what came before, that it is unnecessary to consult the wisdom of the past in confronting the perplexities of the present. A rising tide of distrust of the past, coupled with the self-confidence to develop the new on our own, has had both positive and negative results. The positive results have been the formulation of breakthrough ideas, theories, and technologies that have indeed improved our daily lives and that have allowed culture to advance and to develop. The negative results have been the rootlessness and the alienation characteristic of our times. Severed from the classical sources of wisdom, disinherited from traditional sources of guidance, we are bereft of our historical anchors. Being challenged to "go it alone" in confronting an uncertain future only can exacerbate our already substantial anxiety. To dismiss the wisdom of the past as a disposable obsolescence is neither practical nor wise. To disregard the spiritual resources we have inherited from the past is to squander a much needed and readily accessible heritage. To relinquish cumulative wisdom and experience and to expect to repair our souls on our own is misguided modern hubris. It would be as prudent as trying to reinvent the wheel, as effective as trying to build an electron microscope without the tools or knowledge of physics.

The Renaissance person stands in sharp contrast to the contemporary person. In the Renaissance—a time no less turbulent than our own—people dealt with the perplexities of the present through the recovery of the wisdom of the ancient past. They perceived knowledge as an integrated whole. The Renaissance man was a person at home in a wide range of cultural forms. The person of the Renaissance sought identity as an integrated self, informed by the wisdom of the past. In contrast, modernity has been characterized by the fragmentation of knowledge, the ignorance and the ignoring of the wisdom of the past. This has led to the fragmentation of the self, and the loneliness, anxiety, and rootlessness that have been characteristic of modern times.

With this fragmentation of knowledge, reliance upon experts and specialists has become a characteristic feature of modern life. It is ironic that, in this communications age, increasing specialization has led to the inability of specialists in different disciplines—and even in the same discipline—to communicate with one another.

The Spanish philosopher Ortega y Gasset considered the fragmentation of the modern self as a corollary of the fragmentation of knowledge in the modern period. This situation, in Ortega's view, led to what he called the "barbarism" of specialization. Ortega y Gasset wrote the following about the modern condition, with specific reference to the modern scientist:

> He is one who, out of all that has to be known in order to be a man of judgment, is only acquainted with one science, and even of the one only knows the small corner in which he is an active investigator. He even proclaims it as a virtue that he takes no cognizance of what lies outside the narrow territory specially cultivated by him-

self, and gives the name "dilettantism" to any curiosity for the general scheme of knowledge. . . . The specialist "knows" very well his own tiny corner of the universe; he is radically ignorant of the rest. . . . We shall have to say that he is a learned ignoramus.[9]

The fragmentation of knowledge, indicated by the profusion of specialists and areas of specialization, not only places the individual passively in the hands of these "learned ignoramuses," but reflects the fragmentation of the self in the contemporary world. The self, yearning for cohesion, integration, focused meaning, and unified purpose, lies shattered after having fallen off the wall. All of the king's horses—the specialists—and all the king's men—the learned ignoramuses—cannot put Humpty Dumpty together again, since each only knows a part of Humpty Dumpty. The configuration of the whole eludes them. We literally have fallen to pieces. *The story of Humpty Dumpty may well be the paradigm of our times.*

A major preoccupation of the medievals was the life of the soul. A pervasive characteristic of modern life has been the eclipse of the soul. With the inception of modern physics and philosophy in the seventeenth century, the soul became a superfluous entity in a mechanical universe. The inception of the new science in the seventeenth century was grounded in mechanics. In this view, everything runs according to the mechanical laws of nature, except the human soul. However, it was not long before the soul was perceived as an anomalous entity, superfluous to a mechanistic view of the universe. Hence Descartes's successor in the history of philosophy, La Mettrie, took Descartes's view of animals as soulless machines and applied it to human beings. In his book *Man, A Machine,* La Mettrie asks: How is the human machine different from other machines? His answer: Only the human machine winds its own springs.

The philosophy of scientific materialism, of which La Mettrie's work is but one example, came to dominate Western thought during the modern period. In this approach, science and technology go hand in hand. Science is the theory of which technology is the application.

The demonstrable success of science and technology in providing conveniences for daily living, machines for easing work, drugs and procedures for treating illnesses, techniques for elevating the standard of living, only helped to entrench the philosophy of scientific materialism into the modern psyche. Yet, the benefits afforded by this approach have not come without cost.

Once technology managed to introduce something new to subdue an existing danger or to offer another convenience, a more pressing problem often immediately appeared on the horizon. The introduction of new substances often produced unpredicted by-products that poisoned the environment. New "miracle drugs" often brought with them dangerous and initially undetected side-effects. Weapons produced to provide security often threatened to destroy those whom they were created to defend. As diseases have been controlled, increasingly virulent diseases have appeared to threaten us.

The view of the human being as a machine has become deeply embedded in the modern mentality. For example, in our daily colloquial speech we tend to speak of ourselves as "turned on" and "turned off." We "tune in" and "tune out." We "gear up" and "wind down." We provide "input" and "output." As machines, our claim to meaning became attached to our function. In this regard, Erich Kahler wrote, "Identification of one's function is the admittance ticket granting the right to exist."[10] As Karl Marx observed, "Once machines became more like humans, humans became more like machines."

The French philosopher Gabriel Marcel observed that a world dominated by mechanistic functionalism is one from which mystery, wonder, and the sense of the sacred are lost. When function, efficiency, and output become critical components of personal identity, then intrinsic meaning is lost and is replaced by feelings of alienation and meaninglessness.[11]

It is ironic that technological thinking largely has left us bereft of a sense of wonder while the great scientists of the past were constantly awestruck by the marvel and mystery of existence. Great scientists like Faraday and Newton pictured themselves as little children awestruck by the wonder of creation. Sir Isaac Newton wrote, "I do not know what I may appear to the world, but to myself I seem to have been only like a boy, playing on the sea shore, and diverting myself, in now and then finding a smoother pebble or a prettier shell than ordinary, whilst the great ocean of truth lay all undiscovered before me."[12] Einstein wrote, "The most beautiful experience we can have is the mysterious. It is the fundamental emotion which stands at the cradle of true art and true science. Whoever does not know it can no longer wonder, no longer marvel, is as good as dead, and his eyes are dimmed."[13]

Once the universe and its human inhabitants came to be considered machines, attention shifted from the problem of meaning to the problem of function. Now, the primary issue became "how" and not "why." Now, a preoccupation with method largely replaced a concern for meaning. Now, the functioning of the machine—nature, humans, and fabricated machines—replaced the quest for spiritual meaning. In a real sense, the incessant flow of how-to manuals that populate our bookstores and libraries are the descendants of Descartes's seventeenth-century treatise, *A Discourse on Method.* Unbeknown to himself, Descartes spawned a technology of human behavior. B. F. Skinner and his school of behaviorist psychology is in a direct line of philosophical descent from Descartes. However, the title of Skinner's major study, *Beyond Freedom and Dignity,* probably would have horrified Descartes.

Psychology literally means "the study of the soul." With the technologization of psychology, the psyche, too, became a machine—in need of programming, spiritually dead, tediously predictable, bereft of freedom, evaluated by its functional quality rather than by its claim to intrinsic meaning.

With the establishment of the primacy of method, the technician who understands how to make things work gained supremacy and social status over those preoccupied with the meaning of why things should work in the first place. Technocrats have become the empowered elite of the modern period. Once all problems are assumed solvable through the application of the appropriate technique, it follows that, in order to address any specific problem, it becomes necessary to enlist the services of an individual skilled in the application of that technique. This assumption, so endemic to contemporary existence, has led to the enfeeblement and infantilizing of the individual, assumed to be incapable of addressing his own problems.

I am certainly not suggesting that know-how is unimportant. Rather, what I am suggesting is that know-why is even more important. The crisis of meaning that confronts each of us is at least partially a result of the severance of the how from the why, and the obsession with the how to the exclusion of the why. Without the substance provided by meaning and purpose, the assumption that we can achieve salvation through the mastery of technique palls into irrelevancy.

While technological skill can aid immeasurably in helping to get things done, it never was meant either to address or to replace the deeper problems of human existence. The fallacy of much of contemporary thought is the assumption that method can replace meaning, that skill can usurp purpose, that technological processes can be successfully applied to spiritual problems. As André Malraux wrote, "The basic problem is that our civilization, which is a civilization of machines, can teach a human being everything except how to be a human being."[14]

The self-help and how-to approach to life may enable us to cope with certain types of problems and situations, but it cannot address the deeper human need for meaning and purpose. Manuals that instruct us in how to make love cannot tell us who and why to love. Manuals that lead us to new employment cannot teach us how to find meaning and purpose in our work. Manuals that tell us how to conduct a meeting cannot tell us how to conduct a life of meaning. Manuals that offer insights into how to accumulate money fail to let us know that a person can be rich but not wealthy, or fiscally secure but not personally secure. Learning better methods of communication cannot inform us as to what is worth communicating. Learning how to relate to others fails to convey virtues that give relationships meaning and value.

Writing in the 1960s, Rollo May depicted how-to manuals, written for those who equate sexual expression with technique, as being aimed at "making oneself feel less in order to perform better."[15] Like May, who decries the ideology of "salvation through technique," author Sam Keen observes that "the study of the geography of the erogenous zones may make sex a matter of genital engineering in which anxiety over performance replaces the sweet pandemonium of love. Acquiring living habits and attitudes requires more than a study of the technology of arousal."[16]

We have become, in the words of novelist Jerzy Kosinski, "a nation of videots."[17] Couch Potato is not simply a stuffed toy for our times but a symbol of our era. Not only has public oration become a forgotten art, but more important, the beauty in private speaking has largely been lost; in our conversations we tend to simulate television dialogue. Public relations has become a profession much in demand in our age of "how to," when image has replaced reality. "Private relations" has become a lost art.

Since time immemorial, there have been salespersons of happiness. Today they saturate the airwaves and the print media offering facile and simplistic techniques, strategies and pills promising contentment, security, and serenity. They exploit people's weaknesses, insecurities, and deepest desires with adroitly designed marketing tactics, promising panaceas for a variety of fees. But, just like the purveyors of snake oils a century ago, they hold out empty promises of possessing the key to happiness, health, and fulfillment. And perhaps like the marketers of bliss that preceded them over the centuries, they might even actually believe in the efficacy of what they purvey.

The gospel of salvation through technique is both correlative to and an attempt to undermine the mechanistic view of existence. It is correlative because it follows that if everything is a machine, knowing how to fix it, how to manage it, is desirable and necessary. It is an attempt to undermine the mechanistic view because it affirms human freedom. But if both the universe and the human being are machines that run according to the unalterable mechanical laws of nature, then human beings are nothing more than passive and helpless pawns pushed around by the forces of nature. Human freedom thereby is relegated to an illusion. The human being is cast into despair and anxiety. And no how-to manual, no technological advance, has been found that can address this spiritual malaise.

A feature of modern life is that, for many people, the dogmas of science and the miracles of technology have supplanted religion, philosophy, and spirituality as the main source of guidance about how to live. However, scientific "truth" cannot offer us guidance in how to address the most vital issues of human existence or human behavior. As the philosopher Ludwig Wittgenstein wrote, "We feel that even when all possible scientific questions have been answered, the problems of life remain completely untouched."[18] Scientific and technological development moves at an accelerated pace while we seem caught in a rut of spiritual recession. Indeed, our spiritual concerns seem eclipsed by the onslaught of our technological achievements. Once Albert Einstein's wife was asked what she thought of her husband's theory of relativity, and she said, "Albert has explained it to me many times, but it is not necessary to my happiness."[19] All of the startling advances in science and technology that our age has witnessed are helpless in addressing the vital problems of human existence.

Technology has discovered a way of sedating us in order to cope with life in a fatalistic world. Science fiction writers used to describe societies where pills would be available to produce euphoria, thereby enabling people to cope with disturbing and disorienting realities rather than asking the hard questions about the meaning and purpose of life. Now these fictions have become matters of daily fare. Drugs are rampant in our nation. Indeed, the kingpins of the American drug industry may not be the illegal drug cartels, but the respectable personal physician. Dr. Robert Mendelsohn, known as "the people's doctor," often used to say that physicians are the biggest drug pushers in America. Statistics indicate that physician-prescribed drugs kill more people than illegal street drugs. (It was Eli Lilly who said that a drug without toxic effects is no drug at all.[20]) Yet physicians continue to provide a palliative for every pain. In Mendelsohn's view, the drug culture was not initiated by organized crime or by the South American drug cartels, but by the American "health" industry. The mentality that teaches that for every discomfort there is a pill that can assuage pain or offer euphoria was not instilled by the neighborhood junkie, but by the family physician.

The drug culture, legal or illegal, seems to me a response to a deep human desire for exaltation, transcendence, and euphoria. However, it has become an artificial palliative to block out pain and suffering rooted in a deeper hopelessness when one confronts a life seemingly devoid of meaning and purpose. Drugs are a symptom—not a solution. To paraphrase the Bible: "Man cannot live by Prozac alone."

The individualism that distinguishes the modern period from earlier ones became especially poignant in the United States, where not simply individualism, but "rugged individualism," has held sway. But, as Christopher Lasch explained, rugged individualism has produced the neurotic narcissist. Such an individual lives in a state of restlessness, with perpetually unsatisfied needs. Isolated, deeply lonely, anxious about forming lasting relationships, replete with needs while devoid of passions, possessing much yet having little, with a full schedule but an empty life, the narcissist has everything except a life of focused meaning and purpose. The narcissist may be the high-level manager par excellence, and yet he often is a dis-integrated self.[21] His work is organized while his soul is in disarray. Reflections refract in the mirrors, but there is no self to reflect back upon. Eventually the narcissist may confess to himself, "I'm convinced that something is missing from my life—what's missing is a life."

The experience of the high-level manager reflects the built-in anxieties of organizational life, not the least of which is the conflict between planning and technological development. An endemic feature of organizational management, planning assumes a rational, stable environment and a reasonably predictable future. However, technological development is geared for making the planned future obsolete. Despite the proclivity for control through planning, the executive knows that a blip in the economic environment or a breakthrough in technology may make both his plans and his own self an obsolete resource of organizational existence.

Such negation is not confined to the world of business. Ironically, many of our cultural assumptions—consider for example the cult of rugged individualism and our reliance upon specialists—are inherently contradictory, and are therefore set on a collision course that can only increase existing anxieties. Rugged individualism and the predilection for self-help are crippled by reliance on experts and consultants in the "helping professions" who presume dependence and the need for guidance in virtually every activity in which we are engaged.

The goal of knowing how to do things, of how to perform better, is "success." The American dream is to be successful. But success often does not provide fulfillment. As success is achieved, needs escalate. Like Sisyphus, precisely when we begin to arrive at the mountaintop, the rock rolls down upon us most viciously. As the Nobel Prize-winning philosopher Bertrand Russell wrote, "When sound success comes, a man is already a nervous wreck, so accustomed to anxiety that he cannot shake off the habit of it when the need is past."[22]

According to Christopher Lasch, in his quest for success the narcissist ultimately depends upon others to validate his or her self-esteem. Like Willy Loman in the play *Death of a Salesman,* the goal is to be the best liked. Having dispensed with traditional sources of wisdom for authority and self-confirmation, we have no choice but to look to others for acceptance and validation. The goal of the narcissist is to be known as a winner, as a success. The deepest fear is being known as a failure, as a loser. However, when confronted with the question of the very meaning of the game itself, a spiritual crisis ensues. If playing the game itself provides meaning, what happens when one can no longer play, when one no longer finds meaning in the game, and in the fame it sometimes brings?

Paradoxically, many people who have so much feel so empty. As psychiatrist Viktor Frankl put it, many people "have enough to live by but nothing to live for, we have the means, but no meaning."[23] Memoirs of the rich and famous tell us that neither fame nor fortune guarantees happiness or fulfillment. In fact, it often is the opposite. Fame and fortune, these memoirs reveal, are often dead ends. The testimony of those who have been there is not what we might expect. Consider, for example, the number of famous people who are known to everyone but their own self. Sir Laurence Olivier, perhaps the greatest actor of his time, confessed, "I just don't like me. . . . I don't like my company any more." At the height of her career, actress Kim Novak said, "I was lost. . . . I felt an incompleteness, like an unfinished song." "How come I'm not happy all the time?" asked Eddie Murphy, when fame sent him to new heights.[24] In memoir after memoir the rich and famous tell us that when they go home, they immediately head for the medicine chest or the liquor cabinet. Fame is not based upon who a person finds himself to be. Rather, celebrity is based upon the adage: "You think I am; therefore, I am." Fame bestows a fleeting existence. Celebrity is a fickle companion.

In his study of corporate leaders, Michael Maccoby observes that the onset of middle age often hits the corporate executive with the force of a disaster—especially those trapped by a glass ceiling preventing further upward mobility. Maccoby writes, "Once his youth, rigor, and even the thrill in winning are lost, he becomes depressed and goalless, questioning the purpose of his life . . . he finds himself starkly alone."[25] Or, as Bertrand Russell put it, "Unless a man has been taught what to do with success after getting it, the achievement of it must inevitably leave him a prey to boredom."[26]

Despite the obsession with successful performance, the "American pastime"—baseball—is a game that appeals precisely because limited success is identified with substantial achievement. A batter who fails 65 percent of the time is considered a tremendous success; ironically, the successful person is one who fails more often than he succeeds. A truly successful person is one for whom success is not everything.

Abraham Lincoln is often extolled as the paradigmatic example of the American success story. Rising from a log cabin to the White House, from a rail splitter to the commander in chief, Lincoln seems to represent the epitome of achievement. Yet one can also see Lincoln's life as a litany of tragedy and failure. Lincoln grew up unloved by his stepmother.

His first love died in her youth. Propelled into an unhappy marriage, he moved from business failure to bankruptcy. Elected to Congress, he lost his race to become senator. A number of his children died in their youth. He was afflicted both by a physical disease and by manic depression. While only in his fifties, he was murdered.

From the perspective of history, Lincoln was a success. From his own perspective, he may have been a failure. Indeed, many of the great people of history whom we today consider successes were considered failures by themselves and by their contemporaries.[27] And the converse is also true. Success is relative, transient, and illusionary. As Alan Watts put it, "To succeed is always to fail—in the sense that the more one succeeds in anything, the greater is the need to go on succeeding. To eat is to survive to be hungry."[28]

The Beatles sang of "all the lonely people—where do they all come from?" Not knowing where they come from is precisely why people are lonely. Loneliness is an expression of rootlessness. Severed from tradition, bereft of memories of formative experiences, cut off both vertically and horizontally from a community only exacerbates the loneliness, the alienation, and the meaninglessness many experience.

Roots offer a foundation both for meaning and identity. Twenty-three centuries ago Oedipus cried out, "I must find out who I am and where I came from!" More recently Alex Haley, the author of *Roots,* wrote, "I had to find out who I was. . . . I needed to find meaning in my life."[29]

A further feature of modern thought that has amplified the feeling of loneliness in the world is the separation of the human and the natural worlds. Once part of and partner with nature, the human being has become alienated from the natural dimension. A result has been a feeling of cosmic loneliness, not to mention the reality of ecological catastrophe. Once the view of the sixteenth-century philosopher and scientist Francis Bacon that we ought to "put nature on the [torturer's] rack,"[30] became normative, the irreparable breach between the natural and the human became inevitable. The movement from harmony to hostility, from compatibility to conflict became complete.

The shift in philosophical views of the nature of aesthetics in the nineteenth century is not an earth-shattering event for most people. However, this shift has influenced the subsequent relationship of people to nature. It was the nineteenth-century philosopher Hegel who shifted the definition of aesthetics from a preoccupation with beauty to a preoccupation with art. The human artifact now replaces nature as the focus of our aesthetic interest.[31] As Max Frisch observed, "Technology is the knack of so arranging the world that we do not experience it."[32]

Like many other situations that beset us today, the loss of the self has its roots in the past. Already in the eighteenth century, the philosopher David Hume described the self as a conglomeration of perceptions. The self, in this view, has no unifying center, but is a heap of often unrelated perceptions.[33]

The splitting of the self came before the splitting of the atom. Henrik Ibsen in literature, Paul Cezanne in art, and Sigmund Freud in psychology—each foresaw the coming eruption of the unity of the self. Each predicted the movement from integration to disintegration, and each warned of the need to find a new focus for psychic integration.

The fragmented self that Hume described seems more aptly suited to our own times than to his. The constant flow of stimuli, copiously imposed upon us by a plethora of technical devices, can turn the average person into a heap of disjointed perceptions. In this regard, the paradigm for the self in our times may be MTV and the rock videos it displays. To enter the world of MTV is to abandon the concept of a coherent world; it is to be bombarded by an onslaught of unrelated imagery and sound. We have reached the point in daily life that Ibsen hoped to reach in theater. In Ibsen's words, "The illusion I wished to create was that of reality."[34] The age of virtual reality is upon us.

As the purveyor of images, the camera has replaced the human eye as the conveyor of reality. As Susan Sontag has written, "Reality has come to seem more and more like what we are shown by cameras."[35] In a classroom, action in the classroom was televised on monitors around the room; the actions of the students were in turn monitored by a hidden camera. What the hidden camera saw was the students in the class watching what was happening in front of them on the television monitors around the classroom. The image on the screen was perceived by the students as being more real than what was actually occurring in front of them.[36]

Throughout the centuries philosophers have indicated that the senses are unreliable sources of truth and of perceiving the real. The senses often deceive us; what we perceive is not always what is. Image has become reality; yet, images may be infinitely manipulated and altered. Even history being made around us has become a product of manipulated images. Consider the nightly news on television where the factual world has been replaced by a world constructed for entertainment, profit, and the satisfaction of certain interest groups. For this reason, many ethnic groups have organized their own news programs to tell the news from their perspective. The title of Daniel Boorstin's book *The Image: A Guide to Pseudo-Events in America* seems to capture the contemporary state of affairs.

The acceptability of a wide variety of multiple perspectives on fact can be a liberating viewpoint. However, in our attempt to offer various perspectives on fact and truth, we often undermine our ability to grasp factual truth. If almost every perspective is valid, then none is valid. If everything is true, then nothing can be vouchsafed as being true.

Here we must refer to the eighteenth-century philosopher Immanuel Kant, for it was Kant who revealed that we do not perceive what is, that we do not know things as they are. Rather, we construct models, conceptual artifacts and rubrics, that we impose upon reality and through which we perceive reality. In this view, all we really have are fictions created by the mind. Kant, however, affirmed what many others forget: We must realize that these fictions are tools for dealing with the world, not facts that accurately portray the world.[37]

According to Kant, perception of things-in-themselves eludes us. That is precisely why we are compelled to construct categories with which we can deal with them. We perceive reality through a prism of constructs of our own devising. But, once our firmest convictions and our clearest perceptions are unmasked as artificial constructs, as fictions, where is objectivity and truth to be found? The answer, for many philosophers, was in reason. However, today reason also has been attacked as an unreliable entrée to certainty. Rationality has been shown not to be the guarantor of objective universal truth that it once was assumed to be. Furthermore, various claims to rationality have been unmasked by psychiatry as simply being self-serving exercises, and by cultural anthropology as being culturally determined predispositions.[38] But once the senses have been found wanting in the accuracy of perception, and once reason has become discredited as a reliable source of truth, then we are doomed to a state of epistemological anarchy where anything may be true, where all anchors are cast adrift. As William Butler Yeats wrote:

Things fall apart; the centre cannot hold;
Mere anarchy is loosed upon the world,
The blood-dimmed tide is loosed, and everywhere
The ceremony of innocence is drowned;
The best lack all conviction, while the worst
Are full of passionate intensity.[39]

The spiritual quest assumes that there is a self who can engage in that quest. It requires the integrity of a self who can imbue existence with purpose and with meaning; who can affirm convictions, cultivate virtues, and craft life as a work of art. Yet some contemporary philosophers, literary critics, and psychologists want to convince us that there is no self to engage in that quest, and consequently, that our most firmly held convictions are ephemeral, that our values are illusionary, that our lives are but a mélange of unrelated, meaningless impressions. This approach stifles our attempt to locate our selves. It sabotages our abilities to unfold the potentialities of our pregnant souls by aborting our quest for meaning. Contrary to this pervasive attitude of our times, the Apollo 14 astronaut Edgar Mitchell said, "There seems to be more to the universe than the random, chaotic, purposeless movement of a collection of molecular particles."

This chapter and the one preceding it have focused on how an awareness of the cultural assumptions that dominate our juncture in history
affect the spiritual pilgrimage in which we are engaged. To this point
the question has been, Where are we? In the two chapters now following, the focus shifts to the question of Who are we? There the goal will
be to demonstrate that we are *not* who dominant contemporary cultural trends tell us we are. Indeed, if we would accept the pervasive
contemporary vision of the self as fragmented, sick, hopeless, and helpless, the enterprise of spiritual development would be thwarted at its
beginning.

In the following two chapters, three issues will preoccupy our attention: (1) Why the self is not whom it is being portrayed to be? (2) Why
the integrity of the self is a sine qua non in the quest for meaning and
in the task of crafting life as a work of art? and (3) Who is the elusive
self that contemporary cultural trends have tried to dash to pieces? In
our times, the self, the soul, has shared the fate of Humpty Dumpty. It
is our task to put Humpty Dumpty back together again, lest his fate
become our own.

chapter four

Hide-and-Seek

Once there was a boy who, like many of us, would wake up in the morning and would forget where he put his things the night before. One night, before going to sleep, he devised a solution to his problem. Before he got into bed he took a paper and a pencil and wrote himself a note. The note said, "The eyeglasses are on the table next to the bed. The pants are on the chair next to the table. The shirt is over the pants. The shoes are under the bed. And I am in the bed."

The next morning he awoke and took his list. To his amazement, he found all of his things. But then he went looking for the last item on his list. When he went to find himself in the bed, he was not there. He sighed and said, "I have found everything I was looking for, except myself. So, if I am not in the bed, then where am I?"

*H*ide-and-seek is the oldest human game. According to the Bible, it was invented by the very first human being, Adam. After Adam sins, he hides from God. Deciding to play the new game, God goes to look for him. "Where are you?" God asks.[1] His hideout discovered, Adam emerges.

The biblical commentators asked: If God is all-knowing, why does

God ask, "Where are you?" Surely an omniscient God already knows. The answer: God asks not because God does *not* know, but to stimulate Adam to ask: "Where am I?" When Adam emerges from hiding, he confesses: "I hid myself." One commentator observed that "I hid myself" means "I hid *from* myself." In Hebrew, Adam means "human being." Already here, at the dawn of human experience, we encounter the human proclivity to hide from one's own self, to play hide-and-seek with the often elusive self.

In the quest for the self, there are many obstacles, many detours, many temptations to abandon or to divert the quest. The tests and challenges faced by the heroes and heroines of myth and mythology reflect the fact that a quest is rarely linear, that the route is more often circuitous than direct and nonstop. In the Bible, the Israelites wander for forty years before they get to the promised land. But they get there nonetheless. The experience of wandering prepares them to surrender the slave mentality of Egypt, to appreciate the task of making choices that comes with freedom. Once liberated, they must learn to marshal the necessary strength and determination required to take responsibility for their lives in the promised land. The process of finding the promised land is a paradigm for finding the promised self.

Perhaps Adam did not seek himself because he was not yet conscious that there was a self to find. Indeed, it was not until 1690 that British philosopher John Locke coined the term "self-consciousness." But, fifty years after Locke, his fellow philosopher David Hume previsaged our contemporary predilection to deny the existence of an essential, cohesive self. According to Hume, it is impossible to "catch" the self and pin it down because what we call the "self" is but a "bundle of varied, unrelated perceptions, which are in perpetual flux and movement."[2] By the time we begin to focus on the self, the kaleidoscope already has changed. In Hume's view, the self (like MTV) is a constantly shifting elusive image.

In our times, the search for the self often feels like a blind man looking in a dark room for a black cat that is not there. The quest for the self assumes that there *is* a self that can be found, but this is not an assumption characteristic of our times. The self has become a "missing person" in the topography of contemporary experience. In our times, we have witnessed an attempt to progressively dismantle the cohesive self. The self has become relegated to a composite of imposed images, a bundle of disparate perceptions, a clearinghouse for a database of unrelated relationships.

The shattering of the self into a mélange of multiple personalities reflects the cultural and social tenor of our times. In cultural arenas from literary criticism to the film arts, the existence of the deconstructed self has become accepted dogma, affecting our views of history, meaning, identity, and causality. For example, the postmodernist philosophers, such as Michael Foucault and Gilles Deleuze, maintain that there can be no single personality, only a radical multiplicity of selves. But, in his book *Shattered Selves: Multiple Personality in a Postmodern World,* James M. Glass reveals the uncanny resemblance between the claims of postmodern philosophy about the self and the narratives of people institutionalized with multiple personality disorder. What once was considered insanity now has become accepted as a normal cultural phenomenon. A paradigm for insanity now has become the paradigm for normalcy. The psychological profile of people who should be institutionalized has now become culturally institutionalized as a model for self-understanding.

Ironically, the portrait of the shattered, fragmented, multiple self somehow coexists with the cultural assumption that individualism is highly valued. Yet, in the very culture that values individualism, the self has been hijacked in the name of conformity, adjustment, and socialization. Albert Camus's novel *The Stranger* is a paradigm of our times. The person one meets in the quest for self is not oneself, but a stranger. As Pirandello wrote, "There is somebody who is living my life. And I know nothing about him." A person who lives an ersatz existence, who lives the life of a stranger, who is simply a performer in a script, cannot find meaning in her own life, in her own self, because there is no self, there is no life one can call one's own. For many, the self has become a phantom, and self-discovery has become a task to be avoided.

The fear of finding the self is rooted in the apprehension that there may be no self to find, or in the realization that the self one may discover will be frighteningly alone. As the French novelist André Gide observed, the fear of finding oneself alone is so great in many people that they choose not to find themselves at all. In his now classic essay, *Modern Man Is Obsolete,* the American journalist Norman Cousins wrote that "all of man's history is an endeavor to shatter his loneliness."[3]

It is ironic that when Americans think about societies that stifle self-development and self-awareness, they rarely consider their own. When Americans envision paradigmatic threats to individuality, to self-discovery and self-expression, they tend to think about fascist regimes and about the so-called Evil Empire that was the Soviet Union. Yet Americans often fail to acknowledge the threats to individuality that pervade their own history and culture. Americans often fail to realize that even in our free society with its enshrined tradition of rugged individualism, being one's own self often means being who others want you to be.

In his sociological writings on life in the Soviet Union, published under the pen name Joseph Novak, the novelist and sociologist Jerzy Kosinski vividly depicted the collectivistic mentality that dominated Soviet life. As his description of Soviet society unfolds, Kosinski notes that the group—the collective, the Party—serves as the source of one's identity, self-perception, and values. The individual is viewed as a cog in a giant machine. In *The Future Is Ours, Comrade* one of Kosinski's interviewees articulates the position that one's own identity is imposed from without rather than being generated from within:

No one of us may say that he thinks of himself in *his own* terms, because we evaluate ourselves by the eyes of *the others* . . . on them, our fellow citizens, depends our happiness, our creative development, our tranquility. . . . Therefore, wherever you go, you are in the collective. Wherever your collective goes, there you'll go also![4]

After coming to America from his native Poland in 1957, Kosinski began to observe that, despite the American myth of rugged individualism, a collectivist mentality—albeit of a different type than was present in Eastern Europe—is clearly manifest in America. Kosinski found the collectivist mentality of the American popular culture and consumer society to be indoctrinating, dehumanizing, and oppressive. In his view, the American proclivity toward evaluating the individual by the whims of an often contrived and momentary market differs in content, but not in form, from the Soviet method of defining the individual in terms of his or her present usefulness to the state. In an interview Kosinski observed:

American literature [of the nineteenth and early twentieth century] offered us a vision of a society in which man was free to define himself. The reality of the society was centered around the concept of the self-made man. . . . Americans of that period perceived themselves as protagonists in a drama of life. They were not yet frozen into a specific social milieu or single social role. . . . This is not true any more. Today, even the so-called blue-collar worker has become frozen into middle-class values.[5]

Rollo May locates this shift in the American mentality to the 1920s when a mechanistic view of the self began to hold sway. With the accelerated technological advances of that period, the machine became the paradigm for human existence rather than simply a tool for enhancing human life. The "slave," the machine, became the master. Compared to the power and efficiency of the machine, the person came to be viewed as ineffectual, inefficient, and dysfunctional. The reliability and predictability of the well-functioning machine came to be valued over the unpredictability of human spontaneity and creativity. The unpredictable brought anxiety; the predictable brought the comfort of life without surprises. The social goal became being efficient, being effective, being functional. The great achievements of industrial America during this period owe much of their credit to the introduction of standardized, replaceable parts. Unfortunately, this idea was extended from the factory to the individual. While Russians became cogs in the wheel of the state, Americans became cogs in the wheel of corporate industrialized society.

The identification of the self with the machine cast the human being into a role of dispensability, ineffectualness. As W. H. Auden wrote in *The Age of Anxiety:*

We move on
As the wheel wills; one revolution
Registers all things, the rise and fall
In pay and prices.[6]

In twentieth-century America the company man replaced the lonesome cowboy, the manager replaced the pioneer, the suburban Cleavers replaced the frontier homesteaders. The immediate post-World War II years produced a society characterized by suffocating conformity. The traumas of depression and war shaped a generation in search of security and stability, not of soulfulness or spiritual nourishing. It was an era of rationality and predictability. Bolstered by unprecedented economic expansion, planning presumed growth, investment assumed guaranteed returns. Input of conscientious hard work brought increasing income, increased benefits, an elevated standard of living. At the center of American life was the nuclear family with the dependable, hardworking (and often absentee) father; the conscientious, child-oriented, well-coiffured housewife and mother; and goal-directed, socially popular, and academically achieving children. People who played by the rules succeeded; those who played well the script they were handed flourished. Men who joined a company sublimated their individualities and often their preferred occupational goals in order to take advantage of the newly emerging corporate socialism. The company would take care of them throughout their working years and even after, with generous pension plans in return for fealty and obedience. They would take care of their wives and children for the same kind of behavior. Wives and children became extensions of the corporate image.

The goal was to blend in, to adjust to society, not to be different. Members of ethnic groups tried to divest themselves of features that accentuated their differences. People of diverse backgrounds sought to blend into the melting pot of American middle-class life. Foreignness itself was a foreign concept. People wanted to fit in, to be accepted, to succeed, to be well-liked.

Nonconformity was viewed as a neurosis that, if not cured, was severely punished. Rewards for performance were withheld from those unwilling to conform. The paradigm was the mechanical, well-ordered machine. The company ran this way, each component part and with each employee performing its designed role and function. The family and its members also operated like a well-ordered machine. Life became rational and predictable, but also vacuous, empty. In the words of T. S. Eliot:

> *We are hollow men*
>
> . . . .
>
> *Shape without form, shade without colour*
> *Paralysed force, gesture without motion.*[7]

As the machine became the ideal type in the modern mentality, human existence became more machinelike. Success meant becoming machinelike. Health became equated with the efficient functioning of the human machine. Consequently, the goal of mental health became the programming of the person in a manner that would maximize his social functioning. This approach manifested itself in the goal of becoming well-adjusted. The well-adjusted person was viewed as one who manifests psychological health; the aim of much psychological counseling was to address maladjustments. Like gears of a machine, psychological therapy aimed at functionality, at predictable and efficient behavior. Psychology joined the group-think of technological philosophy that perceived the human being as having been created in the image of his own creation—the machine. Personal problems came to be perceived as machinelike failures requiring repair by a well-trained mechanic, that is, by psychiatrists, psychologists, school counselors, social workers, and other mental-health professionals. One's most intense feelings were not shared with one's most intimate friends but with one's therapist in the therapeutic hours.

In the attempt to create a society of functionally efficient and socially well-adjusted individuals, this approach instead produced a society populated with spiritually dysfunctional individuals, a society populated by people bored with their own company and that of others, bored with tedious predictability. Life came to sound like a prerecorded announcement. Sanity came to consist of sharing the hallucinations of our neighbors. According to Rollo May:

> My thesis is that the problem of identity in the 1950s has now become, more specifically, the crisis of the loss of the sense of significance. . . . In our present stage of loss of sense of significance, the feeling tends to be, "Even if I did know who I am, I couldn't make any difference as an individual anyway." . . . There is, however, a particular dilemma we need to mention which is made more difficult by modern technology. This is the phenomenon of the "organization man.". . . And he is characterized by the fact that *he has significance only if he gives up his significance.*[8]

A recipe for achieving personal meaning that has societal norms for effective functioning as its key ingredients is bound to be unpalatable. The development of the inner life cannot be the product of architects other than the self. In deciding how the inner space of one's life is designed, each person must draw up his or her own plans. The self we are in search of cannot be the self that has been manufactured by others for us. In my search for *my*self, it must be my *own* self whom I find. The search for the self does not begin with a review of bit parts one might play in the drama of life. It begins with the journey inward.

Like the machine, individual identity has become a fabrication, an artifact. Public relations firms labor to create images and identities of corporate and government personalities, and the image becomes the reality. Entire industries are devoted to identity production; identities are fabricated and then marketed. The goal is not to be who you are but to project the image of who you want to become.

The contemporary self is now often perceived not only as an artifact constructed by others but as merely a composite of the relationships it has with others. In this view the self does not exist as a distinct entity, but rather as the clearinghouse for a particular network of liaisons. Deep personal relationships largely have been replaced by networking. Rather than finding oneself, the more pervasive tendency is to expand one's network. From the integral self, we have moved to the relational self. There is no single, coherent self but only a fragmented being, each fragment different than the other, depending upon which relationship is interfacing at a particular time.

Neither personal nor professional life has become conducive to the development of lasting relationships. Contingency rather than continuity, transience rather than commitment, have become pervasive features of our mobile and nomadic society. Already in 1970, in his insightful book *Future Shock,* Alvin Toffler observed that just as we have created a culture of throw-away items, we also have created a culture of disposable people, of transitory relationships defined in functional terms. Rather than relationships between the total personalities of two individual persons, there is the fragmented relationship between two fragmented selves. As John Barth put it in his novel, *The Floating Opera,* even "our friends float past." Or, as F. Scott Fitzgerald described the parties thrown by *The Great Gatsby,* "[They were only] enthusiastic meetings between people who never knew each other's names."[9]

Relationships have now become subject to a kind of cost-benefit analysis. Not only in business or in government, but in the traditionally most intimate relationships and decisions—like choosing a spouse, deciding whether and when to have children, committing to a career— it has become common to evaluate our actions in terms of what they cost us and what benefit they are likely to bring.

Since the Renaissance, the dominant value in society has been competitive prestige measured in terms of work and financial success. This
became especially true of American life in the decades immediately
following World War II, when Americans tended to equate meaning
and self-fulfillment with success. At the core of the quest for success
was what has been termed the "give-and-get" comp act. The harder we
worked—the more we gave—the more we got. If we followed the prescribed paths and obeyed the rules, then we would win the promised
rewards. Success, as characterized by the give-and-get compact, primarily focused around three elements: familial success, successful
pursuit of money, and social respectability. The give-and-get compact
assumed a rational world where specific acts produced predictable results, where prescribed actions led to particular rewards, and where
proscribed actions brought inevitable penalties. Each individual had a
role to play where conformity to that role brought benefits, and where
nonconformity entailed social and economic sanctions. All of this was
buttressed by an almost utopian view of reality supported by a seemingly endlessly expanding American economy.

For men, familial success meant marriage to an attractive woman
who would exclusively pursue a career as a housewife and mother. It
was further desirable that she could also serve as a social asset in her
husband's career. For women, familial success meant marriage to an
actually or potentially financially secure man, preferably with actual
or potential high social prestige. Divorce was a stigma. The working
wife was perceived as an indication that her husband was a failure,
unable adequately to provide for his family. Remaining unmarried was
considered indicative of failure in a woman and irresponsibility in a
man. Childless marriages were considered to be failed marriages.

Pursuit of money was the task assigned to the husband, through
hard work and foraging in the "jungle" of the business world. Money
was not only a means to making life more comfortable, but to other
things as well. Familial success demanded the relentless pursuit of money
on the part of the husband because his primary role was that of provider. Since the identities of his wife and children were inextricably

linked to his, and his self-identity was vested in how well he provided for his family, the pursuit of money became a key element to male identity. Further, money was viewed as a means to power and social respectability. Consequently, how well the husband did in his job often determined how successful he was, and, by implication, how successful his family life would be considered to be by himself as well as by others.[10]

When success becomes the purpose of existence, everything else becomes a means to that end. All else is subordinated to that purpose. In his enormously popular book, *The Power of Positive Thinking,* Reverend Norman Vincent Peale recommended belief in God and prayer as a means of increasing one's ability to be successful. In this view, even God is subordinated to the god of success; even God becomes a means to this end. Subordinating God to anything else is considered idolatry by classical Protestant theology, but in our culture, success became an unquestioned dogma of society. However, as Bertrand Russell reminds us, "Success is only one ingredient in happiness, and is too dearly purchased if all the other ingredients have been sacrificed to attain it."[11] For example, in their classic study of successful business and government leaders, professionals, and artists, Cuber and Harroff found that for a majority of their subjects, sex was almost nonexistent or a source of fear and avoidance.[12] Unable to give or receive gratification, sex was merely viewed as a matter of tension or release, as a necessary nuisance, performed like any bodily function that needs attention from time to time.

Based upon his experience as a revolutionary trying to overthrow the corrupt regime of King Farouk in Egypt, Anwar Sadat—later to become the president of Egypt and to win the Nobel Peace Prize—distinguished between outward success and inner success. Reflecting upon his time spent in prison for his revolutionary activities, Sadat wrote:

Most people are fascinated by outward success. . . . If their external image is, for any reason, shaken, they inevitably are shaken and

may even collapse. . . . Outward success alienates a man from himself. Self-alienation, another name for self-ignorance, is the worst
that can befall a man as it leads to the loss of inner light, and, inevitably, the loss of his vision altogether. A person's inability to see his
way ahead makes him a prisoner within himself. . . . One of the
things Cell 54 taught me was to value that inner success which
alone maintains one's inward equilibrium and helps a man to be
true to himself. . . .[13]

Similarly, psychiatrist Viktor Frankl advised, "Don't aim at success—
the more you aim at it and make it a target the more you are going to
miss it. For success, like happiness, cannot be pursued; it must
ensue. . . as the unintended side effect of one's personal dedication to
a course greater than oneself."[14] Or, as Csikszentmihalyi puts it, "Caught
in the treadmill of social controls, a person keeps reaching for a prize
that always dissolves in his hands."[15] The real issue is inward satisfaction, psychic reward, crafting life as a work of art.

The waiting rooms of psychiatrists and psychologists are filled with
rich and "successful" patients who suddenly wake up—often in their
forties or fifties—to find out that the symbols of success they have
acquired have not brought the happiness, contentment, and self-
fulfillment they seek. Yet people keep believing that changing the external conditions of their lives will provide a solution to their situation. They keep believing that if they had much more money, if they
were in better physical shape, if they were celebrities, they would achieve
their heart's desire. They fail to realize that the quest for success is a
treadmill that never stops. Success is indefinite, open-ended; whatever
success has been attained, there is always more. The "bottom line" is
not the bottom line in life satisfaction. Money, physical fitness, and
fame can be genuine blessings, but only if they are used as means to
crafting life as an art form. Otherwise they are at best neutral, at worst
obstacles to life satisfaction. Life satisfaction comes from within. The
highest happiness consists of intrinsic rather than extrinsic rewards.

The quest for outward success by means of the give-and-get compact worked well in a stable society, where conformity was a para-

mount virtue, where rapid and progressive economic growth could be readily assumed to continue ad infinitum, where the accoutrements of social respectability were easy to quantify and to define, where the nuclear family was the only socially acceptable model, where women were defined as (and defined themselves as) socioeconomic appendages of their husbands. But, as social, cultural, demographic, and economic conditions in America began to change radically, the assumptions and the elements of the give-and-get compact and of what constitutes success began to erode.

The give-and-get compact could only work as long as society could provide the payoffs promised, as long as the getting would be correlative with the giving. Yet recent data shows that an increasing number of Americans are questioning the core, especially the economic core, of the give-and-get compact—the value of giving a particular kind of sacrifice in exchange for a particular set of benefits.

Though changing economic conditions, realities, and expectations undoubtedly have played a major role in the erosion of the give-and-get compact as a foundation of American life, it would be overly simplistic to identify economic causes alone as the only critical factor. Rather, it would seem that a broader change of perspective, of attitude, of cultural assumptions has been taking place. As is often the case, cultural change begins by questioning assumptions previously taken for granted, assumptions tacitly and implicitly presumed to be both unquestionable and true.

The give-and-get compact confused outward success with inner success. It mistakenly assumed that the three elements of outward success—familial stability, pursuit of money, and social respectability—are the means of assuring self-fulfillment. Outward success was considered to be synonymous with self-fulfillment. However, as this view began to erode, its fundamental assumption began to be seen as problematic. When self-fulfillment was believed assured by the attainment of extrinsically measurable factors, it could be readily equated with success. But when self-fulfillment was revisaged to relate to inner satisfaction, to self-expression, to self-development, to experiencing intrinsic rewards, the view that equated success with self-fulfillment—the premise of the give-and-get compact—no longer seemed viable. To the extent that self-fulfillment emphasizes the inner person, external appearances could no longer count as much as they once did. The importance of respectability diminishes, and belongingness loses ground to individualism. As social respectability loses importance, the incentive to pursue it diminishes, and with it the incentive to acquire the accoutrements that it assumes: money, power, position.[16]

With success no longer being equated with self-fulfillment, with money being one of many measurements of wealth rather than the *only* measurement of wealth, with the inception of alternative models for familial living, with the liberation of women from stifling social role-playing, with the attainment of intrinsic self-fulfillment overshadowing the attainment of extrinsically imposed criteria for social respectability, with radical shifts in our socioeconomic expectations— the quest for the self has become something no longer to be avoided. No longer a luxury for people of leisure, the quest for self has become a necessity of life. In times of radical change and of cultural alteration, the stable self can serve as a gyroscope, as a reference point for plotting a life of meaning. It can serve as a secure anchor, even when the ship of daily life is battered by the waves of socioeconomic turbulence.

The ethos of personal satisfaction as an end in itself that replaced the give-and-get compact, pervasive during the 1980s, did not offer a viable alternative. For while it may have made some feel that they had achieved self-fulfillment, needs-fulfillment, and self-satisfaction, the ethos of personal satisfaction still failed to address adequately or directly the deepest of all human needs—the need for meaning. And, despite what Phillip Rieff has depicted as "the triumph of the therapeutic,"[17] that is, the extension of the quest for material advancement and self-interest into the popular obsession with psychological health, Americans largely seem to be more spiritually dysfunctional, increasingly spiritually homeless, and more alienated from their spiritual resources than before. The search for self cannot begin with social expectations, with transient needs, with networking relationships. It cannot be assigned by proxy. It can only begin with the journey inward, with a genuine and committed search for one's own authentic self.

In encountering the self, one discovers the soul—the meaning-generating faculty deeply implanted in the innermost core of our being. As Hermann Hesse wrote in his novel *Demian,* "Each person had only one genuine vocation—to find the way to himself. . . . His task was to discover his own destiny—not an arbitrary one—and to live it out wholly and resolutely within himself. Everything else was only a would-be existence, an attempt at evasion, a flight back to the ideals of the masses, conformity, and fear of one's own inwardness."[18] The way to avoid living a plagiarized existence is to take the risk to become oneself. As a character in Jerzy Kosinski's novel *Blind Date* puts it: "I'm myself—it's the ultimate risk."[19]

Among the obstacles that stifle the quest for self is the presence of anxiety. Anxiety encourages one to divert one's itinerary from the inward journey. Emptiness and boredom are components of anxiety. But just as anxiety can destroy self-awareness, so can awareness of ourselves destroy anxiety and dissipate the components of anxiety. Anxiety smothers the self, while freedom emancipates it to engage in its realization. In freedom is the capacity to become what we truly are. But many people are like the man in one of Mark Twain's stories who sits in a prison for many years, simply because he never realized that the door to his cell was never locked.

Like cowardice, vanity and narcissism are antitheses of courage in that they rest upon the compulsive need to be praised, to be liked, to conform for the sake of approval. Courage is doing what one believes, not out of defiance, stubbornness, or retaliation, but out of an inner conviction that emanates from the innermost self. While anxiety is usually caused by not knowing what to do, not knowing what to do is often preceded by not knowing what to believe. The self is the source of our beliefs, our convictions, our commitments. Rather than being the composite of roles that one might be assigned to play in life, the self is the source of one's capacity to be aware that one is indeed playing roles at all.

Rather than relationships determining the nature of the self, it can be the self that chooses its relationships. The premise for choosing and developing relationships that matter is a commitment to values—to ideas and to experiences that are considered to be valuable and significant. What an individual deems valuable indicates what kind of person he or she is. Authentic existence means living a life, making choices, forming relationships consistent with those values. Such relationships, rather than defining an ephemeral self in flux, fulfill a self already defined. That some choices are considered more desirable than others indicates that a valuing self already exists.

That Adam could not be conscious of the self as long as he dwelled in the Garden of Eden, in the realm of innocence, was an insight not lost on the nineteenth-century German philosopher G. W. F. Hegel. Hegel rejected earlier notions of a static self, but he did not relegate the self to the virtual oblivion of dancing images. According to Hegel, once human beings left the state of innocence they entered history, becoming conscious both of the self and of the flux of historical experience. For Hegel, a person has two choices: to lead a life of leaden, lifeless calm or to move through the flux of life with the hope of reaching a transcendent state. The first choice is virtual death. The second choice is fulfilled living. Life, for Hegel, is characterized by alienation and homelessness. Through self-knowledge, self-consciousness, and self-development, one can find a home for the homesick soul. Spiritual homelessness can be addressed by finding a welcoming place for the soul in that which transcends the self. But first the self must be located, recognized, and developed. For Hegel, the soul is simultaneously essential and dynamic, stable yet capable of growth and change.

Hegel and his successors, such as Marx, stressed the role that alienation plays in modern life. That one is alienated from oneself presumes that there is an authentic self lurking somewhere ready to be found. Alienated living means living without authenticity, being somehow exiled from who one really is. The alienated person is the one who lives a life other than his own, who lives at a spiritual address other than his own. The task is to locate the self, to end the game of hide-and-seek, and to become engaged in the authentic adventure of living—the creation of one's own life as a work of art. A person must reach a point where she says to herself, "Come out, come out, whoever you are." Looking back at her life at the age of 57, Eleanor Roosevelt wrote:

> Somewhere along the line of development we discover what we really are, and then we make our real decision for which we are responsible. Make that decision primarily for yourself because you can never really live anyone else's life, not even your own child's. The influence you exert is through your life and what you become yourself.[20]

As the nineteenth-century British poet Matthew Arnold wrote:

> *O air-borne voice! long since, severely clear,*
> *A cry like thine in my own heart I hear:*
> *"Resolve to be thyself; and know that he,*
> *Who finds himself, loses his misery!"*[21]

Finding the self is a crucial component in crafting the soul, in forging a life of meaning and purpose, in creating life as a work of art. Art endeavors to articulate uniqueness. Artistic creation attempts to bring something unique into existence, or to show us a way of perceiving something already known in a new way. In contrast, science focuses upon universal natural laws rather than upon unique, unprecedented events. The great physicist Heisenberg said, "If I did not discover the Indeterminacy Principle in physics, someone else would have. But, if Beethoven had not written his ninth symphony, no one else could have." Similarly, no amount of the scientific examination of brainwaves can produce a line of poetry.

Science tends to posit "laws of nature," to construct general rubrics into which individual entities can be classified and assigned. Individual entities and events are subsumed by constructed models and categories. From this perspective, it is easy to understand a human being.

Biologically a human person is easy to classify and define. We may readily be able to define the human species in its relationship to the animal world, and we may facilely identify an individual human being as a member of the human species. Yet, such types of definition and classification pall into irrelevancy in an individual's effort at finding and understanding his or her own unique and distinctive self.

As a biological specimen, each individual is a natural being determined by natural laws, but as a human person each individual is unique. From the perspective of the biologist, each human demonstrates the validity of biological laws and facts that relate to the entire human species. From the spiritual perspective, each person is a novelty; each human life is unprecedented, irreplaceable, unique.

The Talmudic rabbis asked why God began the creation of human beings with only one human being—Adam. Surely it would have been more efficient to populate the world by creating a million human beings. But, according to the Talmud, God began with one human being to demonstrate that each person, like "Adam" (whose name means "human being" in Hebrew), is unprecedented, irreplaceable, unique. "A king can make a seal and can stamp many identical coins with this seal. But, God made a stamp based upon Adam, yet each person made with this stamp is uniquely different."[22]

Each person has a body that conducts its activities according to certain known physiological laws and processes. But each human being also has a face, and each face is unique. The face is a window to the soul, to the self. The face reminds us that each human self is the incarnation of uniqueness. Each person has the choice of spiritual development or spiritual suicide, of obfuscating or of manifesting the uniqueness of the self. Definitions of the human being are easy to adduce, yet no human being exists in a definitive edition. Human existence can be reduced to mere vegetation, or it can be elevated to a creative drama. As Hebbel put it, "Life is not anything; it is only the opportunity for something."[23]

What is human about a human being? Little, from the perspective of science: we are easy to classify within the animal kingdom. Our DNA does not vary that substantially from that of our nearest relative, the chimpanzee. As a species we are easy to classify into a variety of biological and sociological categories. Yet, from another perspective, each of us is irreplaceable, none of us can be duplicated. Each of us has a face, a voice, memories, aspirations, and potentialities that belong to us alone. What is human about a human being is his or her uniqueness. The challenge to each human person, to each human life, is to express this uniqueness, to develop the particular potentialities that make each person who he or she is and who he or she may yet become.

There are two dimensions to human existence. On one level each of us is a sample, an example of the species of Homo sapiens. However, on another level each of us is an unfinished work of art, pregnant with possibilities, a seed encapsulating a plethora of potentialities waiting to be born. Each human being's mission during life is to express his or her potentialities for being human, to articulate his or her uniqueness, and to demonstrate the quiet eminence of his or her being by creating his or her life as a work of art.

A friend of mine once was startled after a visit to an art museum. "What surprised you?," I asked. "Of all the paintings I saw," he said, "no two were alike. Each was different." Unlike science, which deals with universal natural laws and general categories, art deals with the unique. The scientist strives to understand what *is* while the artist attempts to create something different, something unique. The challenge confronting each person is whether he will allow his life to become like a photocopy of others, or become a unique work of art.

Each human life hovers between two possibilities: biological classification and artistic creativity. We have the choice of being born as originals and to die as copies, or to be born as unfinished originals and to further develop that originality into a uniquely fashioned work of art. What makes us particularly human is our ability to create each of our lives as a work of art by developing the potentialities that make each of us distinct and unique. Each of us is an artist, commissioned to create one great work of art during our own lifetime—and that work of art is our own life.

How we live *as* human beings is inextricably connected to how we develop spiritually. No one would confuse a human being with an ant or a lizard. Our ability to develop our spiritual capacities, to locate and to enact a nexus of meaning in life, are indicative ways in which we differ from insects and reptiles. In responding to the question: Why craft the soul, why create life as a work of art?, we can pose another question to ourselves: How do we differ from an ant or from an aardvark? That we have the capacity for spiritual development is part of the answer. When we act like an ant, we, in effect, surrender a key quality of what being human means.

The eighteenth-century German philosopher Johann Herder taught that each person has an original and unique manner of being human. The task is to develop it. According to Nietzsche, a person is known by his "style," that is, by the unique pattern that gives unity and distinctiveness to a person's activities. Style articulates the uniqueness of the self. Rather than fitting one's life into the demands of external conformity, rather than living one's life as an imitation of the life of another, one should look to find the authentic self within. One should labor to develop one's own unique style in crafting one's soul. An individual who denies her own individuality articulates life with a voice other than that which is uniquely her own. A person who suppresses his own self is in danger of missing the point of his own existence, of surrendering what being human means.

In the discovery and the development of the self, each person must discover her best entrée to unique selfhood. In absolute terms, one may not be able to be the best person possible. However, in personal terms, one can become the best he or she can become. Becoming "best" relates more to the nature of the individual self than to the nature of bestness. As the British philosopher John Stuart Mill put it, "If a person possesses any tolerable amount of common sense and experience, his own mode of laying out his existence is best, not because it is best in itself, but because it is his own mode."[24] As Nietzsche said, "There is my way. What's your way? There is no *the* way."

The following chapter confronts a vision of the individual self offered by the popular and pervasive view that we are too sick and helpless to attend to the creation of life as a work of art, to developing ourselves spiritually. The doctrines of our therapeutic society stifle our attempts to craft the soul by focusing on the victimization of our body and spirit by forces all around us. Before embarking on the pilgrimage toward meaning, toward self-discovery, and toward spiritual development, we must first cure ourselves of the therapeutic society's attempts to heal us. We must uncover an alternative approach to health and healing more conducive to the creation of life as a work of art than that offered by the society of which we are a part.

chapter five

Are You Sick?

There is a story about three patients in a hospital room. One is an atheist. One is a Catholic. One is a Jew.

The doctor enters the room and tells the men: "Gentlemen, I am afraid I have bad news for all of you. We have completed all of our tests and we've found that each of you is beyond medical help, and that you don't have much time left. Is there anything I can do for you?"

The atheist replies: "Doctor, please call my family, and ask them to come say good-bye to me."

The Catholic replies: "Doctor, please call my priest so that I can have last rites."

And the Jew replies: "Doctor, please don't be insulted. But I would like a second opinion."

*N*o one can deny the startling advances of modern medicine. With the introduction of generation after generation of "wonder drugs," many age-old scourges have been prevented, eliminated, or controlled. Intricate surgical procedures are responsible for many people, who otherwise would have died, being alive today. Computerized technology is now able to locate the presence of disease that previously would have evaded even the most careful diagnostician. Parts of certain organs or even entire organs can be replaced with synthetic or transplanted alternatives. Women who once had little or no chance of becoming mothers can now have children, at almost any age.

It would seem that contemporary medicine is the epitome of an American success story, the quintessence of a modern miracle. Then why is the American health-care industry in crisis? Why is the delivery of health care a primary issue of national concern? Recent American and British studies show that as many as 80 percent of patients feel that their underlying complaint, their reason for going to the doctor, has not been satisfactorily resolved after having been there.[1] Why the pervasive dissatisfaction with health care when health care now accounts for nearly one-sixth of our GNP? In 1990, health-care costs were $666.2 billion, or about 12.1 percent of the GNP; $903.4 billion or about 14.4 percent of the GNP in 1993; and $1.069 trillion, or 15.4 percent of the GNP in 1995.

Physicians often blame lawyers for the current impasse. Patients tend to blame physicians and hospitals. Hospital administrators often pin responsibility on the insurance industry. And, if one cannot decide whom to blame, then there is always the government. Many readily assume that the culprits must be those who profit the most financially. However, I would like to offer my own "second opinion," that is, that the ultimate culprits are not necessarily the people involved in health care, but that the truly culpable are the assumptions, the ideas, upon which American health care rests.

The real problem is not how health care is practiced, but how it is conceptualized. The practice of health care consists of the application of certain ideas and concepts. The crux of the matter is not as much a scarcity of resources as it is an addiction to a particular way of thinking. What is required is the reconceptualization of health care as the necessary prelude to a restructuring of the delivery of health care.

As often is the case, our assumptions act as roadblocks to addressing our critical problems. The therapeutic society hampers our spiritual quest as it impedes our attainment of health. To see how and why this is so, it is necessary to examine two issues. The first is our understanding of the nature of health. The second relates to the impact of the doctrines of our therapeutic society upon crafting the soul. The following discussion of these two issues will lead to the inescapable conclusion that the self the therapeutic society tells us we are is neither who we are, nor is it who we want to become.

Three perspectives on the nature of health underlie much of the delivery of health care in America. All three are put forth as representations of objective scientific truth; yet, while they may be grounded in science, they have been shaped by peculiarly modern cultural predispositions. These three assumptions drive our therapeutic society; they pervade the operation of our American medical-industrial complex. The first flows from the seventeenth-century affirmation of scientific materialism that denies the spiritual dimension, considering it an unnecessary encumbrance. This perspective reduces everything to its physical dimension, ignoring other features, particularly spiritual ones. The second perspective, which flows from the first, conceives of the human being as a machine in need of repair. It understands the human machine as a system embracing subsystems, vulnerable like all machines to system breakdown and dysfunction. Health, in this view, means the restoration and the repair of the broken system, where and when possible.

The third perspective is grounded in a biological model rather than in a technological model. The human being is viewed as an organism that, like all organisms, is a product of its environment. In this view, health is largely defined within an environmental context. Health is threatened by environmental factors, whether they be physical, such as a bacterium that victimizes a person's body, or psychological, such as a bad experience that victimizes a person's psyche. In either case, the patient is considered a victim of a force beyond his or her control. While a crucial component of modern medical practice, this third approach is even more pervasive in the sector of the therapeutic society that concerns itself with mental health. These three perspectives inform the dominant theory of health that drives the practice of American medicine, a theory that has been called the biomedical model.

The biomedical model that compares the human being to a machine considers disease to be a system malfunction that may be corrected or ameliorated with proper diagnosis and reparative techniques. Such techniques often consist of surgical repair aimed at restoring system function and/or the intervention of a chemical or biological agent suited to the restoration of biological function. In this view, health is the absence of disease. Disease is often considered as a deviation from established and measurable values and norms. Spiritual dimensions of the life of the patient are usually disregarded. The psychological is often reduced to the physical and is treated as a biochemical or neurophysiological issue. Health professionals are active while the patient remains largely passive. Simply put, disease is understood as a breakdown of the human machine, and the health professional's task is its repair. Conceptually and procedurally, this model for health care is similar to various models for the repair and maintenance of a machine.

The biomedical model that has dominated much of American medical practice is problematic for a number of reasons. First, it commits what in logic is called the "reductionist fallacy." It reduces a complex entity—the human being—into a simple and one-dimensional being, that is, into a purely physical being, into a being that can be understood and medically treated exclusively in biological and chemical terms. Second, as psychiatrist George L. Engel has pointed out, the biomedical model has "become our own culturally specific perspective about disease, our folk model. Indeed, the biomedical model is now the dominant folk model of disease in the Western world."[2] According to Engel, the biomedical model, like any model, is ultimately a "belief system utilized to explain natural phenomenon, to make sense of what is puzzling or disturbing."[3] As such, it cannot claim to represent objective, scientific truth; rather, it reflects the presuppositions of our culture. While its application to the medical treatment of human beings may prove effective, it nonetheless remains problematic because it fails fully to grasp the nature of the person treated. It embraces too narrow a perspective of health and disease. It is reductionist and exclusionistic.

It reduces the complex nature of the human being to its physical characteristics. It treats the disease rather than the person who is suffering from the disease. While perhaps necessary, it is far from sufficient.

Eric Cassell, a professor of physiology at Cornell University, points out that medical diagnosis is played like a matching game in that an attempt is made to match known, classified diseases with the symptoms of the patient under examination. A problem Cassell identifies with this approach is that the goal of this process is to match symptoms with diseases. Therefore, when the physician asks the patient questions and examines the patient, the goal is not to find out what is wrong with the patient. The goal is to make a match. The patient may be afflicted with a certain disease, but finding out which it may be may only reveal part of what is wrong with the patient.[4]

The approach of scientific materialism that developed in the seventeenth century, which defined the human being as a type of machine and which spawned the biomedical model, may now be both obsolete and undesirable. An alternative model needs to be identified. But we need not forge one. Such a model is already available to us. This alternative has been called the "holistic model." Plato anticipated it. Medieval Jewish and Arab physicians and philosophers already articulated it. As Plato said, "The cure of many diseases is unknown to physicians . . . because they are ignorant of the whole, for the part can never be well unless the whole is well." And, as Plato also wrote, "If the head and the body are to be well, you must begin by curing the soul; that is the first thing."[5]

The holistic model rejects the mind-body, soul-body dualism that Descartes posited at the dawn of modern philosophy and science. The holistic model perceives the human being as a psychosomatic unity, rather than as a machine or as a biochemical unit. This model does not commit the reductionist fallacy of the biomedical model. Rather, it understands the human being as a union of the spiritual and the physical, the physiological and the spiritual. For the holistic model, it is almost meaningless to separate the spiritual and the physical dimensions of human existence. They are interdependent, mutually inclusive. One cannot be understood without the other. Over two thousand years ago, as if in anticipation of the biomedical model, Plato already observed that "the great error of our day is the treatment of the human body alone, that physicians separate the soul from the body."[6]

The Hebrew Scriptures knew only of the person as a psychosomatic unity; soul-body dualism was not a feature of biblical thought. The Hebrew word *nefesh,* often incorrectly translated as "soul," actually meant "the person," that is, the individual as a psychosomatic composite.

The holistic model can offer us a way of self-understanding, of reconceptualizing health and disease, a way of spiritual development, and of achieving spiritual rehabilitation. The holistic approach is an old idea whose time has come again. As Kurt Lewin said, "There is nothing so practical as a good idea."

Unlike the biomedical model, a holistic approach focuses upon the person rather than only upon the disease. As the great medieval Jewish philosopher and physician Moses Maimonides put it, "The physician should not treat the disease but the patient suffering from it."[7] In this view, disease is not merely a systems malfunction but a manifestation of dis-ease, that is, not only a single organ but the entire person may be out of sync. In Hebrew, the word for physician is *rofei,* coming from a verbal root meaning "to ease." Here, care and cure are interlocked.

Similarly, the nineteenth-century Hasidic master Nahman of Bratzlav opposed treating illness on a purely physical basis. In Hasidic thought, physical illness is often considered to be the outward manifestation of an inner spiritual disturbance. To treat the body alone might remove the symptoms but not their cause. For Rabbi Nahman, treating the corporeal aspect of the patient without also attending to his or her spiritual dimension would often prove faulty. Rabbi Nahman described physicians who neglect the spiritual dimension as a modern variety of sorcerer, trying to manipulate natural forces without recourse to the spiritual.

The biomedical model often places the individual under the

controlling influence of the health professional, thereby infantilizing the patient and largely removing the patient from participating in his or her own process of healing. A holistic model perceives the healing process as one of a partnership between the health-care professional and the patient. Not only does the physician, but the patient as well becomes a health-care *provider.* The patient, in this view, becomes obliged to take responsibility for the maintenance of his or her own health.

What characterizes the model advocated here is not only its conceptual base that distinguishes it from the biomedical model, but also its moral posture. The biomedical model's preference for therapeutic invasion—either through surgery, chemical intervention, or other invasive therapies—casts the patient into a completely passive role. This has led to a pervasive mode of social dependency upon therapeutic intervention to deal with the daily problems of life. From this perspective, the patient is disenfranchised from taking any responsibility for his own life, for his habits, for his moral choices, for his personal development. The triumph of the therapeutic is in danger of breeding a passive population dependent upon health providers for the solutions to life's problems, challenges, conflicts, and anxieties. We are in danger of being held hostage by medical terrorists.

The ancient and medieval philosophers maintained that the health of the body is interdependent with the health of the soul. Physical health, in their view, was but a foundation upon which to build the moral and spiritual life. Physical health was viewed as a means to an end, not an end in itself. As the medieval Jewish philosopher and physician Ibn Falaquera put it, "What profit has one in his bodily health if the soul is ill? . . . The malady of the soul is more serious than the malady of the body."[8] A holistic approach to health considers the development of the self as a spiritual being to be a critical component in achieving health and well-being.

According to the World Health Organization's definition, "Health is a state of complete physical, mental and social well-being. . . ."[9] Among the problems with this definition, two may be mentioned. One is that it neglects the spiritual dimension. Second, it would seem to make "health" unattainable. How many people enjoy a state of *complete* physical, mental, and social well-being, and if they do, for how long? Our current medical system knows much about how to diagnose disease but little about how to diagnose health. There is a plethora of diagnostic tests for every conceivable malady, but has a test been devised to screen for health, to identify wellness? From the holistic perspective, a person may be afflicted with a disease and yet be an active participant in the development of his or her life. An individual, though afflicted with a disease, may be restricted but is not wholly disabled in the process of personal development. In this view, a malady may signify a restriction, a limitation, but not a defeat, not an excuse for relenting in the development of the self. A disease may be viewed like any other physical restriction with which a person has to contend in the quest for meaning, purpose, and accomplishing one's goals in life. Some diseases are indeed tragedies, but some may be opportunities to enable and encourage an individual to seek and to find a richer experience in life.

In his book *How to Live Between Office Visits,* Dr. Bernie Siegel tells of an episode on *The Untouchables.* Eliot Ness captures a paraplegic gangster who is sitting in a wheelchair. Ness asks him why he became a criminal, and the gangster says, "I'm handicapped, what kind of job could I get? I had to become a gangster." Ness pulls from his pocket a newspaper announcing Roosevelt's election as president. There is a picture of Roosevelt in a wheelchair. He shows this to the criminal and says, "Well, for one thing, you could have run for the presidency."[10] Stephen Hawking remains immobilized by Lou Gehrig's disease, but is yet able to formulate theories of how everything may have come into being.

The holistic approach poses a direct challenge to the therapeutic mentality that pervades our culture. The triumph of the therapeutic has led to three results that have had a negative impact upon the individual in search of meaning and purpose. The first is the notion that just about everybody is afflicted with an illness or syndrome. Put another way—most of us are sick! The second is that, because most of us are victims of some illness or syndrome, we have become disabled from becoming fully responsible for taking charge of our lives. The third is that we must therefore become dependent upon professional help, rather than upon becoming self-reliant. Ironically, in a culture that has prided itself on its rugged individualism, the prerogatives of the individual have been neutered by making people dependent upon professional help, by defining different types of harmless behavior as one of a wide variety of syndromes, by considering virtually everyone as a victim of some malady, and by considering people incompetent in the performance of virtually every natural function, from eating to parenting, from sexuality to walking.

In his 1978 book *The Psychological Society,* Martin Gross observed that modern America and the Western world in general had taken on "the tone of a giant psychiatric clinic . . . [psychotherapy's] pervasiveness in the fabric of our culture has become near total as it absorbs new disciplines each year."[11] Already in the 1970s, Americans had more professional therapists than librarians, fire fighters, or mail carriers, and twice as many therapists as dentists or pharmacists.

If everyone is a victim, then no one is a victim. If everyone is sick, a victim of some "syndrome," then who is responsible, who is accountable for what they do, for who they are? Some examples:

- A man with an affinity for gambling with other people's money is fired from his job, but is reinstated after a court rules that his compulsive gambling is a "handicap" and thus protected by federal law.[12]
- Fired for consistently showing up late at work, an employee gains reinstatement when he is found to be suffering from "chronic lateness syndrome."[13]
- A woman too obese to sit behind the steering wheel of a car appears on the "Oprah Winfrey Show" to claim that she is a victim of "size discrimination."[14]
- A feminist writer compares the life of a suburban housewife to being a victim of the Holocaust.[15]

- A sociologist calculates that the number of Americans who consider themselves members of oppressed minority groups adds up to 374 percent of the U.S. population.[16]
- Pop psychologist John Bradshaw has claimed that as many as 96 percent of American families are "dysfunctional."[17]
- In the best-selling *The Road Less Traveled,* Dr. M. Scott Peck tells us that "most of us are mentally ill to a greater or lesser degree."[18]

The authoritative *Diagnostic and Statistical Manual of Mental Disorders, Third Edition, Revised,* published by the American Psychiatric Association, discusses the following "disorders": "Self-Defeating Personality Disorder," "Identity Disorder" (epitomized by the person asking: Who am I?), "Narcissistic Personality Disorder," and the ("apparently common") "Adjustment Disorders." It should therefore be no surprise to find the following exchange in a Pennsylvania court record:

Q: Doctor, it's true, is it not, that people with what you have termed a personality disorder exist around us every day in all walks of life; isn't that correct?

A: I'm not sure any of us are spared that diagnosis.[19]

As Sam Keen observes:

The rush to claim victimhood is becoming an epidemic. Criminal behavior is forgiven because experts explain that deviant behavior is caused by hidden social and psychological forces. We are victims of family, gender, class, economics, or hormones. PMS, post-traumatic stress syndrome, or hypoglycemia induced by eating too many Twinkies becomes the cause and excuse for murder. Anything that can be named a syndrome creates a new class of victims.[20]

Considering the pervasiveness of the therapeutic approach and the preferential legal treatment afforded those with illnesses and handicaps, it is no wonder that many want to join these ranks. Once handicaps were considered liabilities; now they suddenly have become desirable. But what is the result: a sick society, a society of infantilized, incompetent, dependent individuals, helpless and not responsible for their actions. There is no longer good and bad behavior, only healthy and unhealthy behavior. In his novel *Satan,* Jeremy Leven has the Devil say, "Modern psychiatry is putting me out of business."[21]

We are rapidly becoming a "no-fault" society. The therapeutic society has replaced moral standards with clinical ones; it has exchanged "being good" with "feeling good." Ethics has been reduced to a matter of personal preference, to doing what makes a person feel good about oneself. This has led to what philosopher Alasdair MacIntyre has called "emotivism," that is, the choice of behavior based upon how it makes a person feel.[22] What MacIntyre contends from a philosophical point of view is stated from a sociological point of view by Robert Bellah.

In his stunning description and analysis of contemporary American life, *Habits of the Heart,* Bellah contends that the relationship of therapist to client has become a model for all relationships. According to Bellah, the therapeutic relationship has permeated both the boardroom and the bedroom. The goal of such a relationship is to empower the individual to be successful. A crucial component in such a relationship is self-acceptance, feeling good about oneself. Paradoxically, such a relationship deals with our most intimate and significant experiences within a framework of contractual relations, businesslike tradeoffs, and procedural cooperation. Relationships only endure as long as personal needs are met, as long as the relational contract is fulfilled. From this cost-benefit analysis approach, there can only be contracts between consenting adults. Real relationships and moral obligations become problematic as they are perceived as thwarting the needs of the participants. Needs replace commitment. The workings of the world are evaluated by whether "this is going to work for me now."[23] As it has been shaped for application in the workplace, this approach ironically strips one's vocation of any intrinsic meaning. Healing the sick, defending the accused, serving the person in need, creating the quality product, surrender their intrinsic meaning to the quest for "feeling good" about one's work. In personal life, relationships and friendships lose intrinsic meaning and become relegated to support groups. As Gail Sheehy writes in her study of *Pathfinders*, at support groups "people generally assemble to express a common frustration, not to transcend it. . . . If the support system becomes a permanent crutch, the person being supported probably has become a cripple."[24]

The manner in which people relate to the wide variety of illnesses, syndromes, and disorders that recently have come to the fore in our therapeutic society bears a remarkable similarity to the way in which many of the medievals spoke about the effects of demons, devils, and evil spirits. In both schemes, individuals are victims of forces over which they have no control. Individuals claim not to be responsible for their deeds on the grounds that they are not fully in control of their actions. Individuals claim that they require some kind of magical intervention by a skilled healer to dispel their malady. Both demons and syndromes prevent people from developing the spiritual dimension of their lives; both are used as an excuse for not developing one's life as an art form.

Demons are believed to be invisible, malevolent forces that surround us and that are poised to injure or to destroy us. Efforts invested in combating them often cause us to be motivated by what we fear rather than by what we find meaningful, valuable, and enjoyable. While it would be naive not to be aware of potential and actual dangers, it may also be counterproductive to fixate upon constructing one's life as a defensive war against possibly harmful elements, a war that we ultimately cannot win. The fear of our health being compromised by external factors inevitably leads to a siege mentality, where opportunities for spiritual self-development and self-expression can become stifled by the paranoia of self-protection. One must, therefore, learn to discern between security and paranoia, between safety and imprisonment. Some become like the person who thinks that if he freezes his entire

mouth with Novocain, he will avoid the possibility of hot food burn-
ing his mouth. But all that is truly avoided are the normal pleasures
that life holds forth.

Like the belief that demons populate our world poised to strike, the
therapeutic mentality encourages us to spend every moment combating a host of forces that are out there to get us at every turn. For example, a number of years ago it was discovered that oats are an effective magical potion against the ever-threatening "demon" of cholesterol. Suddenly the food for horses became the most popular food for
people in America. But subsequent studies have demonstrated that,
with the exception of certain individuals who regularly have high cholesterol levels, oats do not really make a hill of tofu of a difference in
the cholesterol levels of most people. Consider a second example. A
television commercial shows an idyllic scene of children playing in a
meadow. The sun is shining, the grass glitters, the trees sway in a gentle
breeze. Suddenly comes the voice-over: "Somewhere out there, lurking in the grass, is something that can kill." This is not a promo for a
Stephen King movie, but an advertisement for an anti-tick spray. It is
as if every legitimate pleasure is under attack by those ready to warn us
of some form of demonic force waiting to get its malevolent hands on
us. Usually those who warn us of these dangers stand ready to sell us a
product or a service that can help us overcome the apparently immi-
nent peril to our health and well-being.

No wonder increasing numbers of people suffer from anxiety, stress,
phobias, and depressions. If most people believe what they are being
told—that they are sick and dysfunctional, that they are unwilling
victims not only of viruses and bacteria but also of disorders, syndromes, and environmental factors—it is enough to make anyone anxious, fearful, and depressed. And we know for sure that depression is
not good for our health. Among its other results, depression weakens
the immune system.

The modern preoccupation with the body often to the exclusion of
the soul, the concentration upon physical needs often to the exclusion
of spiritual needs, might have been expected to lead to an affirmation

of the carnal and to an anti-ascetic posture. But the opposite is often the case. The preoccupation with the body and with its health as an end in itself has led to an essentially anti-body view, and to a modern form of asceticism. Let's consider some examples.

We are constantly warned about the dangers to one's health of touching someone, because all kinds of diseases are transmitted that way. The only one who urges us to "reach out and touch someone" urges us to do it by bouncing our voice off a satellite way up in space. Yet people need to touch and to be touched, hugged, and caressed. For instance, studies of patients recuperating from surgery in hospitals show that the assuring touch of a physician's hand helps to accelerate recovery and lowers the incidence of postoperative bleeding. Newborn babies in neonatal care units, whose survival is fragile, have a better chance at survival if they are touched, held, and caressed than are those who only receive indicated medical treatment.[25] In the 1920s, the respected psychologist James Watson told parents never to hug or kiss their children, thereby making children untouchables.[26] But a touch often can say more than words can. Being "out of touch" is the first sign of a breakdown in a relationship. There are many studies on physical abuse, but few on the healing application of a caring touch. Studies show that playing with one's children, that making love with someone you love, is better for you both physiologically and psychologically than exercising. One of the reasons things do not make sense is because we are out of touch with our senses. We tend to live life as if it were an out-of-body experience.

Once I arrived at an airport in upstate New York to deliver a lecture. A very charming and attractive woman was there to greet me and to drive me to the lecture hall, some thirty miles from the airport. On the way she told me that she had recently been divorced and that her family was in ruins. Tears streamed down her cheeks as we drove down the New York state thruway. I asked her what caused all of this, and she answered with one word—jogging.

Her husband, convinced that jogging would keep him healthy and young, became obsessed. He would fly all over the country to run in

every marathon. He was literally running away from his family. Whether
he saved his life, his youth, and his health, I do not know. What is sure
is that he lost his family. The divorce was a tempestuous one. It seemed
never to have occurred to him that the stress of a divorce, studies esti-
mate, has the same negative impact on a healthy heart as smoking
more than a pack of cigarettes a day.[27]

Ours has become a pathological society, where people define themselves by the diseases, syndromes, and dysfunctions that afflict them.
People not only have diseases, but tend to make that fact an integral
feature of their personal identities. The disease has the person as much
as the person has the disease. This pathological approach to health and
to identity tends to carry over into how we see the world. What's bad
in society, what tragedies that occur daily, the social and economic
problems afflicting our society is what we usually hear about. The social focus is on disease, pathology, dysfunction—not upon health,
meaning, or creativity.

For example, the unemployment rate is often reported, but how
often do we hear about the employment rate? Obituaries always take
up more space in the newspaper than birth or wedding announce-
ments. If the stock market falls analysts worry that a downward trend
may be developing; if it goes up they worry it might soon need self-
correction. Often when a childless woman over thirty-five becomes
pregnant she wants to celebrate; instead hers is immediately defined as
a "high-risk pregnancy." An air crash merits immediate national news
coverage, but the more than five thousand daily flights in the United
States that take off and land without mishap are barely noticed. The
entire nation can be sunny and warm, but we only hear about the
solitary devastating storm hundreds of miles away.

Some years ago a newspaper was started that only printed good
news. In our pathological society, it was not surprising that it was very
short-lived.

The Duchess of Windsor was wrong when she said, "No one can be
too rich or too thin." The American obsession with dieting is viewed
by many Europeans, including European physicians, as more of a prod-

uct of Hollywood than of medicine, of cosmetics rather than of health. Millions of Americans go on diets each year that, in the long run, do not work. Millions of Americans on diets are literally starving themselves, and are afflicting themselves with malnutrition. Millions of people on diets are not even obese. They are giving up healthy pleasures in the name of health. They are causing physiological damage by yo-yo dieting where weight continues to fluctuate way up and way down. The Duchess of Windsor was wrong. One *can* be too thin—it's called anorexia.

There is little truth in advertising when it comes to dieting. The industry is too big, too powerful. Television commercials show people who have lost more weight than the average person weighs, and then tell us to use the same potions and methods they did to reach our own desired weight. What we are not told is that almost all people who have gone on one form of extreme diet plan or another have gained all of their lost weight back—half of the people within a year; over 85 percent within five years.

The disquieting claim made by one diet program—"Obesity is a death sentence"—does not tell the whole story. Indeed, certain kinds of dieting, especially the ups and downs of yo-yo dieting, may be more of a death sentence than moderate obesity. An extensive long-term study of 11,000 male Harvard alumni showed that being moderately overweight is not correlated with a shorter life span, that the common conception that being obese to any degree is a death sentence, is simply false. Indeed, extensive actuarial studies found the lowest mortality among those who are 10 percent overweight and the highest mortality among the chronically underweight. In the past few decades, Americans have been getting fatter, yet life expectancy has continued to increase.

Besides the direct negative physiological effects of certain kinds of dieting, there are also the direct negative psychological effects that have an indirect negative physiological impact. In the long run, diets are almost always doomed to fail. Failure and its attendant feelings of guilt, a negative self-image, depression, helplessness, and hopelessness are worse for our health in the long run than carrying around a few extra pounds. For a person who has been successful in many endeavors to be constantly defeated by some cookies and cake can be a source of dismay and discouragement. It very well may be that cultural prejudices against the overweight may lead to the individual's developing poor self-esteem, which has more of a damaging effect upon one's health than the extra few pounds he or she is carrying around.

Like so many of our attitudes, our attitude toward our physical appearance, particularly toward weight, are culturally determined. As is often the case, culture dictates to science. Science "proves" what our culture wants us to believe. For example, not so long ago both European and American culture perceived obesity as a sign of health and prosperity. Poor, sick children were portrayed in novels as being scrawny, thin, and presumably tubercular. In the novels of Sinclair Lewis, for example, the rich, the powerful, the healthy are heavy, robust, obese. In those times, bankers were never portrayed as being thin. In those days, the slim, wily person represented the epitome of deception—calculating, maneuvering, exploitative. The heavy person was considered stable, happy, and trustworthy. Would you trust your money to a banker who looks like he's starving? In Buddhism, Buddha is the epitome of enlightenment, but have you ever seen a skinny Buddha? Have you ever seen a skinny Santa Claus?

Contemporary American culture has made slimness into a desired state, into an enviable virtue. Heavy people are portrayed as being lazy, devoid of initiative, sloppy, unhealthy, weak-willed, inefficient, and slow—physically and intellectually. Despite a mountain of laws and regulations protecting people from discrimination based upon race, sex, religion, and ethnic identification, there is little protection against discrimination for people with wide girths. People in our society have been culturally conditioned to disparage the portly. Indeed, the overweight have been culturally conditioned to think that the more they are, the less they are. Since a significant feature of personal identity is sexual identity, our cultural proclivity to equate thinness with sexual appeal inevitably leads to a diminished self-image and personal identity among those who are not thin. The equation of thinness with being sexy has disenfranchised many robust men and voluptuous women from the category of being sexy.

Societal pressures stimulate overweight people to disparage their own physical appearance, to suffer from low esteem where their own bodies are concerned. Such individuals tend to think about how much they weigh, and how much they have been eating, many times each day. They tend to think of these things more than about whether their lives have meaning and purpose.

The "ideal weight" charts that measure whether or not a person is overweight imposes a criterion upon each of us that fails to take many factors into account. For example, genetics seem to be a significant factor in bodily weight. Therefore, what is normal or ideal for the average person might be irrelevant to the actual person. Furthermore, while much attention has been paid to the presumed health risks of being overweight, little attention has been paid to the fact that, while being moderately overweight has not been proven to be a critical early mortality risk factor, being significantly underweight undoubtedly is a major risk factor.

A small but gradual increase in weight seems to be a natural phenomenon of middle-age. For example, the previously mentioned study of Harvard alumni revealed that men who gained about fifteen pounds since graduation were at one-third less risk of death than those in all other categories, including those who either lost or maintained weight since their graduation.[28] A second study showed that those who practiced yo-yo dieting over many years had double the risk of heart disease than those who experienced progressive moderate weight gain over a twenty-five year period. The real issue with regard to diet is not so much how much we eat, but how and what we eat. Already in ancient and medieval times, physicians prescribed diets low in fat and high in complex carbohydrates.[29]

Our cultural obsession with health has created a comparatively new, highly popular, and highly populated American institution—the health club. Working out after, before, and even during work has become, for many, a virtual addiction. People endure physical pain and suffering, jog hundreds of miles that lead nowhere, in the quest for health, weight loss, and thinness. Young singles invest countless hours and dollars to display the results of their physical exertions in the hope of landing a spouse. But what are the results of all this, when we think about it further?

Consider the feelings of failure, guilt, and helplessness of those who do not reach the physical state to which so many aspire as they tread, step, pull, push, and run their way toward often unattainable physiological goals. While the health-instilling value of regular moderate exercise, such as walking thirty minutes each day, cannot be denied, the benefits of stressful exercise, even on a regular basis, remains problematic. It has been calculated that the amount of time spent in daily strenuous exercise, such as jogging or working out, may be equal to or greater than any increase in longevity thereby achieved. If a person began running daily at age thirty, the hours spent on exercising until age seventy-five would add up to between one and two years. Such a person could expect to have lengthened his or her life thereby by between one or two years. The net dividend in life expectancy is zero or less. A distinction must be made between exercising for health and exercising for fitness. Exercising for health can be easily attained by regular, moderate activity—the equivalent of walking thirty minutes a day. Studies show that people who walk thirty minutes a day, six days a week, enjoy a mortality rate almost as low as those who run thirty to forty miles a week.[30]

With regard to diet and exercise, as with so many other things, the therapeutic society casts us as victims of a plethora of hostile forces over which we cannot reasonably expect to prevail, and against which we require professional help to win even minor skirmishes. This tends to lead to feelings of helplessness and hopelessness—feelings that all agree are blatantly dangerous to our health and well-being. This, then, is the irony of the therapeutic culture. By infantilizing us into passivity, failure, victimization, hopelessness, and helplessness, we end up appreciably less healthy rather than more healthy, as a result of the ideology and the ministrations of a therapeutic society that aims at our recovery from disorders and disease and at our achievement of health and well-being. As we have seen, the standard of health utilized in our society is problematic. The definition of health that drives the American health-care industry is specious. Why should we continue to rely upon an approach to health that is not only insufficient, but that actually seems to be harming our well-being? Why kill yourself to save your life?

While the health benefits of some features of the new asceticism may be questionable, two claims are beyond dispute. The first is that feelings of helplessness and hopelessness are bad for our health. The second is that having a sense of meaning and purpose is good for our health. Both the therapeutic society and the biomedical model of health care neglect a critical element in the quest for health and well-being; namely, the nature of the human being as a spiritual as well as a physical being. Health must therefore relate to both dimensions of human life. Health must be holistic, addressing the spiritual as well as the physical, the soul as well as the body. Indeed, the etymological origin of the word *health* comes from the Old English word *hal* and from the Old High German word *heil,* meaning "whole." In Hebrew, the word for health is *beriut,* which comes from a verbal root meaning "to create." Thus, health is not a static state but a dynamic one; it is continuous regeneration, re-creation.

The philosopher Descartes believed that the pineal gland was the missing link between the body and the soul. However, recent cutting-edge medical research has identified our thoughts and emotions as the nexus. A thought or an emotion is translated into a chemical message, which in turn stimulates a distinct organ. Descartes had the right question, but had provided the wrong answer. Our deepest thoughts and emotions—the expressions of our core inner spiritual life—are at the crossroads between the body and the soul. Peptides are the messengers that carry the information from state to state. They make possible the move from thought or feeling to messages transmitted by the brain, to hormonal secretions, on down to cellular action in the body, and then back again to the brain in a never-ending feedback loop. Peptides are found throughout the body, and are highly concentrated in some places, as for example, in the guts. Having a "gut reaction" is more than a figure of speech. According to neuroscientist Dr. Candace Pert, "Intelligence is in every cell of your body." Pert writes that, based upon her research, "I can no longer make a strong distinction between the brain and the body. . . . Indeed, the more we know about neuropeptides, the harder it is to think in the traditional terms of a mind and a body. It makes more and more sense to speak of a single, integrated entity, a 'bodymind.'"[31] Not the pineal gland but the limbic/hypothalamic area of the brain seems to serve as the center of the feedback loop between the source of our emotions and thoughts and the actions of our organs and limbs. It is in this region of the brain where things cross over due to the action of peptides. As Norman Cousins wrote: "Belief creates biology."[32]

For generations theologians have refused to accept the reduction of the human being to a physiological machine, as the natural sciences—especially, medical science—have wanted to do. A number of modern theologians have maintained that, while the mind or the brain is not the soul, it may be influenced by the soul. The recent discoveries of medical science reported by Pert, Bernie Siegel, Deepak Chopra, and others can provide a basis for a revisioning of the soul. If our thoughts and emotions derive from our spiritual dimension, from our innermost self, from our soul, then it may well be our soul that impacts upon the bodymind through the brain. In this view, the brain may not be the address of the soul, but it may be the juncture where the soul and the bodymind meet in an ongoing dialogue.

Understanding the body (or bodymind) and soul as allies leads to a different basis for thought and moral virtue than does the view that sees them as enemies. In the ascetic view, it is necessary to weaken the body in order to strengthen the soul, to neglect the body in order to enhance the soul. In the holistic view, what happens to the soul happens to the body, and vice versa. Cultivation of the spiritual positively affects bodily health. Care of the body enhances spiritual well-being.

Diseases of the soul, such as gluttony and pride, can plague the body. Diseases of the body can afflict the soul.

The bodymind and the soul relate to one another through an ongoing feedback loop. For example, we know that feelings of meaninglessness, hopelessness, and helplessness are corrosive both to the body and to the soul. It is well documented that such feelings weaken the immune system and invite the onset of a variety of diseases.[33] We also know that these feelings sabotage spiritual development, the creation of life as a work of art. These feelings can emerge from the innermost self, from the soul. On the other hand, they may be stimulated as a reaction to awareness of a physical illness and/or they may stimulate or exacerbate an already present physical malady. We also know that feelings of purpose, hope, love, and autonomy are key ingredients in spiritual development. It is also well documented that these feelings are good for our physical well-being and that they are demonstrably helpful attitudes for people afflicted with a variety of diseases.[34] The body is the best pharmacy, and the emotions generated by the soul can stimulate the production of health-inducing or health-restoring chemicals.

Recent studies reconfirm what ancient and medieval physicians, philosophers, and spiritual masters already knew. First, that the person is a composite of body and soul, body and mind, and that what affects the spiritual and intellectual affects the physical dimension, and vice versa. Second, that meaning and purpose are vital for health and well-being. As Deepak Chopra writes:

Healing cannot be understood unless the person's beliefs, assumptions, expectations and self-image are also understood. Although the image of the body as a mindless machine continues to dominate mainstream Western medicine, there is unquestionable evidence to the contrary. Death rates from cancer and heart disease are probably higher among people in psychological distress, and lower among people who have a strong sense of purpose and well-being. . . . When life becomes meaningless, the body's sustaining energy seems to drain silently away like a leaky battery. . . . The greatest threat to life and health is having nothing to live for. . . . There is a secret core of meaning waiting to be discovered in every life, and those who have found it are the teachers I look to for my own future survival. . . . They are the true scientists of longevity. . . .[35]

The overture to the opera of the quest for individual meaning, for the soul's self-expression, is the ability to think for ourselves, to learn to discern truth from fiction, fact from illusion. The chapter that now follows addresses this problem. The secret core of meaning waiting to be discovered will remain dormant and obscure unless we can learn to think for ourselves. To do so, we must liberate the mind from the straitjacket of ideas and presuppositions that strangle its ability to exercise thought freely. We are what we think. Until we can think freely for ourselves and of ourselves, we cannot become who we can become. We cannot proceed on our spiritual journey.

chapter six
Truth to Tell

Once there was a man who had lost his legs and was blinded in an accident. To compensate for his losses, he developed great strength and agility in his hands and arms, and great acuity in hearing. He composed magnificent music and performed amazing feats. Others were so impressed with his achievements that they had themselves blinded and their legs amputated.

*T*here is no such thing as immaculate perception. Instead of thinking for ourselves, we often seem content to act on the basis of what we see others doing rather than on the basis of what we really believe, of what we really think. Misconceptions, missed conceptions, self-deceptions, and rationalizations tend to influence our worldview and our actions.

It is always easier to allow others to program our thoughts, to think for us, than for us to think for ourselves. We often fail to realize that the quest for approval from others is ultimately rooted in a distrust of our own faculty of judgment, that approval means that I care what someone else thinks of me more than what I think of myself. But a critical step in self-understanding and in spiritual development is to think for ourselves. This tendency to assign the proxy of thinking for ourselves to others is a characteristic of modern life. Already in the eighteenth century, Immanuel Kant noted:

> If I have a book which understands for me, a pastor who has a conscience for me, a physician who decides my diet, and so forth, I need not trouble myself. *I need not think*—if I can only pay—*others will readily undertake the irksome work for me* (italics mine).

We become what we think. To refuse to think for ourselves is to accept the labels given us by others. As Kierkegaard admonished, "Once you label me, you negate me."

We tend to allow others to think for us because we often are uncertain of how and what to think for ourselves. Severed from the traditional sources of religious belief, having found no viable alternative in the secular realm, witnessing the collapse and dissolution of modern ideologies, imbued with relativism to the point of being certain only of uncertainty, many people today feel bereft of meaning because they are bereft of conviction. Finding nothing to believe in, they have no foundation upon which to shape a life of meaning, no roots to forge a life of rootedness. As Chesterton so aptly put it, a person who does not believe in something is ready to believe in anything. Indeed, the flexibility that so many admire, may simply be an excuse for failing to affirm anything. As sociologist Philip Slater reminds us:

> When we assert the importance of flexibility, it is because we fear we don't have it. What we *call* flexibility usually turns out to be detachment, non-commitment. . . . What we fear is that if we committed ourselves wholly to any fixed course of action and it proved awkward, we would not have within ourselves the flexibility to respond in a way that would save us. In this we are probably correct since what detachment produces is in fact rigidity.[1]

In determining what to believe, Kierkegaard encouraged each person to take what he called a "leap of faith." We must take the risk of

believing in something that may not be provable, of committing ourselves to people and to activities that may turn out to be disappointing. We must take a chance, take a risk, a leap of faith, of belief, and of
commitment. But what Kierkegaard forgot was that it is necessary to
look *before* we leap, to think before we act.

In the journey toward meaning and toward life satisfaction, we must
not only design a map aimed at guiding us toward our desired destination, but we must also try to be aware of the potential obstacles that
might impede that quest. In charting a journey of discovery, the ex-
plorer must not only start down the road but must be able to detect
the presence of barriers and detours that obstruct progress along the
way. These obstructions are not towering mountains, nor arid deserts.
They are not even physical entities. Rather, they are ideas that we often tacitly and unreflectively assume. They are thoughts and perceptions that we have not adequately thought about, that we have not
sufficiently thought through. Sometimes these are illusions married to
falsehoods that derive from what has been termed "the hypnosis of
social conditioning." When we think about it, we find ourselves fet-
tered to a particular way of seeing the world taught to us by parents
and teachers and infused into us by social pressures and expectations.
However, we can become enabled to discover which of these beliefs are
fictions in which we collectively have agreed to participate. In the preceding chapters, a number of these have been identified and discussed.
In this chapter, we will have occasion to refer to some of them once
again.

Kierkegaard characterized our times as an "age of advertising and
publicity."[2] Ours is an era when we are told by social and cultural
conditioning who to be and what to believe in. We are ready to believe
in advertisements and public relations gimmicks that continuously play
upon our uncertainties, our insecurities, and our gullibilities. We are
told, for example, that a Buick is "something to believe in."

To compound the problem, human beings seem to share a fundamental, yet dangerous, proclivity—the desire to be deceived. Seeking
a palliative for discomfort, preferring promised and packaged certainty

to the insecurity of freedom, we lack immunity to the disease of self-deception. The dis-ease of not being sure of who we are and of what we believe makes us ever more susceptible to the salespersons of delusion who await us at every corner with their huge inventory of slogans and simplistic solutions to the complexities of life in our time.

According to the Hasidic master Rabbi Mendel of Kotzk, more often than not people are prisoners of their own illusions, of their self-deceptions, of their evasions, pretensions, and rationalizations. In his view, such people think they dance, yet they are really paralyzed. The Rabbi of Kotzk asked why we are indignant when deceived by others, while we seem content to live comfortably with our own unconscious desire for self-deception. He would have affirmed the Latin aphorism "Mundus vult decipi," "The world wants to be deceived."

Among some of the Hasidic masters, hypocrisy was a greater fear than heresy. When asked: "Who is a Hasid?, Who is pious?," the Hasidic master Bunam of Przysucha is reputed to have replied, "A Hasid is one who does more than the law requires. The law demands that one not deceive one's neighbor. A Hasid is one who goes beyond the law and refuses to deceive his own self."

In a similar vein, there is the story of a construction worker who would have lunch each day with his fellow workers. Every day he would open his lunch box, take out a bologna sandwich, and complain that each day he had to have bologna for lunch. Tired of listening to his complaint, one of his colleagues said to him, "If you are so tired of balogna, why don't you ask your wife for something else for lunch?"

To which the worker responded, "Oh, my wife doesn't make my lunch. I do."

The moral of the story is that we tend to feed ourselves baloney, but do nothing about it. This story indicates that self-sabotage can readily become a lifestyle.

The Upanishads teach: "For as one's thinking is, such one becomes, and it is because of this that thinking should be purified and transformed. . . ."[3] Changing one's mind means transforming one's self. Making up one's mind helps in making up one's self. Our mentality often is a stumbling block to realizing what we think and in becoming who we can become. In his spiritual classic, *Markings,* Dag Hammarskjold offers himself this advice: "Out of myself as a stumbling block, into myself as fulfillment."[4] The path to meaning must first be paved with a philosophy of life grounded not in the trap of self-deception, but in the pursuit of intellectual integrity. As philosopher John Stuart Mill wrote, "No great improvements in the lot of mankind are possible unless a great change takes place in the fundamental constitution of their modes of thought."[5] Or, as William James, one of the founders of Pragmatism, put it, "The great revolution of our generation is the discovery that human beings by changing their minds, can change the outer aspects of their lives."[6]

Society offers us a variety of scripts for our lives. Society tends to view us—and to encourage us to view ourselves—functionally, to convince us that our value derives from the social functions that we perform. This functional approach to self-understanding has its origin in the mechanistic view of reality that, as was already discussed, has been dominant since the seventeenth century. As Rollo May has noted, "The oversimplified mechanical view of the self really betrayed an underlying failure of confidence in human beings and an implicit lack of belief in the dignity, complexity, individuality, creativity and freedom of the human person."

According to the French philosopher Gabriel Marcel, technolatry is grounded in the following assumptions: that the *only* valid knowledge of reality derives from technical thinking; that technological advancement is an end in itself; that it is the purpose for which humankind exists; that it bestows the human creature with the *only* kind of meaning available, that is, functional meaning within the technological society. For Marcel, however, the acceptance of these assumptions inevitably robs the individual of an intrinsic sense of dignity, sacredness, and self-worth. A mechanistic worldview, warns Marcel, leads to "techniques of degradation," to the inescapable alienation of individuals from one another and from themselves and, to a collectivistic mentality with all of its attendant dangers to freedom, spirituality, and self-expression.[7]

In *The Acquisitive Society*, the distinguished social and economic historian R. H. Tawney in 1920 wrote, "Like a hypochondriac who is so absorbed in the processes of his own digestion that he goes to his grave before he has begun to live, industrialized communities neglect the very objects for which it is worthwhile to acquire riches in their feverish preoccupation with the means by which riches can be acquired."[8] Life in a completely functionalized world becomes a process without a purpose, the utilization of means without clearly defined ends, a journey without a destination. Without meaning, without purpose, nothing ultimately matters.

How we know what we know, how we come to believe what we believe, usually derives from one or more of these three sources: perception, reason, society. Yet each of these has been seriously challenged as being a viable source of truth. Indeed, all three have been identified as being potential obstacles to apprehending the truth. How and why this is so may be described without a lengthy or complicated philosophical discussion.

Already in ancient times, philosophers demonstrated that the senses are an unreliable vehicle to discerning the truth. The senses can be deceptive, inaccurate. Rather than perceiving things as they are, the senses immediately add a layer of interpretation to perception, an overlay based upon one's cultural and social conditioning. In other words, *how* we have been conditioned to see distorts *what* we see. We perceive reality through the lens of how we have been taught to see. More often than not, seeing is not believing because our cultural assumptions, our "mental habits," shape what we see.

Human perception is limited by the equipment we humans have been granted, and by the mechanical devices our ingenuity has constructed to widen the scope of our perception of the world. For instance, the human eye can see only a small spectrum of the various types of rays of light and darkness. Our ears can only tune in to a very limited spectrum of the sound waves that populate our universe. Most animals are more adept than we are at detecting and identifying odors and smells. The abilities of our senses to apprehend the world is not a major strength of the human species.

We normally allow a whole series of illusions to stand between ourselves and reality. Formulated out of genetic instructions, cultural rules, or self-interest, these distortions can be comforting and convincing; yet they need to be seen through, to be penetrated, for the self to pursue the truth. Ancient and medieval mystics and philosophers already knew that reality as it appears to us often is a deceptive illusion. What we see, think, and believe as we confront reality is not what often is actually there. Reality hides behind a set of veils and distorting mirrors. We tend to confuse the veils with what lies behind them. We mistakenly identify an eclipse with the sun. We play hide-and-seek with truth and illusions. A goal of many spiritual disciplines aims at allowing us to pierce the veil of illusion. As the poet William Blake put it, "If the doors of perception were cleansed, every thing would appear to man as it is. . . . For man has closed himself up, till he sees all things through the narrow chinks of his cavern."[9]

Even physics has acknowledged its inability to provide an unambiguous account of reality. Physicists tell us, for example, that what we see as solid matter is mostly space, that what we can perceive is only a small sliver of existing phenomena that register upon the extremely limited capacities of our senses. Biologists inform us that our senses provide us only with the information that we need to help us survive in our particular environment, that the senses relate to the quest for survival rather than to truth. Scientists have come to realize that every instrument, every measurement, gives us only a biased view, dependent upon the instruments themselves; that we, in effect, create our own reality as we try to apprehend it; that our output is always a function of our prior input.

Heisenberg's famous principle of indeterminacy has led us from certainty to skepticism. Once we assumed that the universe could be understood by us—like gods looking at creation from an objectively true vantage point. Now we know that whatever we learn is dependent upon our limited perspectives as observers of and participants in the cosmos. Now we are increasingly aware of how the limitations of the human nervous system, the cultural influences that shape us, and the idiosyncrasies of the symbolic systems that we use determine what we perceive and how we perceive it.

Precisely because of the ultimate unreliability of our senses in apprehending truth, philosophers often have asserted that reason, rather than the senses, should be the human being's preferred vehicle to grasping the truth. But the more they have thought about it, the less convinced they have become. Logic and mathematics were once deemed true but were subsequently unmasked as artificial human constructs, operating within their own independent conceptual universe with no referent beyond themselves. For example, the number 2 does not really exist in the same way as does a table, a chair, or a planet. $2 + 2 = 4$ is true, but does not necessarily reflect any objective reality; $2 + 2 = 4$ is only true *within* a particular mathematical system, otherwise it is a group of unintelligible symbols. Two apples plus two apples are four apples, but the equation $2 + 2$ only represents two numbers, not four entities.

The great German philosopher Immanuel Kant taught that many categories and ideas, such as measurements of time (like minutes) and of space (like meters), are "fictions" that we devise and impose upon reality. In themselves, they do not really exist. Minutes, for instance, are arbitrary finite periods that we impose upon the infinity of time. Meters are arbitrary finite measurements that we impose upon the infinity of space. Kant warned against committing the mistake of equating the artificial and often arbitrary conceptual frameworks that we impose upon reality with reality itself. All we can know, in his view, are the rubrics, the theories, the concepts, the categories that we impose upon reality. But we cannot know reality itself. Similarly, in response to the admonition that he be a realist, the Nobel Prize-winning writer Isaac Bashevis Singer once said, "How can I be a realist when I do not know what reality is?"[10] According to some current theories of physics, there are ten dimensions of reality, but only four are within the scope of our experience. In other words, the perception of most of reality is beyond our grasp, and the aspects of reality that we do perceive, we often perceive without either clarity or accuracy.

Cultural anthropologists teach that our perceptions, our claims to truth, are culturally specific, that is, they do not represent any kind of truth or validity beyond that granted by a particular culture or society. They point out how people from a variety of cultures would perceive the same event or action in completely different ways, how they would interpret it completely differently. Furthermore, anthropologists and sociologists point out that, contrary to the view of some philosophers, reason is not a universal human constant. Different social and cultural understandings of the nature of reason offer different understandings of what is "reasonable." Psychologists tell us further that there is a fine line between reason and rationalization. Neither the senses nor reason seem able to guarantee us an accurate understanding of truth, a reliable perception of reality.

The growing awareness of how diverse cultures apprehend reality threatens our own culture's conviction that it has cornered the market on *the* truth. Once we thought ourselves to have the patent on truth. But as the world "shrinks" we are becoming increasingly aware that truth is not the monopoly of any single individual, philosophy, religion, or culture. Many of our firmest, finest, and most comforting convictions are being unmasked as arbitrary products of our cultural conditioning. Many things we once considered irrefutable facts have been now revealed to be cultural prejudices, intellectual fashions, philosophical fads.

Where does all of this lead us: somewhere or nowhere, to hope or to despair? Are we condemned to the view of abject skepticism articulated by a variety of philosophers throughout the ages? Must we agree with Democritus, who twenty-four centuries ago said, "Nothing is real, or if it is, we don't know it. We have no way of knowing the truth. Truth is at the bottom of an abyss,"[11] or with the Roman philosopher Seneca, who taught that "truth lies wrapped up and hidden in the depths." Are we obliged to confirm the position taken by those philosophers who claim, "There is only one thing I know for certain: that I know nothing"?

Both skepticism and relativism lead to the conclusion that we cannot know anything with absolute certainty, that objective truth is beyond our grasp. Such an approach can easily lead to dismay and anxiety. Indeed, the collapse in recent decades of many philosophical, cultural, and social securities has left us with a feeling of rootlessness, spiritual homelessness, psychological anxiety, and philosophical disorientation. We no longer know who or what to believe, or even how to believe. Being unsure of our very reason to exist, feeling homeless in the realm we inhabit, is precisely what makes the quest for meaning so urgent and compelling. This is the epitome of life in our times. This is the situation that each of us faces. Yet this condition is not hopeless. As the Jewish mystics taught, exile can be the necessary prelude to redemption, alienation the prologue to fulfillment. As many of the existentialist philosophers claimed, to experience anxiety, alienation, and absurdity is a necessary prerequisite for self-knowledge and for self-renewal. Self-doubt can serve as the overture to self-understanding.

Knowing what we cannot know, being aware that absolute truth and complete certitude elude our grasp, can be liberating rather than anxiety provoking. It is better to be aware of our limitations than to labor under the illusion that absolute truth is within our grasp. Better to know that we cannot possess absolute truth than to be possessed by illusory certainty. Better to realize that the search for absolute truth is bound to end in disappointment than to embark on a journey toward an unreachable destination, or to believe we have arrived at our destination while we actually are yet in transit.

It is liberating to know that we cannot know everything. It is liberating to know that the search for certainty, for absolute and objective truth, is bound to be disappointing. As the French philosopher Sartre put it, we are "condemned to freedom."[12] Being freed from the illusions that absolute truth is in our grasp and that cultural conditioning should dictate who we are and who we can become, each of us becomes liberated to formulate and to enact a philosophy of life, a plot for the novel that is each of our lives.

For a period of about 2300 years, philosophers from Aristotle to Hegel tried to provide a systematic and complete account of reality.

They tried to depict reality and truth in nice neat bundles of system-atized knowledge. But to systematize reality and truth is like trying to lay a flat grid on the Swiss Alps. Reality is too amorphous and truth is too elusive to be entrapped by the feeble constructs of the human mind. Only once philosophy shifted its focus from attempting to un-derstand and to systematize everything could it focus adequately on the meaning of human existence. Only once philosophy relented from its attempt to claim a monopoly on *the* truth could it begin to reconceptualize the notion of truth. In the late nineteenth and early twentieth centuries, a new school of philosophy emerged that attempted to do just that. It was called *existentialism*.[13]

Existentialists narrowed their focus to the human condition. Though existentialists differ on many things, virtually all rejected the view that knowledge of objective and comprehensive truth is available to hu-man beings. As the philosopher Franz Rosenzweig put it, "Truth is a noun only to God, to human beings truth is only an adjective." In other words, all we can know is what Martin Buber called "moment truths." We cannot know *the* truth. This insight may be illustrated by the following well-known Indian story.

Once an Indian monarch captured a huge and beautiful elephant. He put this elephant in the great hall of his palace. He invited to his palace four wise men who never had seen nor heard of an elephant. He blindfolded each of these four wise men and led them into the room where the elephant stood. The first wise man walked until he came to the elephant's tusk, which he felt with his hand. The sec-ond encountered the elephant's leg and tried to hold it in his arms. The third found the elephant's tail, and the fourth held onto the elephant's trunk.

The king then led each of the wise men into a separate room and asked each to describe an elephant. The one who had touched the elephant's tusk described the elephant as a huge, curved animal, like a rock. The one who had touched the elephant's leg described the elephant as being like a tree. The one who held onto the tail described the elephant as a hairy snake. And the one who held onto the trunk described the elephant as a fuzzy, long hose.

After reading these descriptions, the king said to the wise men, "What each of you described was both true and false. Each of you truly described what you experienced. Each of you described the part of the elephant you encountered. But each of your descriptions is false because none of you described the whole elephant, the elephant as it really is. None of you grasped the entire truth."

And so the king led the four wise men into the great hall where the elephant stood, and each of the wise men was surprised by what he saw, for by grasping only part of the truth, none had been able to envision what the elephant was really like.

Unlike the wise men in this story, each of us remains blindfolded, able to apprehend only a small sliver of the immense vastness of reality. Limited by historical, biographical, and perceptual perspectives, we are never able to apprehend absolute truth in an objective, complete, total, and accurate way. Even the reflections and echoes of truth that we can apprehend are but a small part of what there is. We should not be vain enough to believe that the "whole truth and nothing but the truth" is available to us. Like each of these wise men, we can, at best, apprehend only part—but we must not deceive ourselves into thinking that by knowing a small piece of reality or truth that we therefore have comprehended the whole.

From Aristotle to Descartes to our own century, philosophers had defined the human being as "the rational animal," as an essentially rational being. The senses, the body, and the emotions were downplayed, viewed as barriers to the apprehension of truth, as factors that stifled the workings of the rational mind. The existentialists, however, took a broader view of the human being, stressing not only the mind but also the body, the senses, the emotions, and the will. As Pascal had put it anticipating the existentialists, "The heart has reasons that reason knoweth not."[14] While classical philosophers had disparaged or even ignored the body, existentialists reaffirmed and celebrated it. The existentialists sought the whole person and not just the intellect. As such, they expanded the limitations on human self-understanding imposed by earlier philosophers. But they simultaneously offered a view of the human person as a more limited being than had their predecessors. Rather than a being who could grasp the totality of reality, they depicted the human creature as one with a limited perspective, as a being limited by history, by experience, by perception, by biology. "All I have are myself and my conditions," wrote philosopher Ortega y Gasset. Consequently, for the existentialists, philosophy, like life, could never become a finished product, could never exist in a definitive edition. Life, like philosophy, came to be viewed as a pilgrimage, a journey rather than a final destination. This view is not antagonistic to the use of reason, but to its abuse and the presumptuousness of its use. Reason is a tool, not a solution. Reason is part of human nature, but not its essence. Reason can offer delusions as well as solutions. Reason should be part of our engagement with life instead of a wedge abstracting life and separating thought from the life of the thinker.

For the existentialists, the conviction that absolute, objective truth is unavailable to us led to a new understanding of the kind of truth one must seek, of the variety of truth that is within our grasp. Soren Kierkegaard, often considered the founder of existentialism, wrote that "the truth consists not in *knowing* the truth, but in *being* the truth."[15] According to Kierkegaard, "Truth exists for the particular individual only as he himself produces it in action."[16] What this means is that each person must live his or her beliefs, commitments, and values for them to be true. In this view, truth is not represented simply by abstract propositions or merely by cerebral affirmations, but by a lifestyle. As the American pragmatic philosophers taught, the truth of an idea cannot be demonstrated simply by reason or by logic, but must be translated into action, articulated in life.

More concerned with being the truth than in knowing it, more preoccupied with self-understanding than in securing a monopoly on absolute truth, the existentialists identified a life of truth as a life of "authenticity," as a life of "integrity." The goal of such a life is "to thine own self be true." From this perspective, truth is not so much what we know but what and how we live. The opposite of authenticity and integrity, to use Sartre's language, is to act in "bad faith."[17] The person who acts in bad faith is a fallacy; it is being who one is not. It is the negation of the self. "Bad faith" corrupts rather than crafts the soul.

Recent developments in psychoanalysis have expressed ideas similar to Sartre's notions of "authenticity" and "bad faith." For example, writing of recent changes in psychoanalysis, Stephen A. Mitchell notes that "in classical psychoanalysis, the central and most important question to be asked of the individual is: What are the patterns of gratification, frustration, and sublimation that shape a person's life? In contemporary psychoanalysis . . . the most important question to be asked has shifted to: How meaningful and authentic is a person's experience and expression of herself?"[18]

In the past, conformity and adjustment were prized as characteristics of psychological well-being. More recently, however, psychoanalyst D. W. Winnicott has claimed that a personality based around compliance and adaptation to externally imposed desires, needs, and ideas generates a "false self," or what Erich Fromm called a "marketing personality."[19] Such a person may be well-adjusted and "normal," but also vacuous and inauthentic. "The false self," according to Winnicott, "however well set up, lacks something and that something is the essential element of creative originality."[20] Some psychotherapists currently find a pervasive diagnosis not to be "maladjustment" or "psychopathology," but "normopathology," that is, the person who—though normal and well-adjusted—is empty, boring, and leading an essentially meaningless and tedious existence, bereft of meaning, individuality, wonder, and creativity, lacking the central features of experience that mark life as valuable, meaningful, and fulfilled. For example, Winnicott has revisioned psychoanalysis as treatment aimed at the quality of the texture of experience rather than at the individual's functional capacity.

Winnicott and others identify "pseudonormality" as the central clinical issue of our times. In Winnicott's view, the key indicator of neurosis is not that the patient manifests signs of maladjustment to society, or the inability to regulate her natural drives. Rather the key indicator is when the therapist is found to be constantly bored during sessions with patients. It is the boring, vacuous patient, and not the creative though peculiar one, who in Winnicott's view is probably most in need of psychological help. This perspective indicates a shift in psychiatric theory from Freud's view of humans as drive-related animals to the more current view of humans as meaning-generating animals. Here the goal is not the establishment of a rational, socially well-adjusted "normality," but the capacity to generate a sense of self, of relationships, of convictions, and of values felt as valuable, as meaningful, and as uniquely one's own. As Mitchell notes, "Creativity, not normality, has become the paradigm of mental health."[21]

Existentialist philosophers like Jean-Paul Sartre and M. Merleau-Ponty recommended that each person choose a "project," by which they meant a cohesive set of goals linked to an ultimate purpose that gives significance to whatever a person does, that makes a person who he or she is. What the existentialist philosophers called the "project" some psychologists have called "life themes" or "propriate strivings." Put another way, what makes a person who he or she is relates to how he or she conducts the pivotal project of human life in search of meaning—the creation of life as an art form. It is to the nature of the quest for meaning that our discussion now turns.

chapter seven

Meaning What?

Once there lived, in Cracow, Poland, a rabbi named Isaac. He was very poor. Isaac lived with his wife and children in a house with only one room. In the middle of the room there was a stove. During winter, when they had money for wood, the heat of the stove would offer warmth and would cook the meager food that barely sustained them from day to day.

One night the rabbi had a dream. He dreamed that in a land called Bohemia, in a city called Prague, there was a bridge under which a river flowed. The bridge was near a large castle. Under the bridge, on the bank of the river, an enormous treasure was buried.

When the rabbi awoke the next morning, he remembered his dream in vivid detail. But the needs of his congregants were pressing, and off he went to the synagogue. Yet, throughout the day, all he could think of was his dream. That night he went to sleep hoping that, in his sleep, he might be free of the dream from the previous night. But once again the dream returned, and it was identical to the dream he had the night before in every way. In the morning he awoke, and the dream, once again, preoccupied him throughout the day.

When the same dream came again that night, he knew it was not simply a dream, but a message, for so tradition taught. He awoke—looked at his exhausted wife and hungry children, shivering in their sleep near the cold stove. The rabbi dressed quietly and left a note that he had gone to Prague to find his dream.

The rabbi traveled through the cold along dangerous roads from Cracow to Prague for three days and three nights. On the morning of the fourth day, he entered Prague. It was not long before he saw the river, and it was exactly as it had been in his dream. He followed the river until he came to a bridge near a huge castle. Both were so identical to what he had seen in his dream that he thought he was in his bed in Cracow, dreaming and asleep.

He looked down from the bridge at the spot where the treasure was supposed to be buried. But, because the nearby castle was the castle of the king, royal guards stood watch on the bridge all day. The rabbi waited all day for the guards to leave so that he could dig up the treasure under the bridge. But, when the sun had set and the guards had left, a new group of guards immediately came to replace them. And so, day after day, night after night, the rabbi stayed near the bridge, hoping for an hour when the bridge would remain unguarded.

As time passed, the rabbi became friendly with one of the guards who stood post on the bridge. The guard was grateful to have a person of culture and learning with whom to converse during the long lonely hours of standing guard at the bridge. One day, the guard told the rabbi that he had a strange dream the night before. The guard dreamed that in a land called Poland, in a city called Cracow, there lived a pious but poor man with his wife and many children. They lived in a one-room house, and in the middle of the room, there was a stove, and under the stove, a great treasure was buried.

Rabbi Isaac immediately returned home. He moved the heavy stove and began to dig beneath it. There, in a large

iron trunk, he found a great treasure. With half of the
money, he built a great synagogue. It still stands today in
Cracow and is called "Rabbi Isaac's Synagogue."

*T*he moral of the story is that the treasure we seek, unbeknownst to us, is right beneath our feet. What we need to do is to dig for it. The place to begin is within our own selves. Spiritual development is an "inside job." The path toward meaning entails an inward journey.

Spirituality is what we do with our inner life, how we cultivate the soul. What for many centuries was called "the soul" is currently often referred to as "the self." The soul, the self, is not a ghost that possesses our body during life. It is the *principium individuationis;* it is that which makes each person who she uniquely is; it is the organizing principle of each person's life. The soul is what keeps us together. A year ago, 98 percent of the atoms that comprise your body were not there. A year from now, only 2 percent of the atoms that comprise your body now will still be part of your body. The body constantly changes—often for the worse, as time progresses. Yet as we age, the soul can develop. But it needs our assistance. The quest for meaning is a critical component of the life and the development of the soul.

The quest for meaning begins with the hope that human life is meaning wrapped in mystery, purpose enveloped by an enigma. The human task is to disclose the mystery, to reveal the concealed, through and throughout the drama of one's life. One must know how to court meaning in order to become engaged to it. Human meaning is a problem, not a question. Questions such as: What time is it? or Who was the sixteenth U.S. president? come from a need to know that is easily satisfied. A problem, however, is the outcome of a situation of perplexity, anxiety, or distress. A question is the product of the mind. A problem involves the whole person. Questions are fleeting, ephemeral. The ultimate problems of existence are perennial, long-lasting. Questions can be resolved by information. Problems require not only knowledge, but wisdom and awareness. Wrestling with problems is a feature of authentic human existence. One can discern a person's depth by the number and the kind of deep problems with which she struggles.

A problem is a homework assignment for the soul. Let us suppose that here in front of you there stands a person who has no problems. Do you know why this person has no problems? Because he is an idiot, that's why. Life means problems, and the deeper the problems a person has, the deeper is that person.

In a certain television commercial, the great basketball star Michael Jordan approaches an aged and wise-looking Asian man, where the question is posed: What is the meaning of life? The answer is then provided: Life is a sport. So drink up.

Simplistic answers—such as this—to life's most essential problems appeal to many people. Many self-help books currently on the market offer equally simplistic responses to the problem of the meaning of life. But at least a simplistic response is a response. On the other side of the spectrum is the view that posing the problem is itself a mistake, that it is foolish even to consider the meaning of life.

Unfortunately, for some the quest for meaning is aborted at conception. Ironically, individuals whom we would describe as having led eminently meaningful lives found life to be devoid of meaning. This includes the great lawyer Clarence Darrow, who described life as "an awful joke" and who wrote, "Life is like a ship on sea, tossed by every wave and by every wind; a ship headed for no port and no harbor, with no rudder, no compass, no pilot; simply floating for a time, then lost in the waves."[1] Similarly, Steven Weinberg, a Nobel laureate in physics, has written, "The more the universe seems comprehensible, the more it also seems pointless." Shakespeare wrote in *Macbeth* that "life is but a walking shadow . . . a tale told by an idiot, full of sound and fury, signifying nothing."[2] Sigmund Freud wrote, in a letter to Marie Bonaparte, "The moment a person questions the meaning and value of life . . . he is sick. By asking this question one is merely admitting to a store of unsatisfied libido to which something else must have happened,

a kind of fermentation leading to sadness and depression."³ The great
scholar of mythology, Joseph Campbell, once said, "I don't believe life
has a purpose. Life is a lot of protoplasm with an urge to reproduce
itself and continue in being."⁴ Some, like Freud, reject life's meaning;
others respond to life's deepest problems with advertising slogans. Yet,
throughout the centuries, human beings have embarked on a spiritual
pilgrimage to locate and to enact life's meaning.

That the spiritual rather than the sexual (Freud) or the quest for
power (Adler) lies at the core of human existence, that the quest for
meaning is a symptom of psychological health rather than of psychological neurosis, has been forcefully argued by a Viennese psychiatrist
who once had been a follower of Freud. His name is Viktor Frankl.
The school of psychotherapy he founded, called *logotherapy*, is, in
Frankl's words, "a psychotherapy in spiritual terms."⁵ It is a form of
spiritual therapy because it assumes that the primary human need is a
need for meaning. Unlike earlier psychotherapy that began with the
search for psychic causes for physical symptoms, logotherapy begins
with a search for the spiritual causes of physical symptoms. In contemporary psychoanalysis, the quest for meaning is only now slowly beginning to move to the fore. As psychoanalyst Stephen Mitchell writes,
"On the level of clinical theory, there has been a marked shift in emphasis from the clarification and renunciation of infantile fantasies to
the revitalization and elaboration of the patient's sense of personal
meaning."⁶

The path that brought Frankl from Freudian analysis to spiritual
therapy led through Auschwitz. During his experience in that place of
unspeakable horror, terror, dehumanization, suffering, and death, in
that place where "no dream, no matter how horrible, could be as bad
as the reality of the camp that surrounded us,"⁷ Frankl's observations
led him to conclude that it was not necessarily the physically strongest
who had the best chance to survive. Rather, the person who found
meaning in a reason or person for which or for whom to survive had
the best chance of surviving and of retaining self-dignity and self-
identity. In this regard, Frankl quotes the German philosopher

Nietzsche: "He who has a why to live for can bear with almost any *how*."[8] Speaking about life in Auschwitz, Frankl continues: "Whenever there was an opportunity for it, one had to give them a *why*—an aim—for the terrible *how* of their existence. Woe to him who saw no more sense in life, no aim, no purpose, and therefore no point in carrying on. He was soon lost."[9]

Based upon his experiences in Auschwitz, Frankl came to the conclusion that the most fundamental drive within the human psyche is not connected with the sexual instinct as the dominant Freudian view claimed, and that it is not connected with any other biological or socially conditioned impulse, as others like Alfred Adler claimed. Rather, Frankl discovered that the deepest moving force, not only within himself but also within every other human being, is the surety of meaning. Frankl asserts that without meaning human beings lose their chief source of strength and become something less than they otherwise could become. For Frankl, the nature of our individual quest for meaning is what ultimately defines us, what essentially distinguishes human beings from all other beings on earth.

Rabbi Pesach Krauss wrote a book called *Why Me?: Coping with Grief, Loss and Change.* He had lost a leg while a boy. After his wife died of a brain tumor, he left his congregation to become the Jewish chaplain at Memorial Sloan-Kettering Cancer Center in New York. In *Why Me?* Krauss discusses the quest for meaning he encountered among the cancer patients to whom he ministered. He writes, "Each of us must find our special meaning in our own way. Nowhere is this more true than in a hospital where there is catastrophic illness. It seems an unlikely place to look for answers to life. Yet it is here, in an environment of great stress and pressure, that many patients pass through the crucible of pain and despair and find their meaning. I see it every day when I make my rounds.

"'Rabbi,' a patient confides, 'before this illness I held a responsible and highly prestigious position in industry. Surely I was a success. I had reached the top. It means nothing to me now. Nothing. I had sacrificed my wife and children to get there. I see now that I was a child; now I am a grown man. I feel tremendous power. I'm born anew. Nothing can frighten me. I see my priorities so clearly. Each day, life is precious.'"[10]

Another patient, a teenager and a high school star basketball player, after undergoing a difficult bone marrow transplant survives and tells the rabbi, "I am wise now and more mature. I've learned a lot. I know what I want and who I am. It's a new ball game now."[11]

A third patient, an elderly woman, says, "Before my illness, I was closed. But now, no more painful aloneness. Now I'm wide open, sharing my life and my feelings—things I have never said before."[12]

On the basis of his personal and professional experience, Krauss concludes that illness can offer a "searchlight to illuminate the dark places of our lives and bring them into the open, to help us live more creative, more fulfilling, more meaningful lives."[13] The "hard knocks" of life can lead to the revealing of doors, to the opening of new possibilities.

Krauss concludes his book with a reference to Viktor Frankl:

> How is meaning realized? According to Viktor Frankl, it is realized through values that are lived and acted upon each moment. These are creative values of giving to the world, experiential values of taking in from it and just plain appreciating the world and all its richness and wonders, and attitudinal values, the positive way we respond to life's hard knocks.[14]

Not only does Frankl offer a new focus for psychology, but his observations and conclusions suggest that not only psychology, but philosophy and religion as well, often have become separated from their essential respective missions. Originally, psychology was a branch of philosophy. Both by definition and by description, *psychology* meant the study of the soul. Once it was severed from philosophy, psychology became a science. Once the focus of psychology became more of a process of empirical discovery rather than an inner quest, psychology became diverted from its initial mission. Science, it should be remembered, aims at understanding things as they are rather than as how they can be. Similarly, philosophy in the modern period, beginning with Descartes, became largely obsessed with method over meaning, logic over life, linguistic analysis over the search for meaning. Except for the existentialists, Socrates' view that "the unexamined life is not worth living" seemed to have been removed from the prioritized agenda of the philosophical enterprise. Albert Camus, the Nobel Prize laureate for literature in 1957, was correct when he wrote, "Judging whether life is or is not worth living amounts to answering the fundamental question of philosophy."[15]

Religion, especially American religion, also has become substantially severed from its spiritual origins. The eminent philosopher and sociologist of religion Will Herberg, whose book *Protestant-Catholic-Jew* became a standard university text in sociology of religion courses, warned that robbed of transcendence, religion becomes "an exalted public utility . . . an idolatrous cult"[16] maintaining the social status quo. According to Herberg, the "religiousness" characteristic of America today is very often simply a way of sociability, devoid of piety and serious personal commitment. Describing the reasons for American religion's failure as a way of dealing with the ultimate issues of human existence, the pre-eminent Jewish theologian Abraham Joshua Heschel wrote: "Religion declined not because it was refuted, but because it became irrelevant, dull, oppressive, insipid."[17] Elsewhere Heschel wrote, "In our passion to advance, we have bartered holiness for convenience, loyalty for success, wisdom for information, tradition for fashion."[18] For Heschel, the true mission of religion is not public relations but "private relations," not social dynamics but dealing with the ultimate problems of human existence, and most specifically, the problem of human meaning. For Heschel, the human being "may, indeed, be characterized as a subject in search of a predicate, as a being in quest of a meaning of life, of all life, not only of particular actions or episodes which happen now and then."[19]

The quest for meaning requires a refocusing of psychology, of philosophy, of religion, and of the self, upon issues that are of ultimate significance. Finding meaning is like the lottery: You cannot win unless you buy a ticket. Worse than not finding meaning is not looking for it. The search itself is part of the answer.

Many people who engage in the quest for meaning fail to find it because they look in the wrong places. Some people predicate their lives on the fallacy that meaning is identical to the satisfaction of needs. But eventually one must confront the problem: After satisfaction, then what? Biological needs demand satisfaction. A spiritual life requires meaning and purpose; satisfaction brings an end to desire. Needs are dead ends. A life of meaning is open-ended. Needs are finite. The spiritual life is a portal to the infinite. It is where the infinite invades the finite.

Animals seem content when their biological needs are met. Human beings require something more. When a human being's needs are met, he is eventually confronted with the peculiarly human problem: Now that my need is met, am *I* needed? Who needs *me*? What is the purpose of my being in this world?

Rather than considering the sacred as a need, needs have become considered as sacred. Suppression of a need has come to be considered a sacrilege that must inevitably avenge itself in the form of some psychological disorder. For example, at restaurants they used to ask if you "want" cream with your coffee. I have noticed that they now ask whether you "need" cream with your coffee. It's as if I might expire instantly without getting cream for my coffee! This change of language indicates a change in perspective. Wants and desires have become needs. At the many meetings I attend, "needs assessments" are performed. The needs of clients, patients, students, and customers tend to drive schools, professions, and institutions. Rarely is the significance, validity, or legitimacy of the need assessed. The fulfillment of any need almost has been aggrandized into a constitutional right. Needs seem to have replaced values and visions as a basis for action. Needs seem to have become ends in themselves rather than means to ends. But neither a person nor a society aimed solely at the satisfaction of their perceived needs and desires will be able to afford themselves for long.

Needs as ends are dead ends. Once one is fulfilled, others appear to replace them, leaving the individual unfulfilled. There is a fixed minimum of needs for all human beings, but no fixed maximum for any human being. Eventually the bank runs out of capital, leaving us as dissatisfied as before.

We are living through a needs epidemic that threatens our spiritual health and well-being. Inauthentic needs engendered by fashion, advertisement, and envy threaten to smother our authentic and natural needs. Need easily turns into insatiable greed. Unbridled desire for unmet artificial needs can become destructive. When needs become ends in themselves, they can cause us to forfeit our freedom. We become imprisoned in a maze of insatiable, ever-expanding desires. Like rats who choose saccharine over a healthy diet and subsequently starve to death, we tend to starve the soul by feeding it junk food.

The social controls of our society want each of us to think of ourselves not as souls in need of nourishment but as mouths in need of gorging. They want us to believe that net worth equals self-worth. Ours is a "consumer" society; the spiritual danger is in being consumed by it. Most advertisements are aimed at motivating us to consume limitlessly. In this regard Robert Bellah has written, "That happiness is to be attained through limitless material acquisition is denied by every religion and philosophy known to humankind, but it is preached incessantly by every American television set."[20] Perhaps MasterCharge changed its name to MasterCard because people had begun to realize that a person addicted to using his MasterCharge was neither master nor in charge of his life. Or, as sociologist Philip Slater puts it, "Why do we want to bribe ourselves to do what we don't want to do?"[21] A similar insight is offered by Sam Keen:

What would satisfy me? My desires seem endless. I want, I want, I want—food, love, sex, entertainment, fame, money, gadgets. I fill my life with things that excite me for a moment. Catalogues come in the mail and I look for something new to desire. I am always wanting. No matter how much I get, I never seem to be satisfied. I am stuffed but insatiable. What would fill this void I stuff with food, sex, trinkets, addictions of one kind or another? How can I silence the concupiscent cravings within me created by the enticements of a consumer culture and follow the path of deeper desire for truth, for meaning? I suspect that when I purify my desires, they will provide me with the most reliable clues to the spirited life.

The change begins the day you notice that you can never get enough of what you didn't want in the first place. You notice the fix doesn't satisfy, the narcotic (alcohol, drugs, success, sex, power, fame, money, possessions) does not anesthetize your pain or restlessness. In the moment when you become disillusioned with your normal satisfactions and ask "What do I really desire?" your soul rather than your ego takes charge of your life.[22]

This is not a new feature of American life. Already in the nineteenth century Tocqueville observed that Americans are "restless in the midst of prosperity." "In America," he says, "I have seen the freest and best educated men in circumstances the happiest to be found in the world; yet it seemed to me that a cloud habitually hung on their brow, and they seemed serious and almost sad in their pleasures" because they "never stop thinking about the good things they have not got . . . they clutch everything and hold nothing fast."[23] The drive for happiness cannot be satisfied through an acquisitive mentality because it inhibits the individual's ability to enjoy what he has by encouraging him to derive pain from the more that others might have.

The quintessential modern person, Goethe's Faust, was given great power by the devil on the condition that he never be satisfied with what he has. While needs fulfillment is important, even crucial, many eventually get caught up in the frustrating treadmill of ever-escalating needs. As our comfort level increases, the sense of fulfillment and meaning that we anticipated seems to keep receding into the distance. When a society is able to deliver needs fulfillment for a time, but then suddenly runs out of steam, a crisis ensues. Listlessness becomes pervasive. People begin to ask: After satisfaction, then what? People inquire: Is this all that there is?

Meaning cannot be anchored in needs because needs are means; meaning focuses upon purpose, upon ends. Meaning can serve as a way of auditing our needs in terms of their being authentic or inauthentic, lasting or ephemeral, real or illusory.

Some people try to find meaning in society. Yet, in the final analysis, neither the state nor society can provide the individual with an "escape clause" to meaning, because both the state and society are entities in search of meaning themselves.

It was the psychoanalyst Erich Fromm who pointed out that society can itself suffer from "collective neurosis," from a crisis of meaning. The process of socialization aims at transforming the individual into a person who functions successfully within a particular social system regardless of its nature, values, or beliefs. The goal of socialization is to make people dependent upon social controls, and to have them respond predictably—like machines or laboratory animals—to certain kinds of stimuli. The quest for individual purpose and meaning becomes subordinated to the values and goals of the society. More often than not, as Erich Fromm observed, this leads to the repression of the awareness of the basic problems of human existence," rather than to an encounter with them and a development of the self as a result of that encounter.[24]

According to some philosophers, the problem of meaning may be posed by asking whether it is better or not that we exist, or whether we do not exist, whether the universe exists or whether it does not exist. This approach was taken by the German philosopher Hans Reiner, who wrote, "Our search for the meaning of our life [sic], is identical with the search for a logically impelled reason why it is better for us to exist than not to exist . . . whether it is better that humankind should exist than there should be a world without any human life."[25] Since we already exist and the world already exists, this view seems to beg the question. Certainly, if we did not exist there would be no one to pose the question.

To students of the Talmud, Reiner's question is very familiar. The Talmudic rabbis posed a very similar question over two thousand years ago. Without doubt, they affirmed both the existence of God and the divine-human relationship, and yet they claimed that neither the existence of God, nor the divine-human relationship, nor the affirmation that it is better that human beings exist rather than not exist, offers any of us a carte blanche guarantee that our own life has meaning.

The Talmud records a debate between the two leading schools of rabbinic scholars, the School of Hillel and the School of Shammai:

> For two and a half years the School of Shammai and the School of Hillel had a dispute. The School of Shammai asserted that it would have been better if human beings had not been created. The School of Hillel asserted it was better that human beings were created. Finally, they took a vote and decided that it would have been better had human beings not been created, but since they already have been created, each person should investigate his past deeds and examine his actions.[26]

For these Talmudic rabbis, the quest for meaning must begin with individual introspection. Often such introspection begins with the confrontation with the reality of our own mortality.

The death of a contemporary often stimulates contemplation of our own death, of the meaning of our own life. As we age, the number of those we know, the number of our contemporaries who expire, tends to escalate at an unnerving pace. Contemplation of the reality of one's own mortality suddenly becomes an uninvited companion.

Contemplating death is not only a confrontation with the unknown, with the inevitability of one's own life coming to a close, but it is also a catalyst for a collision with the problem of the meaning of life. Fear of death is real and natural. But it is inextricably linked to the apprehension that our life may have no meaning, that it may make no real difference whether we have been here or not.

Death is an eventuality. There are some things we can do to forestall it; there is nothing we can do ultimately to avoid it. But there is something each of us can do about the problem of the meaning of life. The first step in doing something about it is becoming aware of the problem—before it's too late. Ironically, confrontation with death often serves as the most powerful stimulant for coming to grips with the meaning of life. Over the door of the anatomy department at Oxford University, where autopsies are performed, is a sign that says, "Here is where death teaches life."

In Leo Tolstoy's famous story "The Death of Ivan Ilych," the protagonist contemplates his death, apparently for the first time. Ivan Ilych then realizes that "what had appeared to him utterly impossible before—that he had not lived his life as he should have done—might after all be true."[27] In contemplating his own death, Ilych discovers that death is a subject that cannot be approached with detached speculation, that death is no abstract philosophical category but an intimately personal matter. Tolstoy wrote:

> The syllogism he [Ivan Ilych] had learnt from Kiezewetter's logic: "Caius is a man, men are mortal, therefore Caius is mortal," had always seemed to him correct as applied to Caius, but certainly not as applied to himself. That Caius—man in the abstract—was mortal, was perfectly correct, but he was not Caius, not an abstract man, but a creature quite, quite separate from all others. . . . Caius really was mortal, and it was right for him to die, but for me Ivan Ilych with all my thoughts and emotions, it's altogether a different matter. It cannot be that I ought to die. That would be terrible.[28]

As an abstraction, death is merely one of the many facts of life. However, when dealing with one's own mortality death becomes a deeply personal issue that must be encountered. How a person deals with the reality of one's own mortality, how a human being confronts the finitude of his or her own life and the inevitability of his or her death, is directly related to how a person chooses to live his or her life, and what meaning a person wants to bestow upon the life one lives. Often it is the crushing awareness that death awaits each of us that leads an individual to consider the quality of life, the meaning of our own stay on earth. Whether our lives have meaning, and what that meaning might be, often remains obscure unless, and until, it is reflected upon in the face of death.[29]

Ironically, awareness of the reality of our own mortality can help serve as an auditor of the authenticity of our needs. The confrontation with the inevitability of death may frighten us, but it also may cajole us to confront the problem of what gives meaning to our lives, of which activities enhance and which activities erode meaning in our lives. Contemplation of death can help teach us how and why to live, how to infuse time with meaning, how to liberate ourselves from preoccupation with trivialities, how to live a life that matters.

In Thornton Wilder's play *Our Town,* there is a character named Emily who had been dead for a number of years. When she is given permission to relive any day in her life, she chooses her twelfth birthday. But as she watches her friends and her family go through the day, living each moment as if life were eternal, she becomes frustrated, sad, and angry, and she says:

> That's what it is to be alive. To move about in a cloud of ignorance; to go up and down, trampling on the feelings of those all about you. To spend and waste time as though you had a million years. To be always at the mercy of one self-centered passion, or another.[30]

Kierkegaard taught that people tend to live in a dreamlike trance, often unconsciously doing what is expected of them without pausing to consider whether their life has meaning and purpose. But in those moments when we are confronted with our own mortality is often when we find ourselves awakened to confront and to respond to life's deepest questions, to life's spiritual dimension. However, one need not become fixated upon the end of life to have an opportunity to reflect upon life's meaning.

Reflection upon life's meaning entails an awareness of what matters to each of us. The quest for meaning is a spiritual exercise aimed at guiding us in life's ultimate challenge—the crafting of each of our lives as a work of art. Each of us is confronted with the task of composing a book. Between its binders is the story of each of our lives. As the medieval Jewish philosopher Bahya Ibn Pakuda put it, "Life is like a book. Write in it what you wish to be known of you."[31] Had Bahya lived in modern times, he undoubtedly would have compared each person's life not simply to a book, but to a particularly modern type of book—the novel.

Think of yourself as the author of the novel that is your life. Then consider yourself as a literary critic writing a review of the novel that is the story of your life. How would you review it? Does it have a plot that offers meaning and coherence? Can you improve upon the chapters already written? How do you previsage the chapters yet to be written? Is the story interesting or boring, adventurous or tedious? How do you feel reading the novel that is the story of your life? How does it compare with what you thought it would be early on in the story? What would you want to add to the story that is not yet there? How would you like the whole story to read once it has come to an end? Does the novel "make sense"? Is the protagonist credible? Is he or she someone you would like to meet, someone you would like as a friend, someone you could trust, someone you could love, someone you would want to spend your life with? Would you buy the novel? Would you recommend it to a friend?

The novel is a literary art form, but life is the ultimate art form. Each individual has the opportunity to create the ultimate work of art—one's own life. This cannot be done by proxy; this task cannot be delegated to another. No one but one's own self can craft the work of art that is one's own life.

Tolstoy was one of the greatest literary artists of all time. As the ominous age of fifty rapidly approached, Tolstoy underwent a deep spiritual crisis. Having composed some of the greatest novels ever written, Tolstoy now turned inward to consider and to review the novel, the story of his own life.

As a writer, able to create, shape, and determine the lives of the characters in his novels, Tolstoy was omniscient and omnipotent. But

in confronting the protagonist in the story of his own life—himself—
Tolstoy felt powerless, uncertain, dismayed. "In my search for a solution to the problem of life," wrote Tolstoy, "I experienced the same
feeling as a man who is lost in a forest . . . rushing about trying to find
a way out, and, though he knows each step leads him still further
astray, cannot help rushing about."[32]

At the time of writing his remarkable inquiry into the meaning of
life entitled "A Confession," Tolstoy was living an enviable existence.
Precisely when, for no apparent reason, life seemed to Tolstoy to be "a
foolish and wicked joke played on me by someone,"[33] he was enjoying
everything a person could expect from life. This juxtaposition of wealth,
fame, and success with a feeling of meaninglessness, helplessness, and
almost suicidal despair only increased his anxiety over the purpose of
life. Fortunately, it also stirred his resolve to find a focus for renewed
meaning and purpose.

Tolstoy describes his life as having "come to a stop."[34] This description of a state of spiritual suffocation, of life in stasis, has been termed
"the general neurosis of our time"[35] by C. G. Jung. In his psychoanalytic practice Jung found that many of his middle-aged patients, particularly those who were "successful," manifested a feeling of the senselessness and meaninglessness of their lives, though they suffered from
no clinically definable physical or mental illness. "The ordinary expression for this situation," Jung wrote, "is: *'I am stuck.'*"[36]

Aware of the onset of physical deterioration, standing immobile at
the pinnacle of success, Tolstoy could only see decrepitude and death
awaiting him. His life had come to an abrupt halt with the eternal
stoppage of life—death—beginning to stare him bluntly in the face.
He asks, "Is there any meaning in my life that will not be destroyed by
the inevitable death awaiting me?"[37]

Tolstoy then begins an exhaustive study of the sciences and the hu-
manities to find an answer to his question. What he discovers is that
"these branches of knowledge were very interesting, very attractive,
but they were clear and exact in inverse proportion to their applicabil-
ity to the questions of life."[38] Having failed to find an answer in study,

Tolstoy then looks for an answer in life, that is, in the lives of those
around him. Not finding an answer in the upper classes to which he
belonged, Tolstoy turns to the common folk, and there—among those
without privilege of birth, without fame and fortune—he finds few
who torture themselves intellectually and psychologically over the
meaningfulness of life or the lack of it. Here he finds an instinctive
and natural affirmation of life that neither reason alone, nor philosophy, nor science can demonstrate convincingly. "It appeared," writes
Tolstoy, "that throughout mankind there is a knowledge of the meaning of life which I had neglected and despised. . . . The knowledge
based on reason, the knowledge of the learned and the wise, denies a
meaning to life, while the great mass of men, all humanity, have an
unreasoning knowledge of life which gives meaning to it."[39] The natural and tenacious lust for life, the struggle not to surrender life, the
celebration of the gift of life among the Russian peasantry, convinces
Tolstoy that the way to find meaning in life is by living it, that the
meaning of life is intrinsic to living. In Tolstoy's view, meaning in life
needs to be recovered more than it needs to be discovered.

A similar observation is found in Will Durant's 1932 anthology, *On
The Meaning Of Life*. Durant wrote to many of the great authors, scientists, religious leaders, and statesmen of his time asking them to
provide an answer to the question: What is the meaning of life? Many
of his respondents could offer no answer. Others responded by pointing to their accomplishments in their work. Apparently dissatisfied
with responses received from famous people, Durant added an appen-
dix to his book written by a prisoner at Sing Sing prison in New York
serving a life sentence. Convict #79206 writes that a person tends to
look everywhere for meaning, except in the obvious place—at life itself. For this man, life is what each person makes of it: "In short, life is
worth just what I am willing to make it worth. . . . It all depends upon
the faith one has in the soundness of his philosophy of life. . . . In the
knowledge that I am an inalienable part of the great, wonderful, upward movement called life, and that nothing, neither pestilence, nor
physical affliction, nor depression, nor prison, can take away from me

my part, lies my consolation, my inspiration, and my treasure."[40]

For Tolstoy, meaning in life can be grounded in five ingredients: (1) the awareness that meaning is intrinsic to life itself; (2) that to experience the meaningfulness of life one must do things that make life feel worthwhile; (3) that once purpose has been discovered and acted upon, neither the foibles of life nor the inevitability of death can deprive one of that meaning and purpose; (4) that witnessing the tenacious hold on the preciousness of life that the average person has offers a strong counterbalance to the speculations of philosophers who often can find no rational basis for life's meaning. If life has no meaning, Tolstoy queried, why aren't there massive suicides? If life has no meaning, then why do people cling to it so dearly? And (5) that meaning in life must be rooted in faith, in convictions, in values. As Tolstoy puts it, "Whatever answers any kind of faith ever gives to any one, every one of those answers gives an infinite meaning to the finite life of man, a meaning that is not destroyed by suffering, privation and death."[41] In the final analysis, George Bernard Shaw observed, each person has a choice in life. That choice is between a life of meaning and purpose, or life as "a feverish selfish little clod of ailments and grievances complaining that the world will not devote itself to making you happy."[42] Or, as William James, one of the founders of American pragmatic philosophy, put it: "Is life worth living? The answer depends upon the one who lives it."[43] In the chapter that follows, nine crucial ingredients for eliciting the meaning implicit in life will be offered. Crafting the soul is how we make explicit the implicit intrinsic meaning of human existence.

chapter eight

Crafting the Soul

Once there was a young man who wanted to become a blacksmith. So he became an apprentice to a master black-smith, and he learned all the necessary techniques of the trade: how to hold the tongs, how to lift the sledge, how to smite the anvil, even how to blow the fire with the bellows. Having completed his apprenticeship, he was chosen to be employed at the smithy of the royal palace. However, the young man's delight soon came to an end when he discovered that he had failed to learn how to kindle the spark. All his skill and knowledge in handling the tools were to no avail.

*I*n the eyes of the world, I am average. But in my own heart, I am of great moment. The challenge I face is how to actualize, how to con-cretize, the quiet eminence of my being."[1] So wrote the eminent Jew-ish theologian Abraham Joshua Heschel. Engaging in the task of craft-ing the soul is how a person can "concretize the quiet eminence" of his or her own being. The meaning of life is a problem to which crafting the soul is an answer.

Within each human soul, meaning flickers as a spark awaiting to be ignited. How one chooses to live, how one fashions one's life, deter-mines whether this spark will be smothered or whether it will burst forth as a flame. Cultivating the soul, the creation of life as a work of art, offers a path toward making extrinsic the intrinsic core of meaning that lays dormant within each human person. The task is not so much to discover the meaning *of* life as to evoke meaning *from* life. When both life and meaning are present, the challenge is to become a match-maker, to affect a sacred union between them. As the author of *The Little Prince*, Saint-Exupéry, writes in his novel *Wind, Sand and Stars*, "Each man must look to himself to teach him the meaning of life. It is not something discovered; it is something molded."[2]

At birth each of us is issued a passport to transcendence, an invitation to become more than we are. At life's end we are asked to justify how we have developed the raw materials—the talents and abilities—granted us at birth. In the art of life, each of us is responsible for creating the greatest work of art that we can. The person who does so thereby becomes his or her own guru. And how do we spell *guru*? Gee, you are you. Your soul, your life, can be crafted into the work of art it was created to become.

Which ingredients are required to produce a great work of art? Which ingredients are needed to craft one's soul as a work of art, to elicit meaning from life?

The first is hard and constant work. Great art is not the product of fleeting inspiration. As Thomas Alva Edison put it: Genius is 1 percent inspiration and 99 percent perspiration. [Actually, Goethe said it first, about fifty years before Edison.] Similarly, crafting the soul requires constant effort. In this regard, a great Lithuanian rabbi compared the spiritual development of a person to the flight of a bird. Once a bird stops exerting effort to fly, once a bird ceases flapping its wings, it falls. Similarly, crafting the soul requires constant exertion, study, reflection, and practice. The spiritual quest can never be a "quick fix." There is no instant spirituality, no prefabrications for life as a work of art. A single peak experience, an isolated twitter of excitement, even a series of "high" moments cannot create a spiritual life. Getting high is easy; remaining soulful is difficult. Excitement comes and goes. Creating life as an art form is a lifelong endeavor.

The second ingredient is study of past masterpieces. An apprentice artist must study the works and techniques of the masters before trying to compose a great work of his or her own. Each aspiring artist studies the works of those accomplished artists who came before. Similarly, those engaged in the art of life must study the lives and teachings of the spiritual virtuosos of the past who have mastered the art of soulcrafting. In crafting life as a work of art, no one is a self-made man. As Mark Twain once said, "A self-made man is about as likely as a self-laid egg." A person's own spiritual quest may become immeasurably enriched by tapping into the substantial resources bequeathed by past tradition and experience. Before one can become a pioneer, one must first become an heir to the legacy left to us by the spiritual masters who have preceded us. We would never buy a house or a car or deal with matters of our health without expert advice, without consulting those with knowledge and experience. Yet we tend to take our most valuable possessions—our souls—and allow them to develop without consultation with the wisdom of the past.

It is our spiritual dimension that ensures our uniqueness, that which makes each of us who we are, and who we can become. There has never been another human being like you, like your beloved, like your child. You may believe that uniqueness is limited to your fingerprints or to your DNA, but if you believe that there is more, that there is an ineffable, sublime essence to being human, that there is a quiet eminence to your unique mode of being, then how will you honor it? How will you nurture and develop it? Souls can grow. The aim of life is to end it with a soul more beautiful than when we began.

A third ingredient is the cultivation of wisdom, the power of discernment, the ability to understand what we know, to evaluate what we have learned. Knowledge is necessary, critical, crucial, but not sufficient. Knowledge of the insights bequeathed to us from the past is enriching, but of little value unless we have the wisdom to employ it.

Scripture tells us, "Wisdom is the principle thing; therefore, get wisdom."[3] Yet Scripture also reminds us that wisdom is rare, elusive, and therefore precious: "Wisdom, where shall it be found . . . it cannot be gotten for gold?"[4] But what is the nature of wisdom? What characterizes this priceless commodity?

It would be a mistake to identify knowledge with wisdom, perception with insight, erudition with understanding. Knowledge is what we know; knowledge is a readily accessible commodity. The computer age literally has placed infinite quantities of information, of knowledge, of data, at our fingertips. Knowledge can be accessed and processed, but wisdom cannot. While the sciences have much to say about knowledge, they have almost nothing to say about wisdom.

There is no wisdom at first sight. It comes out of the crucible of a quest. It emerges out of the dialogue between the mind and the soul, between thought and experience, between concerted effort and the grace of expanded consciousness. It is an acquisition that must be pursued as well as a gift that must be bestowed. As the Talmud states, "One who has acquired wisdom has acquired everything. One who has acquired wisdom, what does he lack? One who lacks wisdom, what has he acquired?"[5]

Like other spiritual traits, wisdom cannot be quantified. It cannot be weighed, measured, or easily defined. Jonas Salk said of wisdom, "It's something that you know when you see it. You can recognize it, you can experience it. Wisdom is the capacity to make judgments that looking back upon them seem to have been wise." Being wise is not something one has, but something one is. An Indian adage says "Wisdom is not the kind of knowledge you acquire but the kind you must become."

The opposite of knowledge is ignorance, but the opposite of wisdom is foolishness. "I search not," said a medieval sage, "for wisdom with the hope of ever coming to the end of it or of attaining it completely; rather I search for it so as not to be a fool. This should be the only motive in the search for wisdom."[6]

The wise person is one who recognizes that wisdom is a journey upon which one embarks, rather than a destination at which one arrives. Wisdom is a quest rather than an accomplishment. According to a medieval sage, "A person is only wise when he searches for wisdom; when he imagines he has completely attained it, he is a fool."[7]

Wisdom begins not with problem solving, but with problem finding. The wise person may be detected by the quality of problems posed, and by the process undertaken to provide responses to those problems. The wise person knows what he or she knows and what he or she does not know. The wise person has the ability to understand what he or she knows. Wisdom entails discernment—the ability to make perceptive judgments rather than expedient decisions. The wise person never claims omniscience, but possesses knowledge while acknowledging doubt. Wisdom is characterized by prudence and perspicacity.

The knowledgeable person is not necessarily identical to the wise person. Knowledge of a specialized subject does not guarantee wisdom. For example, as Rabelais wrote, "The greatest scholars are not the wisest of people."[8] Nor is wide erudition a guarantor of wisdom. The medieval Jewish sage Nahmanides characterized a person with great stores of information who does not know how to apply it to "a donkey carrying books."[9]

A Spanish proverb says "Saber es poder," "Knowledge is power." Centuries later, T. S. Eliot asked, "Where is the wisdom we have lost in knowledge?"[10] It is dangerous when knowledge smothers wisdom, when power eclipses the expansion of wisdom. Ironically, the expansion of power that aimed at achieving security has led to the fragility of security. As Nietzsche warned, "The expansion of power . . . frequently risks or even sacrifices self-preservation."[11]

The intelligent person can recall, analyze, and utilize information, while the wise person will also reflect upon the presuppositions, the meaning, and the limitations of what is known. The intelligent person aims at making decisions on the basis of authority or knowledge or established procedures or social conventions. The wise person will counsel judicial prudence and empathy for others in the process of decision making. The intelligent person will seek to eliminate ambiguity and to overcome obstacles within an established framework.

The wise person will manifest a deeper appreciation of present obstacles and ambiguities.

Wisdom is a means of evaluating the ultimate consequences of events in terms of each other. Wisdom asks us to embrace the path of judiciousness over that of opportunism, to question answers as well as to answer questions, to survey the panorama rather than to rest content with myopic vision, to anticipate long-range consequences rather than to be satisfied with meeting short-term needs. The application of wisdom acts as a prophylactic against short-sightedness. It counsels us against confusing momentary whims with lifelong aspirations, transient pleasures with spiritual fulfillment, needs satisfaction with authentic happiness. Wisdom is basically counsel about how life should be lived.

Plato wrote "All things hang upon the soul, and all the things of the soul herself hang upon wisdom."[12] In other words, without wisdom, advantages like health, wealth, success, power, honor, and prestige are ultimately useless because without wisdom a person will not know how to get benefit from them. For example, according to St. Thomas Aquinas, a characteristic of wisdom is "the ability of seeing through things."[13] The wise person tries to pierce the veil of apparencies, of appearances—of what Plato called "the convenient fictions"[14] that restrict our vision of ourselves and of our world. For Aristotle, wisdom entails being aware of how things happen as a prelude to trying to discern why things happen. Wisdom is the quest for purpose beyond causality, for meaning beyond the mundane. Wisdom points to what to value. A wise decision is a good decision; it is, therefore, a value-laden decision. Wisdom is the bridge between knowledge and action, between belief and virtue. As Plato said, "Wisdom is the essence of virtue."[15] Without wisdom the soul is blind, but without correlative deeds life becomes lame.

Throughout history, and in a wide variety of cultures, the pursuit of wisdom has been associated with joy, transcendence, and ecstasy. According to Plato, the person who cultivates wisdom appreciates both the pleasures of the body and the contemplative pleasures of the mind.

Consequently, the quest for wisdom is intrinsically rewarding. Wisdom is its own reward.

Throughout the ages, wisdom has been linked to ecstasy. In the literal sense, *ecstasy* means "to stand outside." In other words, wisdom entails the ability—at least for a while, to stand outside and apart from ordinary awareness, to transcend the petty problems that tend to make life a game of Trivial Pursuit. We are thereby able to transcend the ordinary, to find the self by losing self-consciousness, to see ourselves and our world from a higher, more expansive plane. We are then able to shift attention from snapshots to the big picture. Wisdom demands commitment to an idea, an ideal, a relationship that transcends the confines of the self. Wisdom informs us that to fulfill the self we must transcend the self, that the path to self-fulfillment stands outside of our selves, that to be who we are we must become more than we are. Paradoxically, the quest for self-fulfillment is doomed to fail if it both begins and ends with the self. Making the self an end in itself inevitably leads to a dead end. While self-fulfillment must begin with the self, within the self, it must lead beyond the self. Paradoxically, self-fulfillment must entail self-transcendence.

Wisdom is the catalyst that leads us to understand what we believe, the conduit that counsels us in articulating our convictions as actions. Knowing what we believe leads us into a waiting room, but not into an inner chamber. Belief is an invitation to action. If our affirmations are not articulated as deeds, they will wither. Belief is like a tree and deeds are like the fruit of the tree. Belief without virtuous deeds is like a tree without fruit—barren, lifeless. Without light, a tree cannot bring forth fruit. Without enlightenment, without wisdom, ideas and convictions remain stillborn.

A fourth ingredient is imagination. We need to transcend ourselves in order to envision who we yet can become. Without imagination, without vision, an artist has nothing to express, nothing to convey. Neither the life of art nor the art of life can move to a higher plane without imagination, vision, dreams. Preoccupation with quantifying and measuring everything, obsession with the credits and debits that constitute the balance sheet of our deeds, stifles the development of a life of spirituality and derails the mission of crafting the soul.

In an episode of *Star Trek: The Next Generation,* a strange malady inexplicably affects the members of the crew. People become anxious and irritable; some go insane. Then they start to die. Medical tests are run, but without results. The cause of the strange illness cannot be identified by any means of medical diagnostic technology. In discussing the situation, the crew members discover that they have something in common, something that they initially had overlooked, something that might be the cause of the affliction. What they find out is that for some reason, the crew members had stopped dreaming. A drug is prepared that reintroduces dreams into the sleep cycle. As a result of taking the preparation, people begin to dream again. The crisis passes.

The moral of the story is that people cannot live without dreams. The same lesson is taught by the biblical prophets: "Without vision the people perish"[16]; and by Shakespeare: "We are such stuff as dreams are made."[17] Or, as Thoreau put it, "I learned at least this by my experiments. That if one advances confidently in the direction of his dreams, and endeavors to live the life he has imagined, he will meet with a success unexpected in common hours. He will put something behind and will pass an invisible boundary."[18]

Like any other creative endeavor, creating life as a work of art requires dreams, visions, fantasies, imagination. In this regard, Rabbi Nahman of Bratzlav interpreted the biblical verse describing the human being as created in the divine image as meaning that the human being, like God, is a being with *imagination,* that is, a being who fantasizes, who imagines, who dreams, and therefore, who can create. Similarly, as Csikszentmihalyi reminds us in his study *Creativity,* "To be human means to be creative."[19]

At the core of creativity is fantasy, imagination. In creating one's life as a work of art, knowledge is important, wisdom is required, but creativity is crucial. As in the creation of any work of art, creativity is a sine qua non. In his studies about the nature of wisdom, psychologist

Robert Sternberg distinguishes among intelligence, wisdom, and creativity. According to Sternberg, whereas the intelligent person will know and use what is already known, and the wise person will strive to understand the nature of what is known, the creative person will strive to go beyond what is known and understood. The creative person will attempt to transcend the conventional, to break through barriers to arrive at novelty.[20] The knowledgeable person aims at preserving what we know. The wise person aims at understanding what we know and at using it judiciously. The creative person attempts to use what we know to transcend what we know in order to create something and someone unprecedented. The life of the authentically creative person is an original work of art.

Creativity is an antidote to boredom, to spiritual incarceration, to suffocating conformity, to stifling predictability. It expands the boundaries of the self, of the soul. It fills vacant voids. The realm of the fantastic is a needed counterbalance to the fatalistic. Fatalism closes off options; dreams open them up. However, dreams are a point of departure, not a destination. Fantasy expands the realm of possibility. But fantasy is the flow that eventually must give way to the ebb.

Dreams and fantasies are like fire; they can illuminate or devour, warm or burn, nurture or destroy. Regretfully, many people's fantasies do not relate to creating their own life as a work of art, nor to composing the script of their own life's drama. Rather, they relate to devising a way of imposing upon their life a script dictated by others and by societal norms. Ironically, fantasy which personifies freedom becomes controlled by social forces that desire to deny individual freedom by casting the individual into a preconceived mold. Strangely, the individual becomes compelled to fantasize about what others want her to be rather than who she might want to become. Fantasies that should emerge spontaneously from within the self often are imposed upon the self from without. For example, we are constantly bombarded with visions of what our fantasies should be in endless commercials. Commercials regularly appeal to our fantasies to be beautiful, thin, wealthy, athletic, and desirable. "I want to be like Mike," says one commercial, suggesting that if you buy a certain product, you will be able to play basketball like Michael Jordan. If you eat a certain yogurt, you will be thin like Cher. If you use a certain perfume, you'll be as desirable as this or that movie star. I always have found it surprising that commercials rarely evoke a desire to become wise—probably because if we were wise, we would not believe the other commercials.

If a person mostly appropriates her fantasies from outside the self, then they are not her own fantasies but those of others. A person must dream her own dreams and must fantasize her own fantasies. To plagiarize the fantasies of others can only lead to a plagiarized philosophy of one's own life—indeed, to a plagiarized life, to living inauthentically, in "bad faith."

Crafting the soul begins with our own vision, with our own dream of who we want to be, of what kind of person we want to become. The next task is bringing about a transition from where and who we are now to where we want to be and to who we want to become and can become.

A fifth ingredient in crafting the soul is the inculcation of humility. Humility is a state of the soul that facilitates the development of life in a creative way. In his authoritative study of creativity, psychotherapist Silvano Arieti writes that "an attitude of humility, of willingness to make even the smallest contributions and to accept a life of commitment and dedication, must be part of the potentially creative person's way of life."[21]

Humility is considered a virtue, partly because it is a vital component in creativity, particularly in the creation of life as a work of art. The truly creative person knows that setting aside the ego is necessary for the creative process to proceed unhampered by one's being overly self-conscious. Such a person realizes that the ego can serve as the greatest obstacle to free creative expression. For example, the great actor must first empty himself out of himself in order to play a dramatic role successfully. When Ben Kingsley won the Academy Award for playing Gandhi, he said that he had to move his ego out of himself in order to allow Gandhi's presence a place within himself. Similarly, in an interview Luciano Pavarotti said that if he thinks about what the critics might say while he is singing, he becomes too self-preoccupied to be able to hit the high notes. Only when he forgets about what the critics might say, only when he suppresses his ego, can he sing his best, can his true artistic self emerge. In the same way, a great artist or author can never produce a great work of art or literature while being preoccupied with ego needs, while worrying about what the critics might write. Great athletes know that focusing on the ego when engaged in an athletic feat only serves to deflect their attention from the task at hand, and leads inevitably to failure. In the art of love, as well, the ego can be an obstacle in the bonding of lovers. As Bertrand Russell put it, "Too powerful an ego is a prison from which to escape."[22]

The opposite of humility is pride. The Bible already warned of the destructive nature of pride. Proverbs says: "Pride precedes destruction and a haughty spirit goes before a fall."[23] Why is pride or arrogance considered a moral vice? Why is it viewed as being so harmful, so dangerous to the creation of life as a work of art? Why is it identified as a corrosive disease of the soul?

The first reason that pride is dangerous is because it is self-deceptive. It fools us into thinking that we are more important than we really are, that we have accomplished more than we have actually attained. It deceives us into believing that we have few or no faults, few or no shortcomings, that our problems are because of the faults and shortcomings of others, or that we are too perfect to have any problems. It stifles the process of moral self-improvement by deceiving us into believing that we are too good to improve. In a sense, pride blinds us when we look at ourselves because it prevents us from seeing who we truly are. It thereby stifles us from becoming who we really can become. It suffocates the actualization of our potentialities by leading us to believe that we could not possibly be better than we already are. The arrogant person is one who is self-indulged and self-deluded. While constantly finding faults with others, he remains oblivious to his own shortcomings.

Second, pride is dangerous because it stifles relationships. The ego stands as an impenetrable barrier between ourselves and others, re-stricting our ability to transcend ourselves in order to be able to forge a relationship with someone else. Narcissus, for example, could not love another because he could not see beyond his own self. Pride is dangerous because it hinders our ability to love, to commit. Pride traps the individual into the isolation, into the prison, of one's own ego.

Third, pride is dangerous because it is self-destructive as well as destructive of relationships. For example, one of the most self-destructive psychological states is depression. Yet certain wisdom fig-ures, past and present, link depression to pride. They understand arro-gance and depression to be two sides of the same coin of ego obses-sion. The arrogant person is obsessed in an exaggerated way with how important he or she is. The depressed person is ego obsessed with how miserable he or she is.

In this view, anger is a form of ego obsession. Anger is considered a disease of the soul. Depression is a form of anger directed against one's own self. Anger can obsess an individual, propelling him or her to act destructively. More often anger controls the individual, rather than the individual being able to control his or her anger. Anger is danger-ous not only because of what harm a person can do to himself, but because of what harm an angry person can inflict upon others. Anger is destructive not only in terms of what it can do but also because of what it can cause that cannot be undone. It is told that a certain rabbi would pray each night before going to bed, "Dear God, one thing I ask of you and that is not to allow me to be angry, for anger is the root of all transgression."

The egocentric person can never find contentment in possessions or in associations because he views everything and everyone merely as extensions of his own ego. For example, a person who constantly refers to "my spouse," "my house," "my career," "my money" sees these people and things not as having value in themselves, but as extensions of his own ego. The arrogant person sees gifts given as entitlements. Never satisfied with what he has, with anything anyone does to please him, he scowls at others, and criticizes others for not being as perfect as he thinks himself to be. An infinitely expanding universe, the ego of the arrogant person can never find satisfaction in what he has. This attitude is self-destructive in the long run.

A fundamental insight of most mystical traditions is that only by losing the ego can we find the self, the soul. Obsessive preoccupation with the ego is bad for our health, both physically and spiritually. For example, in a study of six hundred men Professor Larry Scherwitz, a University of California psychologist, found that those who often used the first-person pronouns "I," "me," and "mine" had the highest risk of heart trouble.[24] After following his subjects for several years, Professor Scherwitz found that the more habitually a man talked about himself, the greater the chance he would have a coronary, that self-obsession may be a greater catalyst for the onset of heart disease than smoking, improper diet, or lack of exercise. No wonder many religious traditions encourage humility. Many mystical schools discourage their adherents from using the word "I," or from spending too much time thinking about themselves. What Csikszentmihalyi writes from the point of view of a secular psychologist restates what many religious traditions have known and taught for centuries: "When not preoccupied with ourselves, we actually have a chance to expand the concept of who we are. Loss of self-consciousness can lead to self-transcendence, to a feeling that the boundaries of our being have been pushed forward."[25]

Finally, let us consider three important antidotes to pride. The first is considering the vicissitudes of life. The rich can become poor, the healthy ill, the powerful weak, the famous obscure. What might engender arrogance today might be gone tomorrow. Sometimes life is like a wheel of fortune—one day we are on top and the next day we are not. A second antidote to pride is a confrontation with the reality of our own mortality. As the Talmud bluntly puts it, "Let a person be humble, for the end of mortals is worms."[26] The third is developing the attitude of gratitude. As a medieval Hebrew proverb puts it, "The arrogant person is always preoccupied with having what he or she wants, while the humble person is grateful for wanting what he or she has."[27]

A sixth component of artful existence is the need to make choices, judgments, commitments—the decision to decide. As was noted above, Kierkegaard translated Socrates' admonition "know thyself" as "choose thyself." In a real way, an individual is the sum of choices made over a lifetime.

Having dreamed our dreams, having become sensitized to the dangers of self-deception, having embarked upon the quest for knowledge and wisdom, we inevitably reach a point when a leap of faith is necessary, when it is time to take a risk, to make a choice, to act—even if it ultimately ends up as not being the optimum choice, the best choice, or the right choice. Not making any choice only leads us to anxiety, to helplessness, to spiritual paralysis. As Bertrand Russell put it, "Nothing is so exhausting as indecision, and nothing so futile."[28] In this regard, consider the old story of Buridan's ass.

The medieval philosopher Buridan had a donkey who, like its master, was a philosopher. One day, rather than offering the donkey his morning bale of hay, Buridan offered the donkey two equal bales of hay. The donkey spent the entire day trying rationally to decide which bale of hay to eat. But the donkey could not decide which bale of hay was the better one. This went on day after day until the donkey, unable to decide, starved to death. In a way, human existence is a game of "you bet your life." We must take the risk of making a choice, even though it might be the wrong choice. Nonetheless, one must make a leap of commitment before starving to death while viewing the repast of options set out before us.

A seventh ingredient in crafting the soul entails the focusing of one's thoughts, choices, commitments, and actions on what matters most, on what is most meaningful. This requires two things: (1) the thoughtful choice of a task, a goal, a project replete with meaning, and (2) the discipline to focus on that task.

As in the creation of any work of art, the creation of life as a work of art presumes our ability to focus, to sharpen our perspective on the world, on oneself, on one's purpose, on what matters most. Focusing one's attention is not an easy task. It is told, for example, that when

Napoleon invaded Poland, he came to the town of Kotzk where the Hasidic master, Rabbi Mendel of Kotzk, lived. Napoleon heard that Rabbi Mendel was a great man, and wanted to know the nature of his greatness. Napoleon summoned the rabbi, who came before Napoleon. Napoleon said, "I have heard that you are a great man. What can you do that others cannot do?"

Rabbi Mendel replied, "I can focus on a single thought for as long as I want."

Napoleon laughed, "And for this, people believe you are great?"

The Rabbi of Kotzk curtly replied, "Try it."

Shocked by this overt challenge, Napoleon turned to his generals and asked each to try it. Each general tried to think of a single thought for five minutes, but each failed. Various things distracted them. Other ideas entered their mind as soon as they tried to focus on a single thought. The generals confessed their failure to Napoleon.

The Rabbi of Kotzk then turned to Napoleon and said, "Surely a man as great as you could do what your generals are unable to do. Try it. For ten minutes, try it."

But, as much as Napoleon tried, he could not succeed. Finally, he turned to the Rabbi of Kotzk and he said, "Yes, it is true. If you can focus upon a single thought for as long as you want, then you are surely a great man."

All meditative techniques are ways to achieve and to sharpen the ability to focus. Meditation aims at two things: focusing concentrated attention on something, and shutting out extraneous "static" filtering into one's consciousness from elsewhere. Put another way, in meditation a person "turns on" to that which is the object of concentration while "turning off" other stimuli and distractions. Various methods of meditation utilize different techniques to accomplish these aims.

The most common form of distraction to be filtered out of the consciousness is self-consciousness. Thinking about *how* one is doing *while* one is doing it deflects attention from the task at hand. A characteristic of the narcissistic personality is always to ask, How am I doing? Instead of worrying about how he is doing, the focused person concentrates wholeheartedly upon the goal at hand. The depth of involvement pushes self-consciousness out of awareness. The mystics often spoke about finding themselves by losing themselves in God. This insight reflects the paradox of intense concentration. By losing self-consciousness, the self becomes amplified and enriched. By surrendering the ego, one encounters the self.

An eighth component relates to the enactment of meaningful goals. Crafting the soul entails the enactment of an action plan to articulate in deeds those ideas, commitments, and values that matter most. But focusing on a goal requires a goal upon which to focus. Accomplishing meaningful goals is a crucial component in enacting life's meaning. Goals provide us with something to live for—a project, a profession, a "calling," a family—and the body and soul respond with vitality. The goal-oriented person wakes up each day ready to devote himself to the task at hand. But meeting particular goals does not occur automatically. Certain requisites must be present. For example, choice, commitment, focus, knowledge, and effort are necessary prerequisites for translating dreams into plans, plans into goals, and goals into accomplished deeds. Yet, by themselves, these requisites are not sufficient to the task. Certain abilities and skills are also required. Sometimes one must undertake a program of long and hard study and practice to acquire and develop the skills necessary to perform a certain task, to accomplish a certain goal. Yet, even before beginning such training, it is first necessary to exercise critical judgment regarding whether one has the innate abilities required for the development of a certain skill. Once there is a confluence among choice, ability, and skill, once the obstacles are apprehended and movement toward the goal begins in earnest, it becomes necessary to focus on the pursuit of the goal.

In striving to achieve one's goals, the truth of the old maxim "As the pain, so the gain" rings true. In fairy tales and legends, the hero must overcome many formidable obstacles to reach the goal. Overcoming these obstacles makes attaining the goal highly valued and precious. Among these obstacles there usually are distractions meant to deflect the hero's movement toward the goal. Such distractions are often more dangerous than the various physical obstacles the hero must overcome, because distractions can completely derail the entire quest toward reaching the hero's goal.

It is not by chance that the most highly admired people are those who have overcome considerable obstacles and handicaps to achieve their goals. What is significant here is that an obstacle may serve as a hindrance or as a challenge, depending upon how it is perceived. Overcoming obstacles and disappointments serves as a test—as in legends— of the protagonist's commitment to achieve the set goal. Obstacles compel us to realize whether and how much we value the accomplishments we wish to obtain. Sometimes it takes a trauma for an individual to clarify his or her goals. However, once there are clear obstacles to overcome, and once one has become committed to surmount them, then one's real goals suddenly become self-evident. For example, these are the words of a twenty-year-old who was injured in an accident and became paralyzed below the waist: "When I became a paraplegic, it was like being born again. I had to learn from scratch everything I used to know, but in a different way. . . . Everybody must have a purpose. After becoming a paraplegic, these improvements became my life goal."[29] The ability to transform tragedy into a challenge, adversity into a goal, sadness into joy is not only essential for survival, but is critical for creating life as an art form. Rabbi Mendel taught that there are three possible responses to tragedy: to scream, to cry, or to transform sorrow into a song. The latter is preferable.

Courage and commitment are required, but as Socrates pointed out centuries ago, the line between courage and foolishness is a thin one. To reach a goal means overcoming a challenge, an obstacle that obstructs clear passage from where we are to where we wish to go. If the challenges are, in fact, insurmountable, then the goal becomes unattainable. Trying to attain it would be foolish, not courageous. One must further evaluate whether the goal fits into one's sense of purpose and value, that is, whether achieving the goal is worth the risk, the potential pain, and the frustration that achieving it might entail.

In choosing goals, balance is important. Opportunities for action must be balanced with one's available capacities and skills. Often people elect unrealistic goals, either in terms of scope (such as a goal to save the world), or in terms of their skills (such as a goal to cure all disease), or in terms of a time frame (such as a goal to manage IBM within three years of receiving an MBA). What then often occurs is that the person becomes despondent and loses confidence in his ability to accomplish *any* formidable goal. According to some psychoanalysts, the missing element of the neurotic personality is recognition and appreciation of an appropriate sense of limits. As psychoanalyst Karen Horney said, "Every neurotic is at bottom loath to recognize limitations to what he expects of himself and believes it possible to attain." While creativity presumes limitless possibilities, the creation of a particular work of art presumes limits—limits of the artist's talent, limits of time, limits of available raw materials from which to work.[30] Similarly, the creation of one's own particular life as a work of art means balancing fantasies with innate and developed abilities, unrestrained dreams with achievable challenges and goals. Being aware of one's real limitations is a source of power rather than of weakness. As poet Richard Wilbur puts it, "Limitation makes for power: the strength of the genie comes from his being confined in the bottle."[31]

Taking inventory of one's potentials while simultaneously accepting one's limitations is always a daunting undertaking, especially for Americans who are ingrained with the myth that you can be whatever you want to be. A more sober approach recommends that you can be whatever you can be. Awareness of one's limitations should not be viewed as an exercise in closing possibilities, but as one of clarifying options. Only once we are aware of what we cannot do or of what we can no longer do—such as because of physical limitations due, for instance, to age—can we begin to focus upon what we can realistically expect to accomplish. For example, it would be both foolish and cruel to expect oneself to become an opera star if one were a monotone. Similarly, an unathletic person could not realistically anticipate winning Olympic medals. Limitless options lead only to anxiety. Limiting possibilities can lead to choice and eventually to satisfying, meaningful action. Accepting one's limitations is not a confession of failure, but an act of inner liberation. Once one knows what one cannot do, one becomes free to set out on the path of accomplishing what one can do, of becoming who one can become.

Two critical components of the spiritual life are the recognition of limitations and the actualization of potentiality. In this task, a person must employ the judgment of neither overestimating their limitations nor of underestimating their potentialities.

One very common way in which individuals fail to accept their own real limitations is by always trying to be perfect. Ironically, the attempt to always be perfect stifles the actualization of their own unique and particular potentialities. Many frustrate themselves and set themselves up for inevitable failure by demanding perfection from themselves. Perhaps they are motivated by the fear that if they are not perfect, they will lose the love, acceptance, and validation they so desperately need and seek from others.

That one always has to be perfect is not only an unrealistic idea, but a dangerous one as well.[32] It is unrealistic because human beings are, by nature, imperfect. It is dangerous because no one can ever fulfill this expectation, and a person who believes she can only sets herself up for frustration and anxiety. And once a person realizes that she cannot be perfect, she might simply give up, and resign from the vocation of spiritual development. "If it's all or none—then if it cannot be all, let it be none," such a person might say.

The artist Salvador Dali once said, "Have no fear of perfection— you'll never reach it." Even God did not create a perfect world—far from it. In the life of art as well as in the art of life, expecting perfection is illusionary, unrealistic. Yet many people live their lives in anxiety and frustration because they fear not being perfect—not being in perfect health, not being perfect spouses, children, colleagues, and so forth. For a person obsessed with perfection, making a mistake is an irreparable catastrophe that will inevitably call down the wrath of others. Yet, for others, making a mistake can be an opportunity for learning something new, for spiritual development, and for discovering the healing power of forgiveness and love. No one would punish a child learning how to walk because the child stumbles and falls. Yet, some people punish themselves as they occasionally stumble on the journey of life. Pencils still have two sides, lead and an eraser, because people are not perfect, because we make mistakes. Being perfect is not part of our nature, but being able to learn from and to correct our mistakes is. A danger of expecting perfection is that the horror of not achieving it can inhibit our actions, paralyze our talents, stifle the crafting of life as a work of art.

No one can do everything. Saving the world is too large a task for an individual to undertake. Trying single-handedly to bring Utopia is bound to end in despondency. When a young man asked Carlyle how he should go about reforming the world, Carlyle answered, "Reform yourself. That way there will be one less rascal in the world."[33]

Most of us will not be what the philosopher Hegel called the heroes of history. Our accomplishments will be more modest, though not necessarily trivial. For example, as Emily Dickinson wrote:

If I can stop one heart from breaking
I shall not live in vain.
If I can ease one life the aching,
or cool one pain . . .

.   .   .   .   .
I shall not live in vain.[34]

Or, as Jung has written, "The least of things with a meaning is worth more in life than the greatest of things without it."[35]

On one side of the spectrum there are those who fail to meet their goals because their goals exceed the ken of their abilities and skills. To strive to reach the unreachable goal only invites frustration and despair. On the other side of the spectrum are those who sell themselves short. These include individuals who seek the security of inaction by underestimating their skills and abilities, who feign humility to avoid responsibility, who are eminently able but who pretend to be disabled when a different but achievable challenge confronts them. Such people either fail to try or try to fail in order to reinforce their fatalistic predictions about their abilities to accomplish their goals. They then wonder why they feel disillusioned, unfulfilled, anxious, and despondent. Yet, in the deepest recesses of their souls, they know that, as Pogo puts it, "We have met the enemy, and they are us." They are somehow aware that, as their life's motto, they have chosen the adage: "There but for me, goes I."

Challenges and goals require appropriate skills. When challenges are high and correlative skills and abilities are low, an activity becomes meaningless and anxiety evoking. When challenges are low and skills and abilities are high, a feeling of boredom and listlessness emerges. However, when challenges are high and personal skills are up to the goal at hand and are utilized to the utmost, we experience a rare sense of heightened consciousness, an enviable sense of accomplishment, a desirable state of self-fulfillment. Psychologist Mihaly Csikszentmihalyi has called such a state "flow." Others have described it as a state of life satisfaction. It is very similar to the transcendence or expanded consciousness described in a wide variety of mystical traditions. There are a number of characteristics of this state that bear consideration when implementing an action plan that articulates one's goals.

In flow, a goal becomes wedded to a specific task. This demands the focusing of attention on a clearly defined goal, knowing what must be done and how to do it. The task must be one we have a chance of completing; otherwise, anxiety and frustration will inevitably set in. Once committed to the task, intense focusing becomes necessary. We narrow our beam of consciousness to a clearly delimited stimulus field. This entails excluding irrelevant stimuli and thoughts from one's immediate awareness, filtering out the static to concentrate on the task at hand. A merging of action and awareness should then ensue. This requires a suspension of doubt and critical reflection about one's current activity. In a sense, the activity becomes incarnated into the individual. The actor and the action become one. As one commences the activity, a lack of concern regarding one's ability to control the situation emerges. One is caught up in the flow of the activity. Already attained skills are applied without self-consciousness, without thought of external rewards. Ironically, when caught up in the flow one does not feel oneself in control, yet one finds oneself able to exercise control over remarkably complex and difficult situations. Acquired discipline merges with spontaneous action in the pursuit of the focused goal. One becomes absorbed in the activity for its own sake. One becomes lost in the activity, too busy to think of oneself, too involved in the task to be self-conscious. Paradoxically, though self-concern disappears during the activity, the sense of self subsequently emerges stronger after the experience. During the activity, one's perception of time is altered. The enjoyment of the activity, rather than the tyranny of the clock, governs one's experience. Extensive periods of time are experienced as fulfilling moments of short duration.

Like music, a flow activity is partly scored and partly improvised. We have control, yet we also lose control. During flow, our acuity is at its sharpest. The realm of our senses is heightened. We look at the same things, yet we are able to see more than before. We listen to the same sounds, yet hear them in a new, amplified, and enriched manner. Our sense of touch conveys a broadened sense of awareness. Our sense of smell becomes surprisingly heightened. Our sense of timing becomes remarkably synchronic. We become in tune with what we are doing, with who we are, with who we want to become. We experience the present in all its fullness. We taste the whole kernel of the moment before it is ground into powder by the imposition of external analysis, judgment, and approval. We perceive relationships between things that escaped us before. Indeed, Arthur Koestler once defined creativity as the bringing together of two apparently unrelated entities or ideas in a new way. A paradigm for flow is lovemaking; certainly the most exalted type of lovemaking exists in the onrush of flow. At its best, lovemaking can be the flow of one person into another. In flow, the boundaries of the self are expanded, voids within the soul are suddenly filled, ego boundaries seem erased as the individual transcends her own self. Chaos is cheated as one fulfills one's sense of purpose.

These features of flow activity can be implemented in almost all realms of experience. They cut across a wide variety of radically diverse activities. For example, flow may be experienced by an athlete in an athletic competition, by an artist drawing a painting, by a writer authoring a book, by a parent playing with a child, by lovers engaged in the sweet pandemonium of lovemaking, by a cook preparing a meal, by an attorney arguing the cause of a client, by a businessperson pursuing a deal, by a hiker climbing a mountain, by a craftsperson engaging in her craft. Flow extends from the martial arts to the marital arts. Few areas of deliberate, creative, or purposeful activity may be excluded from the potential of becoming flow experiences. It all depends upon how they are engaged in. And, ultimately, it all depends on first having faith in a system of meanings that offer coherence and purpose to one's life. Flow is consistent with the observation of the novelist Aldous Huxley, who wrote, "Experience is not what happens to you; it is what you do with what happens to you."[36]

The results of such transcendent experiences have been described by psychologist Marghanita Laski as producing four basic effects: (1) an extraordinary sense of inner harmony; (2) a feeling of deep intensity or focus; (3) illumination, that is, creative thought; and (4) insight, that is, understanding that which was not previously understood.[37] As a result of such an experience, the boundaries of the self are enlarged. We find out something new about ourselves. The loss of self-consciousness during the activity leads not to a loss of consciousness of the self, but rather to the amplification of the self, to the expansion of consciousness, to the awareness of the self's ability to transcend and to transform itself. In this way, everyday experiences may become elevated experiences. Theologians call this "the sanctification of the mundane," the hallowing of those experiences that constitute our daily routine. Flow can transform the mundane into the sacred, the routine into the enjoyable, the tedious into the transcendent.

Rituals are means of transforming the mundane into the sacred. Rituals can sanctify both space and time, places and moments. Besides the religious rituals that one observes, a person can also celebrate personal rituals. For example, some people create a sanctuary for themselves—a hallowed place where they place those objects that remind them of what matters most. Birthdays and anniversaries of significant events in one's life can serve as sacred times upon which to reflect and to refocus one's life around who and what matters most. Bracketing time each week or each day for reflection, for meditation, for quality time with those who matter most, with special projects, can add sacred significance to otherwise dormant moments. Often, all it takes to transform a mundane place or an otherwise mundane moment into a holy place, into a sacred moment, is the performance of a small ritual, a sacramental interlude that can act as a talisman against the tyranny of the clock.

A transcendent experience is also enjoyable and autotelic, that is, it is worth seeking for its own intrinsic (rather than extrinsic or societal) rewards and fulfillment. Such a feeling of accomplishment and approval comes from within rather than from without. As Kierkegaard put it, "Happiness is a door that opens outward."[38]

Csikszentmihalyi describes what he calls the "T-person," the transcendent self, the individual who has taken responsibility for his own evolution. Such a person is original yet systematic, independent yet responsible, bold yet disciplined, intuitive yet rational. Such an individual knows how to create life as a work of art.[39]

Purposeful activity toward a goal can lead to a feeling of inner success, personal accomplishment, and authentic joy. However, it must not be facilely identified with pleasure for pleasure's sake. According to the Greek philosophers, happiness may not be equated with pleasure. They defined happiness as the achievement of the highest values or goals in life, such as realizing one's potential to be virtuous. The virtuous life, the life characterized by the realization of one's potentials, may be fulfilling, self-transcendent, marked by inner success and outer accomplishment. It may be enjoyable, but it is not pleasurable for pleasure's sake. The discipline one must exercise, the training one must endure, the efforts one must invest, the concentration one must expend, require exertion, sometimes pain, and often sacrifice. This can be the road to fulfillment, the road to life satisfaction, but not necessarily the path to pleasure. From this perspective, happiness is not primarily aimed at satisfying our quest for pleasure, but to facilitating our search for meaning, our hunger for purpose, our desire to accomplish significant goals. Pleasure for its own sake dissipates rapidly, addicting us to the desire to recapture it and to escalate it. Pleasure for pleasure's sake only leads us to ultimate dissatisfaction, to eventual unhappiness and lack of self-fulfillment.

A fixation upon physical pleasure can become addictive, restrictive, and can thwart the creation of life as a work of art. There is ample evidence to refute the view that the body knows what is best for itself, that we should do only what feels good, that interference with the pleasures of the body is a conspiracy of puritans who want to make our lives miserable, that pleasure should be satisfied without any fear of the consequences. Yet, the increasing number of drug addicts, alcoholics, sufferers from sexual diseases, unwanted pregnancies, and compulsive overeaters demonstrates that doing what feels good can easily lead to feeling bad indeed. For instance, rats who have a choice between eating and electrically stimulating the pleasure centers of the brain will choose stimulation and will die of hunger—and of pleasure. Similar human behavior shows how easily we, too, can succumb to physical pleasure. Pleasure as an end in itself is a dead end. It offers pleasing physical sensations but not happiness. Pleasure is like a treadmill where satisfaction is transient and must be perpetually and continuously stimulated to be maintained.

Pleasure is a means to an end, rather than being an end in itself. The purpose of pleasure is to stimulate awareness, to heighten consciousness. For example, seeing a pleasurable sight can heighten awareness of the wonder, the marvel, and the mystery of creation. Listening to pleasing music can inspire a person to perform creative deeds. Sexual pleasure can bond a relationship closer than before; it can serve as a way of expressing what transcends words. It can literally "make love." It can make one aware of the gift that is giving. It can demonstrate that in giving we receive more than we give. It can lead one to understand that in doing more than we understand, we come to understand more than we do.

The most creative acts, the most fulfilling experiences, the accomplishments that offer the most profound happiness are often those that are not necessarily associated only with physical pleasure. The athlete who strives for excellence must exercise severe physical and mental discipline, must endure pain, to expand his physical capabilities. The literary or visual artist must endure the anguish, the anxiety, the trying acquisition of difficult skills, in order to produce a work of art. Pain is a feature of childbirth, and the worry and concern that accompanies caring for and raising a child are both trying and stressful. Pleasure is no guarantor of happiness, fulfillment, or spiritual development. It may be a spur, a stimulus, a means, but it can never become an end in itself.

The great British philosopher John Stuart Mill wrote that some kinds of happiness are more desirable and more valuable than others: "It is better to be a human being dissatisfied than a pig satisfied. And if the fool or the pig is of a different opinion, it is because they only know their own side of the question. The other party to the comparison knows both sides."[40]

To sum up much of what has just been discussed, we turn to the insightful observations of Robert Bellah in his study of American life, *Habits of the Heart: Individualism and Commitment in American Life.* At the conclusion of his work, Bellah writes:

> Perhaps the truth lies in what most of the world outside the modern West has always believed, namely that there are practices in life, good in themselves, that are inherently fulfilling. Perhaps work that is intrinsically rewarding is better for human beings than work that is only extrinsically rewarding. Perhaps commitment to those we love and civic friendship toward our fellow citizens are preferable to restless competition and anxious self-defiance. Perhaps common worship, in which we express our gratitude and wonder in the face of the mystery of being itself, is the most important thing of all. If so, we will have to change our lives and begin to remember what we have been happier to forget.[40]

The purpose of life is a life of purpose. Yet many people mistakenly identify the constant and relentless pursuit of goals as behavior that precludes the opportunity for fun, pleasure, and leisure. This is because they fail to realize that meaningful activity, and the psychic rewards that come from the accomplishment of intrinsically fulfilling tasks, are fun and pleasurable as well as meaningful and fulfilling. For the person in flow, there is no better use of work time, leisure time—of any time—than to focus on achieving autotelic goals.

Human beings apparently need purposeful and structured activity to achieve meaning, and to prevent themselves from becoming bored. People report feeling most listless and dissatisfied when they are alone with nothing to do. Paradoxically, when people are most ostensibly free, when they can do whatever they want, they find themselves least able to act. Furthermore, boredom often comes when a person's skills and abilities are greater than the challenges and tasks with which he or she is confronted. The most bored people at work are not the incompetent ones, but those whose abilities exceed the tasks that they are assigned and expected to perform. Bored people who try to fill up time with purposeless activity often find themselves becoming increasingly depressed. It is a vicious cycle. Boredom and depression feed upon each other until a serious psychological and/or physical problem sets in. It is not life that is boring, only people who choose to be bored. As Erich Fromm pointed out, the human being is the only animal who can choose to be bored.

Creative and self-fulfilled people are rarely either bored or boring. On the other hand, the boring or bored person often harbors a sense of meaninglessness, a lack of purpose and direction, a spiritual emptiness, manifesting itself as listlessness and depression. Boredom may be examined by seeing it within the context of leisure. Studies demonstrate that leisure is not the panacea many usually expect, as it often leads to boredom and consequently to depression. Retirement and "empty nesting," once expected by many to be times of liberation, are now dreaded by many because of the threat of boredom. To depict this phenomenon of listless leisure, psychoanalyst Benjamin Ferenczi coined the term "Sunday neurosis."[42] In 1958, the Group for the Advancement of Psychiatry reported that "leisure is a significant danger for many Americans."[43] Vacations have been identified as potentially dangerous for similar reasons. Studies show that in the first few years after retirement, heart attack and cancer rates soar, and early death overtakes people who were otherwise healthy before they retired.

Boredom is often coupled with loneliness. Yet, creative people, while often alone, are rarely lonely. Indeed, the creative person finds being alone for long stretches of time as a desirable state. In many spiritual traditions, what we consider the horror of loneliness is viewed as the opportunity for solitude. Creativity is what an artist does with his or her solitude. However, for the spiritually impoverished person solitude is something to be dreaded. It is a gateway to boredom, an entrée to emptiness. With nothing to do, the mind is unable to prevent negative thoughts from moving to center stage. The dread of being alone can lead to obsessive and sometimes dangerous practices: regular use of drugs or alcohol, frivolous sexual liaisons, compulsive shopping, non-stop TV viewing—whatever dulls or distracts the mind. Yet, a person with control over his or her consciousness, with a focal point of creative attention, can turn the dread of loneliness into the opportunity for creative solitude. Indeed, the greatest (and even the not-so-great) works of art, literature, music, and craft have been created in solitude. Prophets of the great religions, like Moses and Mohammed, experienced their greatest illuminations in solitude. Not only a condition for creativity, solitude can serve as a necessary environment for putting one's priorities in order without the static that comes from outside. Some can experience solitude only when alone. However, more spiritually developed individuals can experience solitude even when in a crowd. A difference between loneliness and solitude is that the lonely person worries that he is in bad company. The person who cherishes solitude knows he is in good company.

Loneliness comes as the result of an absence of adequate external stimuli, whereas enjoying and cultivating the art of solitude comes from the ability to control consciousness and attention when alone.

The creative possibilities of solitude issue from the person who is not dependent upon external stimuli, but who is in control of his or her inner space. The better furnished with ideas, knowledge, fantasies, dreams, plans, projects, and goals the inner self is, the more creatively a person can both enjoy and utilize his or her solitude. The transformation of loneliness into solitude, and of solitude into creativity, is a feature of crafting the soul. Solitude, in the words of Hermann Hesse, is "a sanctuary to which you can retreat at any time and be yourself."[44] Or, as Wordsworth put it:

> *When from our better selves we have too long*
> *Been parted by the hurrying world, and droop,*
> *Sick of its business, of its pleasure tired,*
> *How gracious, how benign is Solitude.*[45]

While the creative person sees solitude as a friend, the spiritually homeless person sees it as an enemy. To bestow upon themselves the illusive deception that they are not really bored and lonely, many people seem prepared to endure a variety of indignities, to allocate substantial resources of time and money for social activities, to initiate an unwanted string of unsatisfying sexual liaisons, to submit themselves to endless hours of vacuous TV programs, to assault their ears with endless hours of cacophonous music—all aimed at dispelling the silence and the loneliness that they otherwise might have to encounter.

Some use frenzied activities as a substitute for confronting their forlorn selves. This exercise in self-deception is based on the view that we are only really alive when we are *doing* something. For instance, being always in a hurry can be a camouflage for anxiety, a pseudo-demonstration of one's sense of self-importance. As Chaucer observed in *The Canterbury Tales,* "Methinks he seemed busier than he was."[46] "To be idle," wrote Robert Louis Stevenson, "requires a strong sense of personal identity."[47]

Some fill the void of their loneliness by fabricating things to worry about as a substitute for confronting their own inner emptiness. Rather

than concentrating upon what matters, rather than confronting the
self, such individuals often become obsessed with worrying about the
unlikely catastrophes they feel certain will befall themselves or those
whom they care about. These people exemplify an old Jewish joke. Q:
What is a Jewish telegram? A: One whose text reads, "Start worrying
now, letter to follow."

As Bertrand Russell reminds us, "Worry and fret and irritation are
emotions that serve no purpose. . . . The man who has become eman-
cipated from the empire of worry will find life a much more cheerful
affair than it used to be while he was perpetually being irritated. . . . A
man who has once perceived, however temporarily and however briefly,
what makes greatness of soul, can no longer be happy if he allows
himself to be petty, self seeking, troubled by trivial misfortunes, dread-
ing what fate may have in store for him."[48]

Others try to overcome loneliness by trying to be liked, by becoming socially popular. In *Death of a Salesman*, Willy Loman advises his
children, "Be well liked and you will never want."[49] Yet Willy Loman,
who was himself "best liked," dies never knowing who he was.

A ninth ingredient in crafting the soul is the cultivation of moral
values. What we value is that which matters most to us, that which
elicits meaning from life. How we cultivate the moral virtues relates
most directly to what kind of person we want to be and how to become that person. Virtues are not absolutes; rather, they are pathways,
guides, indicators. They point the way and offer direction toward a life
of meaning and purpose, toward the spiritual augmentation of the
self, toward the creation of life as an art form. As Nietzsche wrote, "No
people can live without valuing. Valuing is creating. Without valua-
tion, the nut of existence is hollow." Virtue serves as cement for a
society. Without it, the stability of a nation is imperiled. For example,
as James Madison wrote, "To suppose that any form of government
will secure liberty or happiness without any virtue in the people is a
chemerical idea."[50] Or, as Lewis Mumford said, "[The] chief purpose
[of human existence] . . . is the creation and preservation of values:
that is what gives meaning to our civilization, and the participation in

this is what gives significance, ultimately, to the individual life."[51] Virtues, such as wisdom and humility, already have been discussed. However, it is love that is the queen of the virtues because it reveals those relationships, convictions, and commitments that we value most. Love indicates what and who matters most to us, what and who we find most meaningful. Love is the subject of the chapter that now follows.

chapter nine

The Gift of Love

And so it happened that the beautiful maiden named Psyche
fell in love and was loved by Eros, the god of love. Each night
Eros would visit his beloved Psyche, but only on the condition
that she would never ask his name nor look upon his face.
But one night while Eros slept, Psyche awoke, lit a lamp, and
looked upon her beloved Eros, resting in a blissful sleep. Eros
awoke from his slumber, and he knew that Psyche had looked
upon his face. Out of anger Eros fled, leaving Psyche at the
mercy of his mother, the goddess Aphrodite. Yet Psyche would
surrender neither her beloved nor her love. She defied gods
and goddesses and wandered in search of her lover. After an
arduous and relentless search, Psyche found Eros, and was
reunited with him. For her persistent love, Psyche was
granted immortality. Ever since then, Psyche has symbolized
the human soul.

*I*n Greek, *psyche* means "the soul." According to this ancient Greek
legend, it is the soul's vocation to pursue, and hopefully to find, love.
The motto of the soul is: I love; therefore, I am. As philosopher Irving
Singer has written, "For a person in love . . . life is never without
meaning. . . . For love is not merely a contributor . . . to a meaningful

life. In its own way, it may underlie all other forms of meaning."[1]
Discovering who and what one loves reveals who and what one values
most. Identifying one's loves reveals the nexus of meaning in one's life.

Underlying both the fear of death and the realization of life's meaning is a particular type of love: love of life. We love life for the same
reason we love anything else—because we value it highly. Love of life
is rooted in the rapture of being alive, in the realization that life is too
intrinsically precious, too incredibly marvelous, too provocatively wondrous to be squandered, to be wasted away. We are repulsed by death
precisely because we love life. Reverse *live* and you have *evil*. Love of
life can be a prelude to a life of love. As the comedian Eddie Cantor
once said, "Love/live: switch one letter and they are the same."

Despite the paeans to love offered by poets, philosophers, and
theologians throughout the centuries, love has been deflated, dis-
missed, and abused in our times. Many psychologists and biologists
have attempted to reduce it to an endocrinological problem to be
overcome, rather than to a virtue to be cherished. These scientists
facilely reduce love to a physical need, like food and shelter, rather
than identify it as a spiritual aspiration, like beauty and meaning.
They portray love as a trap set by our genes, as a cruel trick of evolution implanted to ensnare us, as an addiction that must be overcome, as an unwanted and unhealthy dependency. The mechanistic
proclivities of modern science encourage us to reduce our deepest
emotions and experiences to a parade of fleeting biochemical urges
and flutters. Many playwrights and novelists portray love as a fanci-
ful desire rather than as an achievable relationship. Following the
tradition of the Greek tragedies, they perceive love as a shipwreck
waiting to happen, as a destined calamity. Some philosophers join in
the chorus with admonitions about the impossibility of love offering
either happiness or meaning. This popular debunking of love was
addressed by an anonymous poet who wrote:

Oh Love! They wrong thee much
They say thy sweet is bitter

When thy rich fruit is such
As nothing can be sweeter.[2]

Many contemporary attitudes toward love are like that of the person who resigned from his fear-of-intimacy support group because he thought that the other people in the group were getting too close to him. Reduced by many scientists and artists to a needless pathology, the search for love is in danger of being replaced by the avoidance of it. As Irving Singer has put it, "We are living during a period in which large numbers of people have renounced their faith in love."[3] Though many people are afraid of not being loved, it may well be that even more they are afraid of loving. For this reason, love, like many of the other virtues, relies upon the virtue of courage. Since love requires commitment without guarantees, giving without the assurance of receiving, intimacy with the exposure of vulnerability, love demands courage—the ability to take a risk, even though it may lead to disappointment and pain.

Perhaps unknowingly, many have become disciples of the Marquis de Sade, for it was he who so greatly advocated and admired the cultivation of *apétie,* that is, apathy, indifference to love. In his novel *The Great Gatsby,* F. Scott Fitzgerald tells the story of a man who no longer cared, who had mastered the art of apathy. His passion for success had effectively smothered his ability to care, to love. On almost every page of the novel, the word *careless* appears. Once one becomes too careless, the soul atrophies. Already in the 1960s, in his book *Love and Will* Rollo May described the progressive onset of apathy and indifference that has come to plague our society. May cites Viktor Frankl's observation that apathy and a lack of feeling are defenses against the anxiety that so many experience. Frankl writes, "Apathy and lack of feeling are also defenses against anxiety. When a person continually faces dangers he is powerless to overcome, his final line of defense is at last to avoid even feeling the dangers."[4] May characterizes our times as follows: "The Victorian person sought to have love without falling into sex; the modern person seeks to have sex without falling into love."[5]

The advocacy of apathy predates our times and the times of the Marquis de Sade. The ancient Greek and Roman philosophers already perceived passion and reason as mortal enemies. In their view, to have passion meant to lose your mind, to surrender reason. They therefore advised a lack of passion, a lack of pathos—a-pathos or apathy—as the desired path in life. This entailed either the surrender of love or the complete intellectualization of love. Following this tradition, Freud perceived passion as a danger to civilization, as the enemy of culture. However, by setting up an artificial dichotomy, by failing to realize that emotion and reason, the body and the soul, the sensual and the spiritual, are partners rather than adversaries, that they complement rather than oppose one another, these thinkers disenfranchised themselves and their adherents from the sweet pandemonium of love.

True love must not only be love but it must also be true. To be true, it must not be counterfeit. It must not be something else pretending to be love. Yet many people tend to identify counterfeit copies with the genuine article. The very pervasiveness of so much counterfeit love demonstrates not only the existence but also the high value of love. Why try to counterfeit that which has no high value? Just as networking is not synonymous with developing relationships, so are relationships not necessarily synonymous with love. A relationship can function well for years, like a well-oiled machine, while the parties who comprise the relationship remain strangers for all that time.[6]

Many people make the mistake of seeing love as primarily a matter of being loved rather than of loving. They then focus on strategies aimed at making them lovable. One such strategy equates power, riches, success, and a good physical appearance with making one lovable. While this strategy, if successful, may make a person attractive, there is no reason to believe that it will also make that person lovable. In the struggle to attain these supposed accoutrements of lovability, it may well be that love will pass you by. It is not only important for you to be in love, but for love to be in you.

What makes a person attractive often depends upon the culture and its current fashions. For example, not so long ago, smoking—especially by women—was synonymous with sexual attraction. In our consumer culture people often come together when they believe they are getting the best commodity the market has to offer, considering the limitations of their own exchange value. Often, as in buying real estate, potential future market value plays an important role in closing the deal. However, while a cost-benefits analysis strategy may help induce an initial attraction, a relationship based upon a balance sheet can be many things, although loving is not one of them.

Love is not a contractual matter of give and get. It is not a listing on any commodities exchange. In a cost-benefit approach to relationships, we tend to appraise the other in terms of the benefits we hope to derive from association with them, and of those of our needs they are expected to fill. Love, to the contrary, creates a value in the beloved and in the loving relationship that goes beyond appraisal. Love is rooted not in appraisal but in bestowal, not in what we can receive but in what we can give. Love is an inextricable part of eliciting meaning, because through loving we find a person whose very being bestows meaning upon our lives. In love, by bestowing unquantifiable value upon another, we bestow meaning and value upon ourselves. In the masquerade ball where a wide variety of pretenders come attired as love, we can unmask dependency pretending to be love. When love parades itself as an unspoken bargain to keep a person from loneliness, what often occurs is a heightened sense of emptiness and loneliness.

It is a common teaching of philosophers and psychologists that self-love must be attained before love of others can be accomplished, that one must love one's own self before one can or should love another. However, it is also true that while self-love can lead to love of another, it also can degenerate into narcissism.

Self-love can readily become an obsession that never transcends the self. It can easily become egocentricity pretending to be love. Furthermore, if self-love is the love of the self, are there then two parties involved: the lover and the beloved, the self who loves and the self who is loved? To be sure, there is a fine line between self-love and narcissism. Self-love that never goes beyond the self can turn a person into a dead star in the galaxy of the forlorn. Like a black hole, such an individual will take and take from another while giving nothing in return. Rather, it is the self who loves. Love need not necessarily begin with self-love, but it must begin with the capacity of the self to love, and with the development and the expression of that capacity. By learning to love, a person issues himself or herself a get-out-of-jail-free card from the prison of the self, from the loneliness of his or her own heart.

Freud equated self-love, indeed all love, with narcissism. His view that self-love is undesirable echoed certain traditional Christian views that saw self-love as sinful, as pride, and as not really love at all. St. Augustine and St. Thomas Aquinas, however, held forth the hope that there could be a form of self-love that is not the same as pride, that does not inevitably become narcissistic. This, for them, is a form of self-love that is beneficial and not corruptive because it leads to the love of God and to the love of other people. Self-love can serve as a means to love of others instead of always being an end in itself. Self-love can become a pathway rather than a destination. Plato maintained that a person who truly loves himself is not one who is egocentric or narcissistic, but is one who wants what is truly good for oneself, which means eliminating selfishness and cultivating the moral virtues. Thus, self-love is both a danger and an opportunity. It can be a prelude to narcissism or an invitation to love of another, a stop sign or a step to self-transcendence.

Freud mistakenly identified self-love with narcissism because he misread the legend of Narcissus. Narcissus was not in love with himself, but with a reflection of himself. Narcissus was too preoccupied with his image to attend to his own real self. Preoccupation with a reflected image either of one's own self or of another is more akin to infatuation than to love. Both self-love and love of another entails the internal acceptance of the self as it is, rather than the gaze at an ephemeral, refracted, glittering image.

Self-love can serve as a vehicle either to narcissism or to altruism, to vice or to virtue, to self-absorption or to self-knowledge, to obsession with the self or to concern for others. Love of others and love of self exist in a feedback loop. Loving others gives us a reason to love our-selves; self-love can extend the capacity to love beyond ourselves.

It is not through loving the self that self-esteem and self-love are ultimately attained. Instead, through loving another, through exercis-ing our capacity to love, self-esteem, self-worth, and self-validation can be achieved. The person in love with another—rather than the person in love only with his or her own self—suddenly feels compelled to take better care of himself, to further develop her innate abilities, for the sake of the beloved. The person in love with another feels the exhilaration of meaning, purpose, validation. The awareness of the capacity to love is not so much a feature of self-love as it is a feature of love of another.

Psychologists tend to define love as the fulfillment of the person's emotional needs. From this perspective, which begins and ends with the needs of the self, it is not surprising that self-love is deemed a necessary prerequisite to other kinds of love. However, what is forgot-ten is that at the core of love is not only one's creature needs, but one's need to be needed. Love often entails a subordination of one's own needs and interests to a person or to an ideal outside of the self. As Erich Fromm wrote, "Immature love says: I love you because I need you. Mature love says: I need you because I love you."[7] Love is not the immediate gratification of one's every impulse and need. It is shaped instead by needs, concerns, and cares that transcend the self. What often is forgotten is that to be loved a person not only needs to be needed. A person must be wanted as well.

Love must originate within the recesses of the self; but love that re-mains cloistered within the self will become stillborn. Such love is like a bachelor dancing with himself at his wedding to himself. "The main condition for the achievement of love," wrote Erich Fromm, "is the overcoming of one's narcissism. The narcissist orientation is one in which one experiences as real only that which exists within oneself. . . . The opposite pole to narcissism is objectivity; it is the faculty to see people as they are, objectively."[8]

Love of another is not only spiritually nutritive, but a catalyst for physical health. Studies have found an elevated immune response among people who recently have fallen in love. The old adage, "If you don't want to catch cold, fall in love," has a physiological basis. Paradoxically, love that focuses upon the well-being of another affects our own well-being in the most profound ways. Love is a health-generating and a meaning-generating emotion.[9]

Often what passes for love of another may merely be egocentricity in disguise. If who or what I love is only an extension of my own ego, then my love of the other is a mirage. Parents, for example, often express their love for their children through considerable self-sacrifice. Yet such behavior may in fact be self-serving rather than self-sacrificing. The parent who projects his or her own frustrated goals and desires upon the child, the parent whose aim and intention is that the child live out and fulfill the parent's own inadequacies, that the child achieve successes in precisely those areas where the parent experienced only failures, is ultimately motivated not by love of the child but by the parent's own needs for ego self-gratification.

Whether it be love of a parent for a child or love of any person for another, the starting point is not one's own ego needs, one's own ego gratification, but the recognition, the awareness, the acceptance, the concern, and the care for the other in all his or her uniqueness and singularity. Ultimately, love is not dependency, but interdependency that flows from attending to the expression of our own uniqueness as it relates to the one we love and to the uniqueness of the one we love. There is interdependence even in the case of a newborn child whose very life and sustenance is dependent upon its mother. The child needs the mother to survive, but the mother needs the child to love and to suckle. As the Talmud puts it, "More than the calf needs to suck, does the cow need to suckle."[10] Love is a declaration of interdependence.

In love three new beings are created. Love changes the shape of the self; it extends the contours, the boundaries, the identity of the self. Thus, a new person comes into being. If the beloved reciprocates, the beloved as lover also becomes someone new, and renewed. And, in the matrix of love, where each lover maintains individuality while the boundaries between each become obscure and penetrate one another, a third new being is created, a being called "we."

Love is intimate interdependence and commitment. Even in the deepest intimacy, each participant retains his or her individuality. Indeed, it is precisely in the bliss of such moments that the individual both realizes himself and transcends himself, becoming who he is by becoming more than he was. Interdependence means the acceptance of the other as a separate and autonomous person whose own self-interests are equally important and worthy of respect.

Love need not be a merging, a union, to be real. But love needs to be a blending, a harmony. Love is a spiritual event. It amplifies who we are. It points toward who we can yet become. As was already discussed, creating life as a work of art depends upon the individual's ability to establish the uniqueness and singularity of the self. Love is a way of eliciting the uniqueness of the self while simultaneously transcending the self.

Just as love cannot be centered only in the self, it cannot effectively be directed to all persons. The view that love of one person must either include or must lead to the love of all people is a fallacy. If I love everyone, then I love no one. If everyone is special, then no one is special. If I love all children equally, then in what way is my love for my own child unique and particular?

In his now classic work, *The Art of Loving,* Erich Fromm identifies certain elements common to all forms of love: care, responsibility, respect, and knowledge.[11] Care is the capacity to "make" love, to give love. Care is giving. Responsibility, as the word suggests, is the ability to respond, to accept love. Responsibility is the opposite of spiritual frigidity.

In sexual relations, dysfunction is often characterized as impotence and frigidity. Impotence afflicts men and frigidity afflicts women. However, seen from a spiritual point of view, neither impotence nor frigidity need be gender specific. Impotence may be depicted as the inability to give love, to "make" love, to create love. Frigidity may be described as the inability to receive or to accept love, the inability to experience penetration by the inner core of another or to take the risk of penetrating into the inner core of another. Indeed, the gender-specific manifestations of sexual malfunction may be physical expressions of a deeper spiritual problem.

Respect comes from *respicere,* "to look at." Respect means seeing the other person as he or she is. It means being aware of his or her objective individuality, distinctiveness, and uniqueness. Respect implies an absence of exploitation. Respect means wanting the other person to unfold and to develop for their own sake. It means acceptance of who the other person is and can become instead of considering the other either as a servant of our needs or as an object of our dependencies. To respect a person, that is, to see that person as he or she is, is not possible without knowledge.

In biblical Hebrew the verb *yada* means "to know," "to love," and "to experience." Love entails the intimate knowledge and experience of another as he or she really is. Self-disclosure, revealing one's innermost core to another and receiving the disclosure of the other to his or her own self, is how knowledge becomes part of a loving relationship. Loving another not only augments one's love of one's self, but it also augments one's knowledge of oneself, and self-knowledge is the mainspring of the spiritual life. Disclosing oneself to another presumes two features of a loving relationship: trust and the ability to communicate. Trust is critical because in love one is exposed and vulnerable to another. Communication is vital because it is the entrée to intimacy. It is the art of sharing convictions, hopes, joys, fears, and dreams. Ironically, in our age of high-tech communication, the art of communication is becoming increasingly scarce.

The social self is the self society trains us to be, wants us to be. The successful social self is one that is adept at public relations, at networking. The social self is conditioned to behave as it is expected to behave—predictably, rationally. The social self is a superficial projection of who we are that can never be too revealing. It is make-up, a made-up self donned for appropriate social occasions. For some, make-up becomes the face, the image becomes the reality. The core withers away.

The real self is lost in the refraction of mirrors. What love provides is an opportunity for the authentic self to come out of hiding, to reveal itself, to express itself, to become manifest. Love is an invitation to discover our core, who we really are, who we can become.

Love is a virtue rooted in uniqueness—the uniqueness of the lover, the uniqueness of the beloved, and in the particularity of their relationship. Precisely for this reason, it is appropriate to depict love as a spiritual event. As Viktor Frankl wrote, "Loving represents a coming to relationship with another as a spiritual being."[12] This is why love and narcissism, why love and infatuation are two different things. Love is a joining at the core, at the soul. Infatuation never penetrates to the core. Infatuation is a delight that focuses upon what the other has rather than upon who the other is. A person may be infatuated with another's physical appearance, social status, social graces, riches, and possessions, but not with the uniqueness of who the other person is. Infatuation may develop into love, but it cannot be equated with love since it is not grounded in a recognition of the uniqueness of the other. One way to distinguish between infatuation and love would be to apply this test of singularity: Suppose someone with whom you are truly in love is lost to you forever—either through death or departure and permanent separation. You are then offered a double of the departed person—with the same looks, the same voice, the identical gestures. Would this, or any replacement, be satisfactory? If the answer is "yes," then you are infatuated; if "no," then you probably are in love.

Often callous people say to a young parent who has lost a child, "Don't worry. You can still have more children." A new pet is offered a child as a replacement for one that died. But an individual who is truly loved can never be replaced. There are no substitutes because love is always rooted in the uniqueness of the beloved, in what makes the other incomparable and irreplaceable. Infatuations are replaceable because the characteristics we perceive in one person may be found in another. Infatuations are usually with a person who fulfills a "type" being sought, rather than an individual being loved. Infatuations often objectify the other in terms of something they have (such as a good body, fame, or fortune) rather than in who they really are. Infatuations focus on what a person *has* while love focuses upon who a person *is*. Infatuation is the twin of narcissism because it is rooted in our own selves, in our needs and desires, rather than in the acceptance of the uniqueness of the other.

In infatuation, jealousy plays a major role. In true love, it does not. Jealousy is rooted in the assumption that one can be replaced, duplicated by another. Love is rooted in uniqueness and irreplaceability. If I am jealous because I am afraid of being replaced, then I neither love or am being loved. Jealousy, according to the poet John Dryden, is the jaundice of the soul.[13] If I accept my own distinctiveness and that of my beloved, then I cannot be jealous because replaceability is not a real option.

That we can continue to love someone even after their death, when their physical presence no longer remains with us, demonstrates that love primarily relates to the distinctive spiritual essence of the person rather than to their physical presence. This is an important factor to realize with regard to the erotic or romantic relationship, where preoccupation with the physical, with the sexual, is so acute. Even there, especially there, the spiritual is paramount. The body is a vehicle for the expression of the soul. Beneath the veneer of the body the soul waits, ready to reveal its innermost core to another.

The act of physical penetration is penultimate to the event of spiritual penetration, entering the core of another person's being. In a sense, the physical is a vestibule, an invitation, to the spiritual. The physical act of "making love" must do just that. It must offer expression to the soul to articulate in gestures that which transcends words. Making love is a serenade two souls sing to one another. In infatuation, the pleasure principle governs; pleasure is the goal. But, in love, pleasure is a means to an end. That end is revealing one's core to another in intimacy, as passion coupled with commitment. In that act of disclosure, a person sees a glimpse of his or her own realized, actualized self—who he or she can become—and also revealed is the core of the beloved in all of his or her disclosed particularity and uniqueness. The goals of love and of making love are: to see who we are, and who we can become; to experience the uniqueness of another; to disclose our self to another; to have another disclose themselves to us. Though not always achieved, the goals remain. As the German poet Goethe said, like all ideals, love is "set up like the bull's-eye of a target, always to be aimed at, even if it is not always hit."[14]

While many psychologists continue to consider love as a "pathological addiction" (ala Stanton Peele), other psychologists such as Robert Sternberg have begun to take a more positive view of love. According to Sternberg, there are three primary ingredients in love. They are intimacy, passion, and commitment.[15] Each is not always found in equal measure, but each must be present for true love to occur. Without passion, love is impotent, but with passion alone love easily fizzles into infatuation. Without commitment, love is a passing fancy, but with commitment alone love can degenerate into a vacuous impersonal duty. Without intimacy, love becomes a distant relative, but with intimacy alone love becomes a barren tree. Only with intimacy, passion, and commitment together can there be consummate love, can love flourish and thrive.

Freud reduced sexual desire to a physical need like a hunger that needs to be fed, like an itch that needs to be scratched, like a thirst that needs to be quenched. Once the physical need, desire, and tension is adequately attended to, satisfaction occurs. On the purely physical level, Freud may have been right in analogizing sexual satisfaction to the relief of an itch. But like all attempts to reduce a complex phenomenon to a simple one, Freud committed what philosophers term "the reductionist fallacy." What Freud failed to factor in was the presence of love in the sexual act. In this regard, the teachings of the sixteenth-century Jewish philosopher Leone Ebreo are relevant.[16]

Ebreo's Italian treatise, *Dialoghi d'Amore,* had a substantial influence upon the works of great writers, such as Cervantes and Milton. (In the introduction to his *Don Quixote,* Cervantes advises his readers that if they wish to understand the nature of love, they should study Ebreo's book.) In this work, Ebreo makes an important distinction between lust and love, between the biological need for sex and the spiritual desire for love in the erotic relationship. According to Ebreo, when the sex act is motivated by physical desire alone, it can be readily satisfied by sexual relations. (As Freud might have put it: Satisfaction occurs when the itch is scratched.) However, in love the sex act only increases the desire for the other because the love generates more love, passion rooted in love generates more passion, intimacy propels the desire for increased intimacy, commitment engenders deeper commitment. In physical desire, the hunger disappears once it has been satiated, satisfied. In love, neither party can be with the other enough, know the other enough, make love to each other enough, love one another enough. For Ebreo, lust is the offspring of desire while desire is the offspring of love.

Love that remains a heart condition is destined for dissolution. Love must be translated into deeds for it to flourish. For instance, love must be wedded with a compassion that is not only a sentiment but a constellation of deeds. Compassion is a willingness not only to care about but also to take care of someone else. For love to be real, it must be expressed in deed. In this regard, consider a note a teenager once sent his girlfriend:

Dearest Jane,
   My love for you is higher than the highest mountain and deeper than the deepest sea. My heart skips a beat each time I think of you. I cannot live without you. I ache every moment to see you.

Love, John

P.S. If it is raining Saturday night, I can't take you out because I don't want to catch cold.

It is important to study, learn, and practice techniques of sexual relations. When skill is correlative with desire and emotion, fulfillment can ensue. When skill is lacking, frustration will occur, especially when love and desire are at a peak. Desirable but not sufficient, skilled sexual technique will not necessarily engender love, nor guarantee satisfaction. Technique is a means to an end, not an end in itself. When sex becomes reduced to technique, it becomes a matter of genital engineering in which anxiety over results replaces a chorus of harmonious souls.

Were a major in love offered at a university, courses in lovemaking would be required of students electing this course of study. Not only would they have to learn sexual techniques, but they would also have to learn about care, concern, empathy, compassion, friendship, trust, humility, and freedom, as well as about hate, envy, jealousy, and malice. Malice, for example, is the opposite of love in that it aims at destroying another's autonomy. But the best way to learn how to love is not by taking a course in love, or by mastering a how-to manual. It is by exposure to a loving person, a loving relationship. Think about who you have known or heard of who knew how to love and observe the lives of those persons. You will then learn how to love.

A major in love would have to include various types of love, including friendship. While modern thought has largely focused upon eros, that is, erotic love, earlier philosophy dealt not only with eros, but also with *philia,* the love between friends. Whereas erotic lovers can, and should, also be friends, friendship can also stand on its own as a form of love devoid of an erotic component.

Aristotle wrote that "without friends no one would choose to live, though he had all other goods."[17] Dag Hammarskjold described friendship as deliverance from the "anguish of loneliness."[18] William Blake wrote, "The bird a nest, the spider a web, man friendship."[19] The Talmud says, "Either friendship or death."[20] Friends are beloved, cherished, valued. The love in friendship, like the erotic form of love, includes the components of intimacy, passion, and commitment, though they may not be expressed in the same way as they are in erotic love. Friendship embraces the features of love delineated by Erich Fromm: care, responsibility, respect, and knowledge. Like other varieties of love, friendship also demands empathy, understanding, and compassion.

The intimacy of friendship is an intimacy of mutual disclosure. A friend is someone with whom we can share our most secret feelings, our deepest fears, our greatest joys, our most noble achievements, our most fervent hopes, our cherished values, our dreams and fantasies, our most devastating failures, our most heartwrenching sorrows and traumas. With friends we can be ourselves, become aware of our uniqueness, elicit our individuality as well as that of our friends.

As individuals whom we cherish, friends cannot be confused with acquaintances, with professional relationships, with people who are part of our "network." True friendship is a rare commodity. We constantly hear or read about enormously successful professional and business people, about popular celebrities, who confess how starved they are for real friends, how lonely and isolated their lives have become, how nostalgically they recall the friends of their youth, left behind in the march toward success.

A true friend is not one who simply reaffirms our public persona, who never questions our dreams and desires, who always approves of our actions, who tries to stifle our autonomy by exploiting or controlling us. Rather, a friend is someone who recognizes our uniqueness, our autonomy, our self-hood. A friend is someone with whom we share an adventure of mutual and reciprocal self-development, self-realization, and self-transcendence. Like all virtues, like all deep relationships, like all types of art, like all types of love, friendship requires patience and cultivation, tolerance and care, intimacy and commitment, discipline and desire.

As Plato already observed, one can learn much about a person's character from the friendships he or she seeks and sustains. Like all of the moral virtues, friendship and love both reflect the self that each of us is and point to the self that each of us can yet become. Like all the moral virtues, love and friendship indicate who and what we value, who and what matters most to us. Like the other virtues, love offers us an anchor for behavior, a foundation for the development of our moral habits. The virtues act as a check against following sometimes destructive momentary whims. They enhance a person's capacity for moral judgment in difficult situations. They offer a framework within which to be flexible in choice, depending upon the particular situation. They act as guides in sorting out ethical dilemmas. They help define who we are and who we want to be. And, like all the moral virtues, love, friendship, compassion, patience, humility, and the others are critical building blocks in crafting the soul, in manifesting the meaning of our lives. As William James, the great American pragmatist, wrote:

> A man's character is discernible in the mental or moral attitude in which, when it came upon him, he felt himself most deeply and intensely active and alive. At such moments there is a voice inside which speaks and says: *"This* is the real me!"[21]

William James also wrote that "the greatest use of life is to spend it for something that will outlast it."[22] The chapter that now follows examines how meaning generated during life may be perpetuated after life, how the contemplation of life after death can spur us to craft life in such a way that death does not entail oblivion. Or, as Tolstoy put it, "Is there any meaning in my life that will not be destroyed by the inevitable death awaiting me?[23]

chapter ten

What's Next?

A skeptic once came to see the Rabbi of Kotzk in order to mock him. The skeptic facetiously asked the rabbi, "It has been said that you can perform miracles."

"Yes, I can," answered the rabbi.

"Then show me one," scowled the skeptic. "Show me how you can resurrect the dead."

"I'd prefer to show you how I can resurrect the living,"
responded the rabbi.

*I*ncreasing numbers of films, radio shows, television programs, magazine articles, and books are discussing and exploring belief in a life after death. In some scientific quarters, evidence is being relentlessly sought to prove the existence of a hereafter. A debate rages as to whether reports of clinically dead people who have been returned to life actually describe an afterlife, or whether their experiences merely reflect the results of biochemical changes in the brain stimulated by severe physiological trauma. Past-life regression therapy has begun to gain scientific respectability. But here, too, it is debated as to whether subjects under therapy recall actual past lives, or whether they merely believe, without any real basis in fact, that they have lived before. While the existence of the afterlife continues to be debated, surveys consistently show that the vast majority of Americans believe in some kind of afterlife existence.

Social commentators have observed that increasing interest in America in a life after death comes as a result of the aging of the baby-boom generation, the largest segment of the American population. About every seven minutes, someone in America reaches the age of fifty. As these people age, and as they begin to see their parents' generation die off, they come to the realization that their generation will be next. Furthermore, baby boomers are also now beginning to see members of their own generation die; heart disease and cancer have begun to claim some of their contemporaries, suddenly and unexpectedly. Knowing they might be next, the question of what—if anything— *is* next, takes on a pervasive relevance and immediacy. As in all other matters, the immense size of the baby-boom generation assures that its concerns will become central to the agenda of American public policy; for example, in the escalating public debate over end-of-life issues, such as voluntary euthanasia.

Preoccupation with life after death stimulates a stark confrontation with the limitations of living. This not only includes the reality of one's own mortality, the awareness of death as the ultimate limitation upon our physical existence. It also includes coming to grips with a plethora of limitations on many aspects of living about which we seem powerless to do anything. Death is not only an end to physiological existence, but an end to our ability to create life as an art form, a closing parenthesis to our ability to implement life's meaning, a separation from that and those who matter most to each of us. Death is not only an end to life, but an end to living—and all that entails.

For generations Americans have viewed their environment and their possibilities as being limitless. They have perceived life in terms of endless space, inexhaustible natural resources, an ever-expanding economy, boundless opportunities for personal growth and socioeconomic success, and ever-advancing scientific and technological achievement. In a culture focused upon seemingly inexhaustible growth and limitless consumption, death and afterlife concerns are repressed as inevitable nuisances. When the general sense is "it can't get better than this," there is little impetus to wonder, "what's next?" However, when confronted with limitations in many areas of life, it becomes inevitable to be concerned with the ultimate limitation—death.

In recent decades Americans have had to shift their mentality to accommodate new realities with which they now have to contend, including an acceptance of limitation and constriction in a wide variety of areas, such as the limitations of the biosphere, the exhaustibility of certain natural resources, the rationing of health care, "glass ceilings" and downsizing in the world of work, new restrictive laws and governmental regulations, limiting of national military options and initiatives, economic restrictions, and so forth. As the limitations upon daily living have become increasingly evident, limitations on life itself have become increasingly poignant.

Despite the many experiences of genocide and mass death that have characterized life in the twentieth century, much of twentieth-century thought has attempted to repress death, just as the nineteenth-century Victorians tried to suppress sexuality. For example, we regularly use euphemisms to avoid death in our daily speech. The deceased person is often referred to as the "departed," or as one who has "passed on." The grave is called a "resting place" for one who is "asleep" or "on a journey." The corpse is taken to a "parlor" where cosmetic techniques can make a person look "lifelike." Condolence calls often become cocktail parties characterized by false levity rather than by authentic grief. Nonetheless the pervasiveness of not only death, but of mass death in our times, has prevented any longstanding evasion of the sobering reality of death and dying. Yet, despite the emergence of an academic discipline concerned with death (thanatology), and in spite of an accelerating personal and societal awareness of end-of-life problems and issues, it should not be assumed that either our society or our times are the first in human history to confront either death or the question of what may be beyond it. Already in the first known human writings, those of ancient Sumeria and Babylonia, these issues haunted our distant forebears.

Long before the human mind gave birth to the legends of the Greek and Roman gods, long before the idea of one God entered the world, the earliest recorded legends told of Gilgamesh and his quest for immortal life. On ancient Babylonian clay tablets, fragments of the story remain. Though Gilgamesh never found eternal life, the story of his search has survived down the centuries. Whether or not there actually was a man named Gilgamesh is not important. What is significant is this story of the quest for immortality, which is the story of men and women throughout the centuries, from the time that scribes first pressed their styluses upon clay tablets to inscribe the tale of Gilgamesh.

The story of Gilgamesh, in all of its details, was widely known in the ancient Near East. It influenced the literature and thought that came after it. Its echoes are found in Hebrew Scriptures, especially in the story of Noah and the flood. But its main theme has little to do with the worldwide catastrophe of the great flood. It has more to do with the catastrophe of the inevitable death of the individual person, and with the perennial human desire to discover immortality, or at least to find meaning in life.

The epic tells of the great warrior Gilgamesh and of his friend, Enkidu. Once enemies, they became the closest of friends. Together they encountered and slew the great bull that belonged to the gods. The gods were angered, and they condemned Enkidu to death.

Gilgamesh watched in despair as his friend Enkidu took ill, as his health deteriorated, and as he died. Gilgamesh sat in the presence of his dead friend in sorrow and in mourning. After leaving his friend's corpse, Gilgamesh traveled to see his ancestor Utnapishtim, the Babylonian Noah, who had survived the great flood. From his ancestor, Gilgamesh hoped to learn the secret of life eternal.

On his way to visit Utnapishtim, Gilgamesh met Urshanabi, the boatman, who asked him:

Why are your cheeks wasted?
Why is your face sunken?
Why has evil fortune entered your heart?

There is sorrow in your belly.
Your face is like that of a man on a long journey.
Your face is weathered by cold and heat
because you roam the wilderness in search of a wind puff.

Gilgamesh replied that he looked that way because of the death of
Enkidu:

My friend and loved one . . .
We overcame everything together:
We climbed the mountain,
Captured the Bull of Heaven and killed it,
we entered the mountain and slew lions.
But, my friend, whom I loved dearly,
Who underwent with me all hardships
The fate of mankind overtook him.
Six days and seven nights I wept over him
until a worm fell out of his nose.
Then I was afraid.
In fear of death I roamed the wilderness.
The cause of my friend lies heavy in me.
I wander the steppe.
How can I keep still?
How can I be silent?
The friend I loved has turned into clay.
Me, shall I not lie down like him,
never to move again?

Arriving at the home of Utnapishtim, Gilgamesh asked for the secret of eternal life:

Where can I go?
A thief has stolen my flesh.
Death lives in the house where my bed is,

And wherever I set my feet,
there Death is.[1]

Utnapishtim was unable to impart to Gilgamesh the secret of eternal life. But, to try to assuage Gilgamesh's despair, Utnapishtim offered the next best thing—the secret of a plant that grants youth to the aged, a plant called The Old Man Will Be Made Young.

Gilgamesh traveled to the lake where the magical plant grew. He dove to the bottom of the lake and pulled up the plant. While he rested on the beach, a snake came and stole the plant. In despair, Gilgamesh journeyed back to his land of origin.

Like every great epic story, the story of Gilgamesh is of perennial relevance. Like Gilgamesh, many of us are shocked into despondency and despair by the death of someone close to us. Jolted into the shocking awareness that death is an inevitable fate each of us must yet endure, we tend to search desperately for immortality. We try to find a way to escape and to overcome death. Finding that there is no escape, we tend to find ways of deluding ourselves into believing that the inevitable can be indefinitely postponed by regressing back to our youth or by masking the process of aging. Yet eventually we discover that youth cannot be recaptured, that youth is no guaranteed remedy against death. Like Gilgamesh, we are condemned to accept the inevitability of aging and of death.

Death frightens us because, like Gilgamesh, we fear lying down and not being able to move again. In other words, we fear not only the end of life, but also the end of movement, of possibility. We fear becoming bereft of a future. We are afraid of an end, not only to our life, but also to the meaning of our life. We fear the abrupt limitations that aging and death inevitably hold forth. Contemplation of death inevitably leads to a rendezvous with the reality of our individual finiteness, with the finality of life that death represents. However, contemplation of death can also lead to a profound consideration of what of our life can be perpetuated beyond our death. Another term for life after death is *self-perpetuation.* In thinking about life after death as self-perpetuation, the focus of our attention comes to dwell upon the life each of us has lived, and can yet live. We are inevitably drawn to consider how we have lived and what aspects of our life might be perpetuated beyond the grave.

Self-perpetuation assumes three things: (1) that there is a self; (2) that in some way it can be perpetuated; and (3) that human life has some purpose that extends beyond the grave. In the task of crafting the soul, one must begin with one's own self. Where else is there to begin? But the quest that ends where it begins has ventured nowhere at all. One insight shared by the spiritual masters of the past is that the quest for meaning must include self-transcendence. Though the self is the necessary point of departure, it cannot serve as the final destination. The great human achievements in history, the lasting milestones in culture, the values that we cherish, are rooted in that which transcends the individual. By forging a link with that which is more than one is, by reaching out beyond where one is, by spending life for something that will outlast it, a person can become more than he or she is. We begin with the self in order to transcend the self. The aim of the spiritual life is to be who we can become by becoming more than we are. Self-perpetuation after death presumes self-transcendence during life.

It is of little comfort to know that the atoms that comprise our bodies may have been in existence for millions of years and that they may survive our deaths by millions more. Indeed, the atoms that comprise our bodies are constantly changing during our lifetimes. It is of little comfort to know that when our corpses decompose, they will replenish the earth with certain nutrients and chemicals. These ideas are not comforting because neither one's atomical nor one's anatomical structure is one's real self. Our bodies are a crucial part of who each of us is, but we are more than our bodies.

Self-perpetuation relates to the continuity beyond each of our deaths of that which makes each of us who he or she is. Self-perpetuation relates to the continuity and the perpetuation of each of our own selves, of each of our own souls. But in order for self-perpetuation to occur, there first must be a developed self, part of which at least can achieve perpetuation. Unless a person has developed his or her own self during life, unless we have attended to the articulation of our life's meaning by crafting our soul, by creating our individual life as a work of art, we are doomed to oblivion. As Erik Erikson put it, "I am what survives me."[2] Life provides an opportunity and a challenge for the self to be perpetuated beyond life. The perpetuation beyond life that a person can achieve is largely one that needs to be acquired during life. Self-perpetuation is mostly determined by what and how much one has invested during life in the ultimate future options exchange.

There are many forms of self-perpetuation. The most obvious is self-perpetuation through one's children. Genes are a living embodiment of immortality. If we have done a good job of parenting, children carry not only our genes and our genealogy, but also our memories—memories of the life we have shared with them, and memories that we have transmitted to them. If we have done a very good job of parenting, children also can perpetuate our values, virtues, and deeds. They can continue some of what we have begun, but left an unfinished song.

Parenting is an important strand in the weave of the fabric of each of our lives. However, each of our lives is like a vast garment composed of many strands, many stitches. The medieval Jewish mystics taught that each deed a person performs adds a stitch to a garment that, upon death, comes to represent our life. The nature and the quality of each deed determines the beauty or the ugliness, the neatness or the sloppiness, the brilliance or the blandness of the stitch. According to this teaching, when a person dies the soul is draped for eternity in the garment woven from the deeds that together have constituted one's life. In this view, our eternal attire portrays the life each of us has lived. From this perspective, life should be lived with a vision of how each of us might want our life portrayed when the final stitch is woven. Put another way, our life determines our afterlife. How we have lived determines what of each of us can be perpetuated. The imprint we have made upon others, upon society, upon humanity, upon culture, offers a visa to a form of self-perpetuation.

Preoccupation with the afterlife is not an exercise in moral and social escapism. Concern with our existence in the next world need not obfuscate our moral and social obligations and commitments in the here and now. Actually, the opposite is truly the case—concern for our existence and status after death can serve as a powerful stimulant for forging a life of meaning, for creating life as an art form, in the time now at our disposal. This life offers an opportunity to develop the self, to cultivate the soul in order to perpetuate something of each of our lives beyond death. This is precisely what the poet John Keats meant when he wrote that "the world is a vale of Soul-making."[3]

The spiritual life is like a tree with its roots above, pointing to that which transcends us. The spiritual life aims at transcendence while it affirms a meaning beyond absurdity, the presence of the lasting behind the screen of the ephemeral. Consideration of the afterlife directs our attention toward that which is lasting, toward that and who can survive us. In this regard, Dostoyevsky wrote, "If you were to destroy in mankind the belief in immortality, not only love, but every living force maintaining the life of the world would at once be dried up."[4]

Thoughts about self-perpetuation can lead to actions aimed at making life more meaningful, more beautiful, more saturated with significance. Yet, so doing does not necessarily satisfy our curiosity as to what might yet await us. Various religious traditions not only accept the belief in an afterlife as an article of faith, but also offer a variety of views of what the nature of that afterlife might be like.

So far, no incontestable scientific evidence for or against an afterlife exists. But this should not be surprising. If life after death is a completely different dimension of existence than the one we presently inhabit, and if scientific measurement only relates to our present dimension, then is it understandable why the dimension of afterlife existence cannot be detected through scientific investigation. Precisely because we tend to conceive of everything on the basis of our own experience (which is only natural), we tend to think of the afterlife in terms of time and space, which may be irrelevant. While everything we experience in this dimension exists in time and space, something beyond our current experience, something beyond this life, may be beyond time and space, and beyond the ken of our current range of experience. In other words, we can accept belief in an afterlife as a matter of faith, but we can have no concrete, verifiable, or understandable information regarding what kind of existence it might be. Since the afterlife may be a totally different atmosphere, a completely different dimension of existence than we experience here, even if we knew what it were we could not express it, since all of our language is predicated upon our experience of this world of time and space.

Just as a person blind from birth cannot conceive of the splendor of colors that the sighted constantly see, so a person restrained by the dimensions of our normal everyday existence could not conceive of the dimension of existence that may still await each of us. Consider, for example, an analogy with an astronaut. In space, the astronaut is totally dependent upon a space suit for existence in space, but it is not so of the astronaut in the totally different atmosphere of the earth. Similarly, the body may be merely a capsule designed for life in this world, required for life in this world. In the totally different atmosphere of the next world, it might not be required. Or, to use another analogy, can the caterpillar conceive of what life is like as a butterfly? For the caterpillar, a cocoon may mean death. For a butterfly, it means a new beginning.

From this perspective, consider the notions of heaven and hell. If the afterlife is a different dimension of existence than our own, it is useless to conceive of heaven and hell in terms that assume time and space. It is pointless to think of heaven as a place of earthly delights and of hell as a place of physical punishment. It might be better to think of heaven and hell as *states* of being rather than as *places*. In this view, a person does not *go* to heaven but *becomes* heaven. As a state of being, rather than a specific place, heaven and hell would both be accessible during our lifetimes. Indeed, various religious and mystical traditions speak about the possibility of experiencing some aspect of the future life during this life. For some traditions, this can only be achieved in paranormal experiences. Such experiences come as the result of mastering a variety of difficult meditative and other types of spiritual disciplines. Through such mastery, a person becomes enabled to ascend to a higher level of consciousness that some religions equate with that which is achieved in the completely spiritual state of afterlife existence. Yet some religious traditions deign it possible to experience a taste of the bliss of the afterlife through normal experiences. For example, the Talmud tells us that "three experiences offer a foretaste of the World to Come in this world. These are: the beauty of a sunny day, the bliss of sexual intercourse, the harmony with nature achieved through Sabbath observance."[5]

That heaven and hell are states of being that relate to how a person has led his or her life is expressed by a Hasidic text. According to this text, heaven and hell are not places but matters of perspective. When the righteous arrive in paradise, they perceive themselves to be in heaven because there they find a continuation of the spiritual life of study, prayer, and moral virtue that they practiced while alive. However, when the wicked arrive in paradise—not having cultivated the spiritual life while alive—they perceive it as hell. In this view, heaven and hell are not places but a matter of perspective, based upon how one has lived one's life. Similarly, a story is told of a man who reaches the next world and he sees his very elderly friend sitting on a sofa with an incredibly beautiful young woman on his lap, spending eternity. "So, this is heaven?," the man exclaims. His friend replies, "For me it's heaven, but for her it's hell."

Anthropologists tell us that a people's idea of the afterlife represents the projection of its highest values. For example, for Native Americans, heaven is a happy hunting ground; for Vikings it is Valhalla; for Arabs it is an oasis; and for Jews it is a house of study. (Once when I mentioned to my students that classical Jewish writings portray eternal life as being an eternal student, one of my students said, "If heaven means being in school forever, I'd rather go to hell.") In this context it would be interesting to speculate about what a particularly American view of the afterlife might be. A celestial shopping mall, perhaps. From the perspective of the cultural anthropologist, heaven is a projection of what we value most. Consequently, during life we create our own heaven by implementing and by living that which we value most.

Different traditions pose not only various views on the nature of heaven, but different visions of the nature of life after death. Such views include a disembodied afterlife in which the spirit survives the death of the body and seeks repose in some supernal realm. There is also the idea of resurrection, where the body is reinfused with the soul and lives again. There is the idea of transmigration of souls which claims that a soul lives many times, each time in a different body. A variation of this theme is reincarnation, where the soul can inhabit not only human bodies (of both sexes), but also the bodies of animals and plants, and even of inanimate objects like sponges and stones. These different views of the nature of life after death cannot either be scientifically verified or denied. They are matters of faith. Yet, even if a person does not want to accept either the general idea of life after death or the claim that life after death exists in one of the forms just noted, or in another form, it is still possible to glean some ideas about the nature of life in this world from variations on the theme of what kind of existence may await us in the life after death. From seeing how the afterlife is envisaged we can locate some insights on how to live this life, some views on what matters most, some perspective on crafting a life of purpose and meaning. For example, even if one does not accept the notion of resurrection and transmigration of souls, there are four ideas such a teaching suggests that are compelling:

1. We are who we were. No person is a tabula rasa, a blank slate, as Aristotle claims. No person is a creation out of nothing, *creatio ex nihilo.* Rather, each person carries a history and that history helps shape his or her destiny and identity.

2. As Yogi Berra said, "It's not over 'til it's over," that is,

there are always new possibilities, new opportunities; the unfulfilled life, the disadvantaged life still has a chance.

3. One can interpret transmigration as meaning that in a single life, one can be many people. I am not talking about multiple personalities, but multiple possibilities, multiple careers, multiple lifestyles within a single life. The doors to change and improvement, as well as to change and decline, are always open. What we choose and what we do determines the life or lives we lead during our time on earth.

4. The ideas of transmigration and reincarnation point to an important insight, that is, each person is more than he or she thinks he or she is. Our lives are much richer and deeper than we dare to imagine.

Reflection upon the idea of the resurrection of the body also offers valuable insights on the nature of our present lives. Though we may not accept the faith-claim that the body is resurrected to live again, this claim includes a number of ideas that we may yet find appealing. First, it articulates the individuality of the human person both during life and after death. The individual, even after death, need not be lost in a crowd. Second, the idea of resurrection is an affirmation of the human body, for it is the body that is resurrected. The carnal can serve as a vehicle for spiritual self-expression. Third, one need not wait until after death to experience resurrection. It can happen every day.

I am sure you have used the expression "I'm dead" when you are tired. After a rest, you feel revived. Similarly, composers, writers, and artists often admit to feeling dead after completing a great work; after a period of hibernation they return to their creative work and feel revived. Or people go through traumas and tragedies or periods of life where they feel numb and deadened—physically, emotionally, spiritually. If they are lucky, they discover that this temporary "death" is but a prelude to a resurrected existence. It seems to me that only a person open to new possibilities, to new opportunities, can find the idea of the afterlife appealing and promising. A closed-off person who lives in a state of suspended animation would not find such an idea engaging. Ironically, such a person is already dead in a way. It is precisely this kind of person who needs resurrection during life. As the German poet Goethe wrote, "As long as you do not know how to die and come to life again, you are but a sorry traveler on this dark earth." And, as the Christian theologian Thomas à Kempis said, "Learn to die so that you may begin to live."

In sum, how we live determines whether part of us will achieve perpetuation after death. Life is a quest for that which transcends and survives this life. Crafting the soul aims at creating something worth enduring, something of ourselves that merits self-perpetuation. In the enterprise of creating life as a work of art, it is wise to be guided by Robert Browning's poetic admonition that "reach should exceed grasp, or what's a heaven for?"[6]

chapter eleven

Spiritual Rehabilitation

It is told that the Rabbi of Lublin once stopped in the middle of the street to watch a man removing rust that had accumulated over many years on a wheelbarrow. The rabbi watched the man for a long time, and finally the rabbi asked the man why he was working so long and so hard to remove the rust. The man replied, "Unless I remove the rust, I can no longer use the wheelbarrow. But, rabbi, why does what I am doing interest you so much?"

Said the rabbi, "Souls also accumulate rust. Like the wheelbarrow, if they acquire too much rust, they cannot do what they were made for. While I have been watching you, I have been trying to figure out how I can repair rusty souls."

*L*iving is easy, but not simple. Life flows onward, caught in a perpetual tension between pairs of complementary opposites: up and down, day and night, good and evil, privilege and privation, joy and sorrow. Each is meaningless and incomprehensible without the other. It is self-evident that for there to be *up,* there must be *down.* But, when we are up, we neglect to think about being down. When we are down, we are often too preoccupied with our depressed state to think about being up.

Despite our desire to progress, life nonetheless proceeds in a perpetual ebb and flow, with ups and downs. Both around us and inside
us, there are cycles of growth and decay, success and failure, expansion
and contraction, creativity and destructiveness, vibrancy and dormancy,
progression and recession. It should not be surprising that the spiritual
life also embodies shifts between opposite states of the soul. Spiritual
equilibrium tends to give way to spiritual imbalance, spiritual exaltation suddenly transmutes into spiritual recession.

The mystical masters of many traditions recognized these natural,
seasonal shifts in the life of the soul. Jewish mystics called them "bigness" and "smallness." Christian mystics spoke about "beatitude" as
contrasted with "the dark night of the soul." Past masters understood
that, despite our desire that life remain on a constant progressive course,
spiritual development does not progress down a linear primrose path.
They knew that the life of the soul cannot be put on automatic pilot.
They realized that it is natural for the soul to have ups and downs.

They also understood the potential dangers of spiritual recession.
They were keenly aware that once the life of the soul has been cast off-
balance, it becomes increasingly susceptible to a wide variety of spiritual maladies. They apprehended that in such a state the soul could
easily lapse back into its past undesirable addictions, into a vortex of
confusion and disorientation. No matter how substantial the individual
spiritual development already achieved, no matter how well a person
had progressed in the task of crafting the soul, there always lurked the
omnipresent danger of losing it all when the susceptible soul sank into
a low ebb. From their own experience, they taught that the higher the
rise, the harder the fall.

The Jewish mystical masters viewed "smallness" both as an invitation to catastrophe as well as a possible prelude to even greater spiritual strength. It all depended upon how the individual weathered the
crucible of spiritual recession, with how well the individual could cope
with a depressed soul, with how well one could undergo the necessary
process of spiritual rehabilitation.

On the one hand, these mystics taught that spiritual descent could serve as a necessary preface to an unprecedented and a renewed spiritual ascent. In their words, "ascent first requires descent." Yet they cautioned that too deep of a descent, that an ebb that is not linked to a subsequent flow, can become perilous. For these mystics, the spiritual life—indeed, life itself—is both precious and precarious. As Rabbi Israel of Rhyzen put it, "Life is like being a person dressed in white garments, with a bottle of ink on his head, walking a tightrope that transverses an abyss. One small wrong move, and the ink spills, soiling his garments, and himself. One big wrong move, and unable to recover his balance, the person may fall and be lost in an abyss."[1]

Besides the natural ebb and flow of life, there are always also those unpredictable events that can propel us either into ecstasy or despondency. Life is a blind date with a future populated by random events, by blessings and tragedies, by treasures and traumas, by luck good and bad. Buffeted by chance circumstances that can either enhance or diminish our quality of life, we are constantly at risk of being cast adrift, of being severed from our moorings.

Whether it comes as a result of the normal ebb and flow of life, or whether as the result of happenstance, as a product of chaos invading our daily lives, spiritual imbalance—spiritual recession—requires spiritual therapy, spiritual rehabilitation. The soul needs to ascend from the depths in order to later climb to greater heights than had been previously attained. The spiritual life needs to regain its balance so that it does not slip and fall further down. The venture of spiritual rehabilitation can become the most significant adventure undertaken by the soul, by the self. From the crucible of confusion, from the depths of disorientation, from the sickness of the soul, a resurrection, a rebirth, a renaissance of the self can ensue. From what seems at the time to be a purgatory, one may experience a passage to a renewed and strengthened spiritual condition. Paradoxically, losing a battle can lead to winning the war.

A crisis in life may be a disguised opportunity for renewal. Stagnation can give birth to generativity. A period of increased vulnerability may transmute into a realization of heightened potential. Just as up and down are part of the same continuum, so are destructiveness and creativity, death and resurrection. No one can make an omelet without breaking the eggs.

At various junctures of life—some awakened by an internal alarm clock, others generated by powerful events that intrude unexpectedly upon our lives—we encounter times of crisis. Sometimes when the fibrillations of the soul become dangerously erratic, it becomes necessary for the soul to be shocked in order to regain its normal pulse. How we navigate the passage into our own future from times of crisis and imbalance often shapes the narrative of the subsequent chapters of the novel which is each of our lives.

Spiritual rehabilitation is a path toward regaining one's balance. It is a catalyst for initiating a passage from crisis to renewal, from "smallness" to "bigness," from the dark night of the soul to the replenishment and the expansion of one's spiritual inventory. In some circles, psychology is returning to its original mission of spiritual rehabilitation. Psychology is beginning to recapture its etymological meaning—"discourse on the soul." We increasingly find psychology and spirituality often dealing with the same problems while using different vocabularies to do so. Thus, spirituality and psychology become complementary approaches to a multisided truth. Most people today often prefer psychoanalytic therapies and psychological vocabulary to the substantial offerings provided by traditional spiritual insight. They prefer "psychic integration" to "salvation," "alienation" to "sin," but the issues are the same. As Susan Howatch points out in her novel, *Mystical Paths,* "Psychology's the grass-roots intellectual language of our time, and if you can translate Christianity into *that* everyone will finally understand what the preachers are twittering on about in the pulpit—and then with understanding will come spiritual enlightenment. . . . The real journey—the journey all people are required to take to achieve integration, self-realization and fulfillment—the 'eternal life' of religious language—is the journey inward to the center of the soul."[2]

Spiritual rehabilitation is what theologians through the centuries have called *repentance* or *atonement*. Not only these concerns, but now even these terms are infiltrating the psychoanalytic vocabulary. Describing recent reconceptualizations of psychoanalytic self-understanding, Stephen Mitchell writes, "Psychoanalysis becomes a struggle to find and to be oneself in the process of *atonement* and reconciliation in relation to others, both actual others and others as internal presences."[3]

In Hebrew the term for repentance, for spiritual rehabilitation, is *teshuvah,* which literally means "return."[4] Spiritual rehabilitation is a process of return, of renewal, of replacing spiritual disintegration and fragmentation with "at-one-ment." It is a return to balance from being off-balance, a return to one's moorings after finding one's life precipitously set adrift. It is a regaining of health by the previously ailing soul. It is a recapturing of commitments somehow discarded, a making of desirable new commitments somehow previously obscured. It is a reaffirming of cherished relationships that had begun to unravel and a forging of new relationships that can serve to resuscitate the soul. It is a journey back to the self. It is a return home for the soul. It is therapy for the spiritually homesick.

A Hebrew word for sin is *hait,* which literally means "missing the mark." But to miss there must first be a mark. To return means to return somewhere, to someone, to something that had been there before. The spiritual rehabilitation of the self presumes that there is a self that can be rehabilitated. What theologians call sin, what psychologists call psychic disintegration, what existentialist philosophers call inauthenticity or acting in bad faith, is a condition that makes spiritual rehabilitation desirable. When a person somehow is "not himself," when an individual has forgotten who she is, when a person seems to forget life's mission, then spiritual rehabilitation becomes necessary.

To sin is to act without authenticity. It is to exile the soul from its own home, to become diverted from one's mission, to become a messenger who has forgotten the message. It is an act of self-alienation, of becoming someone other than who we are. It is to play a scene in the drama of our life that is miscast. According to Jean-Paul Sartre, to act in bad faith is to be who one is not, to betray the project that offers meaning to our lives, to subvert one's own integrity, to become a heretic to one's own convictions. Acting in bad faith is to live life as a fallacy, as a contradiction in terms.

In theological parlance, sin is a spiritual illness; repentance is a spiritual remedy. As a medieval Hebrew text puts it:

Just as the body is subject to health and sickness, so is the soul. The health of the body is indicated by its good deeds, and its sickness is indicated by its sins. Just as physical illness is cured by its antithesis, so is the sick, sinful soul restored to health by its antithesis. What is the antithesis of sin? Repentance and good deeds.[5]

One of the rituals practiced by millions of people is the periodic medical check-up. Whether because they feel ill or just because they want to be checked for indications of potential or developing illness, many people undergo a physical examination and a wide variety of tests. Similarly, many spiritual disciplines encourage periodic spiritual check-ups. These are times of introspection, of self-examination, of trying to discern whether the soul is well or ill, whether it requires any particular treatment, whether some spiritual illness is waiting in line ready to become manifest.

The components of a spiritual examination are similar to those of a physical examination. For example, standing naked before a mirror in an examining room, there are no garments to hide one's deformities, no clothes to cover blemishes, no ways of camouflaging unwanted protrusions. Similarly, a spiritual examination begins with a confrontation with the naked truth of who we really are, with what our spiritual profile looks like, with how the results of our deeds have shaped and altered the contours of our spiritual physique. A spiritual check-up begins with seeing ourselves stripped of our pretentions, of our vanities, of the accoutrements we tactically employ to look good to others. Here we are bared of self-illusions, of delusions; in this naked state, no one can honestly fool himself or herself. Such self-reflection compels us to confront the credibility gap within the self. It forces us to ac-knowledge things we have done that have defamed our own character, that have impugned our own integrity. It requires us to question an-swers we glibly have accepted, to scrutinize motivations we have tended to rationalize, to purify noble intentions we sometimes have polluted, to control impulses of the ego we may have let undermine us.

Toward the beginning of most physical check-ups, we stand on a scale to record our weight. But there is another scale, and that is the scale of our deeds. On one side of the scale are those deeds of which we are proud, deeds of virtue, deeds that help make our life a work of art. On the other side of the scale are those deeds of which we are not proud, the memory of which makes us queasy, the recollection of which leads us to reconsider how we have behaved at certain times, to certain people, in certain circumstances. These conscience-jolting deeds are those that inform the diagnosis of our spiritual state, that suggest a spiritual regimen or treatment aimed at restoring our spiritual bal-ance. Reflection on past and current deeds that deflect from the cre-ation of life as a work of art should lead to a feeling of regret. Aware-ness of our faults, recognition of our having missed the mark, is a critical step in the process of spiritual healing.

This feeling of regret must embody two components: remorse and resolve, that is, remorse over what we have done, and resolve to alter our course, to improve our behavior, and, if possible, to right the wrong. Both remorse and resolve are necessary. Remorse without resolve is ineffectual. Just feeling bad about having done something changes nothing. Without resolve to rectify one's behavior, remorse alone is merely an ephemeral emotion that cannot help ensure that we will take the necessary steps to heal our soul, to stop missing the mark. Furthermore, resolve without remorse is also incomplete. We might, for example, resolve to change our behavior for self-serving reasons, rather than because of sincere contrition. If we remain unaware of why our deeds had been unworthy and undesirable of repetition, there is no possibility for spiritual rehabilitation. There is only a mechanical imposition of behavior modification. The symptoms of the spiritual malady have been addressed, but not its cause. In such a case, a relapse becomes likely.

After the scales, there is usually the taking of blood pressure. What is being determined is whether pressure is too high or too low. Similarly, in a spiritual examination, one should ask oneself: Is my pressure too high—not only the pressure *in* me, but the pressure *on* me? Or is my pressure too low? Am I listless due to lack of adequate stimulation, because I am not challenged enough by the tasks with which I am confronted? Can I carry my own weight? Can I bear the weight I am carrying? Am I carrying too much? Am I not carrying my load? Am I doing too much, am I working too hard, am I putting myself under too much pressure? Am I letting others pressure me too much? Could I pass the stress test that each day requires? Is what I am doing important; is it meaningful; does it matter? Am I preoccupied with trivialities while neglecting what is really important?

From taking the blood pressure, we usually move to the examining table. There, the first question often asked is: Do you have pains anywhere? Hearing this question always reminds me of the story of two Russian peasants at a tavern getting drunk. One says to the other, "Ivan, do you love me, are you my friend?"

"Yes, Igor, I do love you. I am your friend."

A few drinks later, Igor asks again, "Ivan, do you love me, are you my friend?"

And, again, Ivan says, "Yes, Igor, I do love you. I am your friend."

And a few drinks later, they are both very drunk, and Igor asks again, "Ivan, do you love me, are you my friend?"

And again Ivan answers, "Yes, Igor, I do love you, I am your friend."

But this time Igor, who has lost all inhibitions, starts to cry, and he says, "Ivan, I think that you really are *not* my friend. I think you really do *not* love me, because if you *did* really love me, and you really were my friend, you would know what causes me pain."

Do we always know when those we claim to love are in pain, are suffering, are in need of our care, of our concern? Do we always remember that the words "care" and "cure" are related? That knowing another's pain, and caring, often helps to cure that pain, that suffering? And how many of us are aware of our own pains, of our own hurts which are in need of care and of repair?

Like physical pain, so emotional pain, psychological pain, spiritual discomfort may be a signal, a warning that something is really wrong with us or is about to become really wrong with us, and that it must be treated before it worsens and causes lasting damage. Do we feel these pains, do we listen to what they are telling us, do we confront them, do we deal with them? Or do we ignore them and just hope they'll go away? And which are those pains? The pains of disappointment, the pains of not meeting our goals, the pains of failing relationships, the pains of fading hopes and dreams, the pains of becoming ever more distant from those to whom we want to be closer, the pains of being distant from those whom we love.

While examining the topology of the body, we inevitably find scars. All of us carry these little visible reminders of past pain, of previous injury, that occasionally fester and remind us of what we had suffered. These scars never go away. But if they begin to fester, they should be attended to immediately, lest the wounds of the past overcome us in the present. The scars we carry are reminders of the past, but they are also warnings for the future.

An instrument with a small light attached is used to examine the mouth, the ears, the tongue. Similarly, in a spiritual examination, we should illuminate and reflect upon what we have done with our ears, our mouths, our tongues. We are encouraged to recall the times we refused to hear, to listen, as well as the times we only allowed ourselves to hear what we wanted to hear. We become compelled to become aware of how we can hurt ourselves and hurt others by what we say to them. Words are weapons that can injure. Words have power that can destroy people, especially people we care about. Not by chance does the Bible say that even life and death are in the power of the tongue.

Bad words can shatter good relationships. Gossip can destroy a good reputation. In the Talmud it is asked why human beings have earlobes. The answer is so that when we begin to hear evil gossip, we can put the earlobe over our ear so as not to hear it.[6] The Talmud further says that a gossiper is like a murderer, except a murderer kills one person, but a gossiper destroys three people—the one who speaks gossip, the one who hears gossip, and the one about whom the gossip is said.[7]

Long before psychoanalysis, many religious traditions realized that confession is a vital element of spiritual therapy. Confession was known to be therapeutic long before Freud. As the old adage puts its, "Confession is good for the soul." Both classical Judaism and classical Christianity recognized that confession can make us feel better by "getting it out," by making us listen to what we are saying and thereby becoming aware of what we have done. The first thing an alcoholic who joins Alcoholics Anonymous must do is to say, out loud, "I am an alcoholic." As for the alcoholic, so for all of us—confession is a crucial step to recovery, to spiritual rehabilitation.

Among some of the Hasidim there was a custom to confess one's sins to a wise man and to receive advice as to how to rectify one's fault. However, other Hasidim followed a practice of identifying their best and closest friend. At regular intervals, each person would go to a private place with his closest friend and bare his soul. He would confess his misdeeds, reveal his inadequacies, his fears, his hopes, his dreams, his fantasies. And then the friend would do the same. Yet, as crucial as regret and confession are, the ultimate test of whether the process of spiritual rehabilitation has been effective is whether balance has been restored, whether one's subsequent deeds engender the fruits of introspection.

In a physical examination, a little hammer is used to test our reflexes. But there are emotional as well as physical reflexes that require attention. For example, it is important to learn better how to control some of our responses to people and to situations—for instance, how to control our anger, especially when losing our temper hurts those whom we love; when speaking without first thinking inflicts a wound on one whom we hold dear; when argumentation precludes talking things out; when we automatically close ourselves off, rather than open ourselves up to the care and to the concern of someone we cherish.

The stethoscope is placed on the chest. The electrocardiogram machine is used to see how the heart is. Similarly, in a spiritual examination it is important to see how the heart is functioning in the emotional and in the spiritual sense. We worry a lot about hardening arteries, but not enough about hardening hearts. We worry about arterial sclerosis in the brain that could bring on a stroke, but we worry little about arterial sclerosis of the mind, about a hardened mind, closed to new ideas, new experiences, new learning, new joys, new relationships, new possibilities. The great medieval Christian mystic Hildegard of Bingen taught that sin means the drying up of the sap of life. In her view, the soul of the sinner is one that has become cold, hard, brittle, and dusty. Similarly, a Hasidic teaching is that more than one should fear becoming old, one should be continuously apprehensive about becoming stale.

In preparation for certain medical tests, it is necessary to abstain from food and drink. As a result, hunger is often present during a physical examination. There is not only physical hunger but spiritual hunger as well—the hunger for love, friendship, justice, beauty, and meaning.

Then come the tests of bodily fluids—of blood and urine. Similarly, in a spiritual examination we need to know what's floating around inside of us. Is our compassion, love, integrity level too low? Is our envy, hate, hostility level too high? Are we spiritually anemic? What regimen must we undertake to bring our internal forces into balance?

There are stimuli that motivate us to undergo a spiritual examination. But there also are obstacles that hamper spiritual rehabilitation. One such obstacle is what a medieval philosopher called "self-excuse," that is, failing to acknowledge our shortcomings by blaming others for our faults. This sabotages the process of spiritual rehabilitation because it stifles our ability to recognize our faults, to take responsibility for them, and to initiate an action plan for overcoming them. Another obstacle that hampers our spiritual recovery is addiction to bad habits. The premise of spiritual rehabilitation is the freedom to alter and to improve our behavior. Habit restricts our freedom to improve our behavior.

Often, habit has a person more than a person has a habit. In this regard, the Talmudic rabbis remind us that bad habits, that undesirable actions, that sins, begin like a traveler passing by our home. Invited in, they become guests that overstay their welcome. Then they become residents. Finally, they can become masters of the home, that is, of the self, of the soul. In this view, a bad habit, an undesirable action, can not only stifle desirable changes in behavior; it also can suppress our creative potentialities. It can smother the potentialities pregnant within us to create life as a work of art.

As self-excuse and habit obstruct one's spiritual rehabilitation, other factors can act as catalysts to improve our spiritual standard of living. Ironically, one such factor is contemplation of death. The recognition of human finitude, the confrontation with the reality of our own mortality, can serve as a cause not of fatalistic morbidity but as a stimulant to spiritual self-awareness and self-improvement. The often quoted Talmudic adage "If not now, when?" is taken by the medieval commentators to mean that since all one really has is *now*—the present—since the future is always uncertain, the task of spiritual realignment cannot be deferred.[8] It must be treated with immediate urgency. The process of spiritual rehabilitation must commence here and now, rather than being postponed to a future that may never come, to a future in which it may be too late to begin.

A second factor in stimulating the process of spiritual rehabilitation is by evoking memory—by remembering who we are, by reaffirming what matters most to us, by recommitting to those values that shape our lives and ourselves. A person who has lost his memory has lost his mind. To remember is to re-mind. Bereft of crucial memories, a person becomes dis-membered. Recollection of what matters is an act of re-membering, a reversal of disintegration and an entrée to the reintegration of the self.

A third factor is reminding ourselves of what we have to be grateful for. Evoking the attitude of gratitude enables us to emerge from self-pity and depression to recognize the state of grace that characterizes our lives. The attitude of gratitude teaches us not to take for granted that which has been granted us. There are five major ways of doing this. One is by becoming fully aware of what we have. The second is realizing that it is more important to want what we have than to have what we want. The third is by being grateful for the catastrophes that might have happened from which we have been spared. The fourth is by envisioning our life without who and what we often take for granted. The fifth is by envisioning what matters most and how impoverished our lives would be if those things, those people, those relationships that matter most to us were taken away.

Sometime try this simple exercise. Think of all those whom you love and all those who love you. Then imagine what your life might be like without them. Or try what I call the Fiddler on the Roof exercise. In *Fiddler on the Roof* Tevye reminds us that in Jewish tradition there is a blessing for everything—for eating bread, for seeing beauty, for smelling a wonderful fragrance, for waking up in the morning, for getting dressed, for health, even for a successful venture in the washroom. There is a blessing for just about everything, for so very many things that we usually look past. And this is precisely *why* there is a blessing for everything—to evoke our awareness of the many, many blessings that we so often overlook. Being aware of these blessings is a stimulus to evoking the attitude of gratitude. Realizing what the withdrawal of any of these blessings would mean to the quality, and even the quantity, of our lives can only stimulate our awareness of how much we have, and of how grateful we ought to be.

For example, in Chicago, where I live, there are many homeless people. They stand on the streets begging for money and for food; some hold signs asking for help for themselves and their families. Mostly, people just ignore them and pass them by. But there is one homeless man who stands in front of an office building in downtown Chicago who people rarely deny. They inevitably reach into their pockets and hand him some money. They smile at him and go on their way. I did not understand why he evoked such a response, until I read the sign he carried. It simply said, "I was like you, but you might one day be like me." In reading his sign I was reminded of the Yiddish proverb "If you cannot be grateful for what you have received, then be thankful for what you have been spared."

Helen Keller often would ask people what they would want to see if they knew they would become blind three days later. We tend to take things for granted until we lose them or feel threatened with losing them. Until short of breath, we take breath for granted. Until ill, we take health for granted. Until unloved and rejected, we take love and acceptance for granted. Until hungry, we take food for granted. Until confined, we take freedom for granted. Until we become aware of the sufferings of others, we often remain unconscious of the gifts, of the bounties, that sprinkle our daily lives with blessing.

One day when I was shopping at the local supermarket I noticed that the store manager was detaining a black man on suspicion that he had stolen something. The man had been walking around the store for hours without a shopping cart, without a shopping basket, without buying anything, and people became suspicious of him. When I got a little closer, the man motioned for me to come over and talk to the store manager on his behalf. As I approached I recognized the man as a former student of mine, an Ethiopian Jew. I asked him what was the problem, and he told me that he was being detained on suspicion of theft and for loitering. So I asked him, "Why are you wandering around the supermarket?" And he said, "You know, in Ethiopia, we always were starving. Because of the long drought, we never had much food and I grew up always being hungry. Here—look at all of this food around us. When I have free time I like to walk around the supermarket, simply to look at the abundance of food around me. Because then I know I'll never have to be so hungry again. Because I am so grateful to be here in America, a land where people do not have to starve." For those who once were deprived, the attitude of gratitude often comes easily.

Often people make the mistake of believing that the world is there to make them happy. Self-pity inevitably leads them to the refrain: "It's just not fair." But if everything were fair, the world could not exist for a day. Birds could not eat worms, the weather could not be disagreeable to some yet agreeable to others. Expecting the world to treat you fairly is like expecting a bull not to charge at you because you are a vegetarian. Such advocates of the attitude of entitlement usually subscribe to the compulsion to blame others for everything they dislike about their lives. If asked to make a list of everything that is wrong with their lives and to assign responsibility to each of those situations, most would be blamed on someone else. But the process of spiritual rehabilitation asks us to take responsibility for our own actions and deeds, and to accept the fact that life is difficult. Once one has accepted that life is difficult, and often unfair, it suddenly becomes less difficult.

Spiritual rehabilitation is grounded in optimism, in hope, because it assumes the possibility of improvement. As an old myth reminds us, hope has two daughters: anger and courage—anger at the way things are, and courage to change the way things are. Similarly, spiritual rehabilitation is rooted in hope—the hope that an individual will be angry enough at oneself to rehabilitate one's self and courageous enough to undertake what must be done in order to achieve it.

As already was mentioned, in Hebrew the word for *repentance* means "return." The process of spiritual rehabilitation is a turning, a returning to that which matters most, a retuning of the discordant soul. Return means, for example, the healing of a fissure in a loving relationship, the repair of a breach that never should have occurred, of an act of alienation that never should have taken place. The highest kind of return is not one motivated by fear of punishment or of retribution, or on the basis of a cost-benefit analysis, but one motivated out of love. Return is an opportunity for healing, for mending, for building, for creating something unprecedented. As the Jewish mystics would put it, "From the descent can come a higher ascent than existed before." Often it is not until we find ourselves in the depths of the valley that we are able to recognize the beauty of the view from the top of the mountain.

Return is an opportunity for once again becoming a part of the life of a community from which one may have moved apart. It is an invitation to move from "I" to "we," from self-encapsulation to communion. However, many confuse membership in a group with living in a community. A group of people is an association, not a community. A community is bound together by values, goals, dreams, a common mission. A community is an interweaving of individual lives with one another. In a community, lives are not lived in solitude but in solidarity. And the smallest community, the most vital community, is the family. Community begins with family, where lives intermesh in an intimacy that cannot be wrenched apart one from the other. But, while community may begin with the family, it cannot end there. The family is a foundational brick in the structure of society, but it is not society in its totality. In forging a feeling of community, the adage "Think globally, act locally" rings true. Like charity, community begins at home. Community helps define where and what is our home.

Finally, return means the return of the soul to its home. Spiritual rehabilitation culminates with an end to alienation, a termination of spiritual homelessness, a recognition that the soul has found its way home. Home is both a place as well as a state of being. Home is a metaphor for where we belong, for the center of our world, for the core of meaning, for that which matters most. The old folk saying "Home is where the heart is" rings true. Home is where one can be oneself, where those with whom one wants to be dwell. It is a focal point of utmost significance. It is where we feel rooted. It is a haven for the soul. In the film *Sleepless in Seattle*, the protagonist, Sam, has lost his young wife to a terminal illness. Asked to describe his love for her, he says, "It's like finding a home you never knew you had."

Finally, the process of spiritual rehabilitation, like the broader task of crafting the soul of which it is a vital part, may be compared to a game of checkers.

The Rabbi of Rhyzen once entered a room where he found his closest disciples playing checkers. When the students saw their master, they were deeply embarrassed, for they knew they should have been studying sacred texts rather than squandering their time playing games. But the Rabbi of Rhyzen was not angry. He approached his disciples, and he said, "I am glad that you are playing checkers, for if you have learned the rules of checkers, you have learned something important about life. There are three rules in checkers which are also three rules for life:

1. *You should move only one step at a time.*
2. *You should move only forward, but not backward.*
3. *When you have reached the highest rung, you may move whichever way you want."*

Notes

Chapter One

1. For another version of this saying, see Elie Wiesel, *Souls on Fire* (New York: Random House, 1972), 158.
2. Matthew 16:26, Mark 8:36, Luke 9:25. I follow here an old standard translation.
3. This is a nonliteral translation of Blaise Pascal, *Pensées*, para. 68. See also Blaise Pascal, *Pensées*, trans. A. J. Krailsheimer (London: Penguin Books, 1966), 48.
4. Hermann Hesse, *Reflections*, trans. Ralph Manheim (New York: Farrar, Straus and Giroux, 1974), 35.
5. Harold Kushner, *When All You've Ever Wanted Isn't Enough: The Search for a Life That Matters* (New York: Pocket Books, 1986), 20.
6. Quoted in Viktor E. Frankl, *Man's Search for Meaning*, trans. Ilse Lasch (New York: Washington Square Press, 1963), 121.
7. Mihaly Csikszentmihalyi, *Flow: The Psychology of Optimal Experience* (New York: Harper and Row, 1990), 3, 1.
8. Carl G. Jung, *Modern Man in Search of a Soul*, trans. W. S. Dell and Cary F. Baynes (New York: Harcourt, Brace, 1933), 61.
9. Stephen A. Mitchell, *Hope and Dread in Psychoanalysis* (New York: Basic Books, 1993), 67.
10. See Matthew Fox, *The Reinvention of Work* (New York: HarperCollins, 1994), 14, quoting Dr. Larry Dossey.
11. Regrettably, I could not locate the translation of Tolstoy from which I

copied this quote. However, for an alternative translation of Tolstoy's "A Confession," (sometimes translated as "My Confession") see Leo Tolstoy, "A Confession," in John Bayley, ed., *The Portable Tolstoy* (New York: Penguin Books, 1978), 678–79.

12. Leo Tolstoy, "The Death of Ivan Ilych," trans. Aylmer Maude, in *The Death of Ivan Ilych and Other Stories* (New York: New American Library, 1960), 148.

13. Quoted in Mitchell, 210.

14. Irving Singer, *Meaning in Life* (New York: Free Press, 1992), 5.

15. Talmud, Mishnah-Abot 1:14.

16. See Moses Maimonides, *Eight Chapters,* trans. Joseph I. Gorfinkle (New York: Columbia University Press, 1912), 84.

17. Soren Kierkegaard, *Either/Or,* trans. Walter Lowrie (Garden City, NY: Doubleday,1959), vol. 2, 263.

18. Arthur Lovejoy, *The Great Chain of Being* (Cambridge: Harvard University Press, 1936), 7.

19. Matthew Arnold, "Stanzas from the Grande Chartreuse," in Matthew Arnold, *Selected Poems* (New York: Penguin Books, 1994), 113.

20. Quoted in George Seldes, ed., *The Great Quotations* (New York: Pocket Books, 1967), 615, from Thoreau's *Walden.*

21. Rollo May, *Love and Will* (New York: W. W. Norton, 1969), 43; William Barrett, *The Illusion of Technique: A Search for Meaning in a Technological Civilization* (Garden City, NY: Doubleday, 1978).

22. Csikszentmihalyi, 5.

23. Quoted in Arianna Huffington, *The Fourth Instinct: The Call of the Soul* (New York: Simon and Schuster, 1994), 45.

Chapter Two

1. Quoted in Wayne Teasdale and George Cairns, eds., *The Community of Religions: Voices and Images of the Parliament of the World's Religions* (New York: Continuum, 1996), 238.

2. Quoted in Bryan Appleyard, *Understanding the Present: Science and the Soul of Modern Man* (New York: Doubleday, 1992), 134.

3. From Woodrow Wilson's war message to Congress, April 2, 1917, quoted in Seldes, 277.

4. Jacob Bronowski, *The Ascent of Man* (Boston: Little, Brown, 1973), 53.

5. Arnold, "Dover Beach," 103.

6. See William Safire, ed., *Lend Me Your Ears: Great Speeches in History* (New York: W. W. Norton, 1992), 813–14, 812.

7. The National Commission on Excellence in Education, *A Nation at Risk: The Full Account* (Cambridge: USA Research, 1984), 5.

8. Quoted in Kushner, *When All You've Ever Wanted*, 166.

9. See Algernon Charles Swinburne's 1871 poem, "Hymn to Man."

10. Jean-Paul Sartre, *The Condemned of Altona*, trans. Sylvia and George Leeson (New York: Vintage Books, 1961), 58, 177.

11. Marc Connelly, *The Green Pastures* (New York: Holt, Rinehart and Winston, 1967), part one, scene six, 69.

12. Source unknown.

Chapter Three

1. Quoted in Rollo May, *The Cry for Myth* (New York: Dell, 1991), 154. For another translation, see Dante, *The Divine Comedy*, trans. C. H. Sisson (New York: Oxford University Press, 1993), 47.

2. Rollo May, *Man's Search for Himself* (New York: W. W. Norton, 1953), 14.

3. William Barrett, *Death of the Soul* (Garden City, NY: Doubleday, 1986), 46.

4. Nathan A. Scott Jr., *The Broken Center: Studies in the Theological Horizon of Modern Literature* (New Haven: Yale University Press, 1966), 8.

5. Jean-Paul Sartre, *Being and Nothingness*, trans. Hazel E. Barnes (New York: Philosophical Library, 1956), 439. See also Robert D. Cumming, ed., *The Philosophy of Jean-Paul Sartre* (New York: Random House, 1965), 277.

6. Ford's words are usually rendered in this way; however, what he actually said was, "History is more or less bunk." For this quote and notation of its origin, see e.g., Seldes, ed., 476.

7. See citation and discussion in May, *The Cry for Myth*, 102.

8. Philip Slater, *Earthwalk* (Garden City, NY: Anchor Books, 1974), 139.

9. José Ortega y Gasset, *The Revolt of the Masses* (New York: W. W. Norton, 1957), 110–12.

10. Quoted in Scott, 190.

11. See Sam Keen, *Gabriel Marcel* (Richmond, Va.: John Knox Press, 1967), 10–13.

12. Quoted in Appleyard, 42.

13. Quoted in Bernie S. Siegel, *Peace, Love and Healing* (New York: Harper and Row, 1989), 254, from Einstein's *The World as I See It.*
14. Quoted in Huffington, 60.
15. Rollo May, *Love and Will*, 55.
16. Sam Keen, *To a Dancing God* (New York: Harper and Row, 1970), 58.
17. Jerzy Kosinski, "A National of Videots," *Media and Methods* 11:8 (April 1975): 24–32, 52–53.
18. Quoted in Appleyard, 15, from Ludwig Wittgenstein's *Tractatus Logico-Philosophicus.*
19. Quoted in Appleyard, 35.
20. Quoted in Robert S. Mendelsohn, *Confessions of a Medical Heretic* (Chicago: Contemporary Books, 1979), 39.
21. See Christopher Lasch, *The Culture of Narcissism* (New York: Warner Books, 1979), 92–96.
22. Bertrand Russell, *The Conquest of Happiness* (New York: Book League of America, 1930), 70.
23. Cited in Huffington, 234.
24. All quoted in Huffington, 74.
25. See discussion in Lasch, 94, citing Michael Maccoby's *The Gamesman: The New Corporate Leaders* (New York: Simon and Schuster, 1976), 102.
26. Russell, 52.
27. For example, Martin Buber describes the biblical prophets as failures who succeeded. See Buber's essay "Biblical Leadership," in Will Herberg, ed., *The Writings of Martin Buber* (New York: World Publishing, 1956), 222–24.
28. Alan Watts, *The Way of Zen* (New York: Pantheon, 1957), 116.
29. Oedipus and Alex Haley as quoted in May, *The Cry for Myth*, 47–48.
30. See Barrett, *Death of the Soul*, 42.
31. Ibid., 98.
32. See May, The Cry for Myth, 57.
33. Barrett, *Death of the Soul*, 44–46.
34. Quoted in Lasch, 161.
35. Quoted in Lasch, 97.
36. See Kosinski, "A Nation of Videots."
37. See Barrett, *Death of the Soul*, 70–75.
38. For different perspectives on the nature of rationality, see e.g., Bryan Wilson, ed., *Rationality* (New York: Harper and Row, 1971).

39. William Butler Yeats, "The Second Coming," in Alan Swallow, ed., *The Rinehart Book of Verse* (New York: Holt, Rinehart and Winston, 1952), 322.

Chapter Four

1. Genesis 3:9.
2. See Barrett, *Death of the Soul,* 46.
3. Quoted in May, *Man's Search for Himself,* 27.
4. Jerzy Kosinski (pseud. Joseph Novak), *The Future Is Ours, Comrade* (Garden City, NY: Doubleday, 1960), 35, 27.
5. See Geoffrey Movius, "A Conversation with Jerzy Kosinski," *New Boston Review* 1:3 (Winter 1995): 3–6.
6. H. Auden, "The Age of Anxiety," in *Collected Poems* (New York: Vintage Books, 1976), 476.
7. Quoted in May, *Man's Search for Himself,* 16, from Eliot's poem, "The Hollow Men."
8. Rollo May, *Psychology and the Human Dilemma* (New York: W. W. Norton, 1967), 37.
9. Quoted in May, *The Cry for Myth,* 136.
10. This description of American life reflects the sociological analysis done by Daniel Yankelovich. See his *New Rules.*
11. Russell, 49.
12. Cited in Slater, 119.
13. Quoted from Sadat's autobiography in Gail Sheehy, *Pathfinders* (New York: Bantam Books, 1982), 516–17.
14. Quoted in Csikszentmihalyi, 2.
15. Ibid., 19.
16. On the give-and-get compact, see e.g., Yankelovich, 225–33.
17. See Phillip Rieff, *The Triumph of the Therapeutic* (New York: Harper and Row, 1966).
18. Hermann Hesse, *Demian,* trans. Michael Roloff and Michael Lebeck (New York: Bantam Books, 1968), 108.
19. Jerzy Kosinski, *Blind Date* (Boston: Houghton Mifflin, 1977), 110.
20. Quoted in Gail Sheehy, *Passages* (New York: Bantam Books, 1976), 377.
21. Matthew Arnold, "Self Dependence," in Matthew Arnold, *Selected Poetry and Prose* (New York: Holt, Rinehart and Winston, 1953), 56.

22. Talmud, Sanhedrin 37a.
23. Quoted in Frankl, *The Doctor and the Soul,* trans. Richard and Clara Winston (New York: Alfred A. Knopf, 1955).
24. Quoted in Charles Taylor, *The Ethics of Authenticity* (Cambridge: Harvard University Press, 1991), 128.

Chapter Five

1. See Deepak Chopra, *Quantum Healing* (New York: Bantam Books, 1989), 22.
2. George L. Engel, "The Need for a New Medical Model: A Challenge for Biomedicine," *Science* 196:4286 (April 8, 1977): 129–36.
3. Ibid., 130.
4. See Chopra, 140.
5. *Charmides* in *The Dialogue of Plato,* trans. B. Jowett, 2 vols. (New York: Random House, 1937), vol. 1, p. 6, sec. 156–57.
6. Ibid.
7. Moses Maimonides, *Treatise on Asthma,* trans. S. Muntner (Philadelphia: Lippincott, 1963), 89.
8. Shem Tov ben Joseph Ibn Falaquera, *The Book of the Seeker,* trans. M. H. Levine (New York: Yeshiva University Press, 1976), 31.
9. For the text of and discussion on the World Health Organization's (WHO) definition of "health," see e.g., Tom L. Beauchamp and LeRoy Walters, eds., *Contemporary Issues in Bioethics,* Second Edition (Belmont, Calif.: Wadsworth Publishing, 1982), 48-59.
10. See Bernie Siegel, *How To Live Between Office Visits* (New York: HarperCollins, 1993), xix.
11. Martin Goss, *The Psychological Society* (New York: Random House, 1978), 6–7.
12. Charles J. Sykes, *A Nation of Victims: The Decay of the American Character* (New York: St. Martin's Press, 1992), 3.
13. Ibid.
14. Ibid., 8
15. Ibid., 123
16. Ibid., 13
17. Cited in Harold S. Kushner, *How Good Do We Have To Be?* (Boston: Little, Brown and Co., 1996), 88–89.
18. M. Scott Peck, *The Road Less Traveled* (New York: Touchstone, 1978), 17.

19. Quoted in Sykes, 130.
20. Sam Keen, *Hymns To an Unknown God* (New York: Bantam Books, 1994), 106–107.
21. Quoted in Sykes, 146.
22. Alasdair MacIntyre, *After Virtue* (South Bend, Ind.: University of Notre Dame Press, 1984), 11–12.
23. See Robert Bellah, et al., *Habits of the Heart* (Berkeley: University of California Press, 1985), 121–38.
24. Sheehy, 227.
25. See Robert Ornstein and David Sobel, *Healthy Pleasures* (Reading, Mass.: Addison-Wesley, 1989), 38–46.
26. Ibid.
27. Ibid., 24.
28. Deepak Chopra, *Ageless Body, Timeless Mind* (New York: Harmony Books, 1993), 199–201.
29. On dieting, see e.g., Ornstein and Sobel, 85–94.
30. On exercise, see e.g., ibid., 105–13; Chopra, *Ageless Body,* 201–203.
31. See Siegel, *Peace, Love and Healing,* 36; also note Chopra, *Quantum Healing,* 70–71. On the interaction between beliefs and healing, see e.g., Herbert Benson, *Timeless Healing* (New York: Fireside, 1996), and Larry Dossey, *Healing Words* (San Francisco: HarperSanFrancisco, 1993).
32. Quoted in Chopra, *Ageless Body,* 56.
33. On the impact of negative emotions on the immune system, see e.g., Daniel Goleman, *Emotional Intelligence* (New York: Bantam Books, 1997), 166–77.
34. Ibid., 177–85.
35. Chopra, *Ageless Body,* 20, 72, 195.

Chapter Six

1. Slater, 192.
2. Soren Kierkegaard, *The Present Age,* trans. Alexander Dru (New York: Harper and Row, 1962), 35.
3. Quoted in Erich Fromm, *The Art of Loving* (New York: Harper and Row, 1989), 125.
4. Dag Hammarskjold, *Markings,* trans. Leif Sjoberg and W. H. Auden (New York: Alfred A. Knopf, 1964), 131.
5. Quoted in Csikszentmihalyi, 9.

6. Quoted in Huffington, 20.

7. See Keen, *Gabriel Marcel,* 8–13.

8. R. H. Tawney, *The Acquisitive Society* (New York: Harcourt, Bruce, and Howe, 1920), 183–84.

9. William Blake, "A Memorable Fancy," in *William Blake: A Selection of Poems and Letters,* ed. J. Bronowski (Baltimore: Penguin, 1958), 101.

10. Singer said this to me in a conversation in June 1978.

11. Quoted in Mihaly Csikszentmihalyi, *The Evolving Self* (New York: Harper Collins, 1993), 56.

12. See chapter 3, note 5.

13. On existentialism, see the now classic work of my teacher, the late William Barrett, *Irrational Man: A Study in Existential Philosophy* (New York: Doubleday, 1958).

14. Blaise Pascal, *Pensées,* 154. This translation, which differs slightly from the one in my book, is the way this citation has been traditionally rendered in English.

15. Soren Kierkegaard, *Training in Christianity,* trans. Walter Lowrie (Princeton, NJ: Princeton University Press, 1944), 201, emphasis mine.

16. Ibid.

17. Sartre, *Being and Nothingness,* part 1, chapter 2, 47–73.

18. Mitchell, 132–33.

19. See ibid., 23.

20. Quoted, ibid.

21. Ibid., 25.

Chapter Seven

1. Quoted in Paul Edwards, "Meaning and Value of Life," in *The Encyclopedia of Philosophy,* ed. Paul Edwards (New York: Macmillan, 1972), vol. 3, 468.

2. William Shakespeare, *Macbeth,* act V, scene 5.

3. Quoted in Edwards, 477, from Freud's letters.

4. Joseph Campbell, *The Power of Myth* (New York: Doubleday, 1988), 229.

5. Frankl, *The Doctor and the Soul,* 9.

6. Mitchell, 67.

7. Frankl, *Man's Search for Meaning,* 45.

8. Ibid., 121.

9. Ibid.

10. Pesach Krauss, *Why Me?: Coping with Grief, Loss and Change* (New York: Bantam Books, 1990), 168–69.
11. Ibid., 169.
12. Ibid.
13. Ibid., 170.
14. Ibid.
15. Albert Camus, *The Myth of Sisyphus and Other Essays,* trans. Justin O'Brien (New York: Alfred A. Knopf, 1955), 3.
16. Cited in Daniel C. Matt, ed., *Walking Humbly with God: The Life and Writings of Rabbi Hershel Jonah Matt* (Hoboken, NJ: Ktav, 1993), 12. My friend and colleague the late Hershel Matt was a very close disciple of Herberg.
17. Abraham Joshua Heschel, *God in Search of Man* (New York: Harper and Row, 1955), 3.
18. Abraham Joshua Heschel, *The Earth Is the Lord's* (New York: Henry Schuman, 1950), 106.
19. Abraham Joshua Heschel, *Who Is Man?* (Stanford: Stanford University Press, 1965), 54.
20. Quoted in Huffington, 78.
21. Philip Slater, *The Pursuit of Loneliness* (Boston: Beacon Press, 1971), 148.
22. Keen, *Hymns to an Unknown God,* 16.
23. Cited in Bellah, 117.
24. See Erich Fromm, *Escape from Freedom* (New York: Avon Books, 1965), 157–231.
25. Quoted in Edwards, 474.
26. Talmud, Eruvin 13b.
27. The translation used here is currently not accessible to me. For an alternate translation, see Tolstoy, *The Death of Ivan Ilych,* 148.
28. Ibid., 131–32.
29. According to many of the existentialists, classical Western philosophy failed to confront the reality of death, and, therefore, largely avoided dealing with the meaning of life. For many of the existentialists, however, philosophical speculation should begin with a contemplation of human finitude and inevitable death, and should consequently be drawn to focus on the quest for meaning. For instance, the Jewish existentialist philosopher Franz Rosenzweig depicted classical philosophy as an attempt to

"rob death of its poisonous sting and Hades of its pestilential breath" by retreating into consideration of universal categories of abstract thought, rather than dealing with the individual existential shock occasioned by the awareness of one's own mortality. Rosenzweig, who suffered from Lou Gehrig's disease (ALS) was keenly aware of the limitations, both in time and in space, of the human body. For Rosenzweig's critique of classical philosophy in this regard, see Franz Rosenzweig, *The Star of Redemption*, trans. William H. Hallo (New York: Holt, Rinehart and Winston, 1970), 3–6.

30. Thornton Wilder, *Our Town*, in *Three Plays by Thornton Wilder* (New York: Bantam, 1966), act III, 63.

31. Bahya Ibn Pakuda, *The Book of Direction to the Duties of the Heart*, trans. Menahem Mansoor (London: Routledge and Kegan Paul, 1973), 370.

32. Tolstoy, "A Confession," 681–82.

33. Ibid., 679.

34. Ibid., 677.

35. Jung, 61.

36. Ibid.

37. Tolstoy, "A Confession," 683.

38. Ibid., 682.

39. Ibid., 683.

40. Will Durant, *On The Meaning of Life* (New York: Ray Long and Richard R. Smith, 1932), 138, 144.

41. Tolstoy, "A Confession," 704.

42. Quoted in Singer, 140.

43. Quoted in Singer, 86. The actual citation from James's essay, "Is Life Worth Living?" is "It depends on the liver." I have rephrased it so that the reader will not think that James's main referent here is to a body organ; however, in typical Jamesian style, a double meaning is intended here by him.

Chapter Eight

1. Heschel, *Who Is Man?*, 35.

2. Antoine de Saint-Exupéry, *Wind, Sand and Stars*, trans. Lewis Galantiere (New York: Harcourt Brace and World, 1967), 33.

3. Proverbs 4:7.

4. Job 28.
5. Talmud, Nedarim 41a.
6. Solomon Ibn Gabirol, *Choice of Pearls*, trans. A. Cohen (New York: Bloch, 1925), 26–27.
7. Ibid.
8. Cited in Robert Sternberg, ed., *Wisdom: Its Nature, Origins, and Development* (New York: Cambridge University Press, 1990), 42.
9. On this Hebrew expression, *"hamor nosei keilim,"* see Israel Davidson, *Otzar ha-Mashalim ve-ha-Pitganim* (Jerusalem: Mosad ha-Rav Kook, 1969), no. 2851, 171, n. 39.
10. Quoted in Sam Keen, *Apology for Wonder* (New York: Harper and Row, 1969), 129.
11. Quoted in Sternberg, 41.
12. Cited in Sternberg, 14.
13. Ibid., 21.
14. Ibid., 32.
15. Plato, *Epinomis*, 977.
16. Proverbs 29:18, translation mine.
17. William Shakespeare, *The Tempest*, act IV, scene 1.
18. Quoted in Sheehy, *Pathfinders*, 69.
19. Mihaly Csikszentmihalyi, *Creativity*, (New York: HarperCollins, 1996), 318.
20. Sternberg, 142–60.
21. Silvano Arieti, *Creativity* (New York: Basic Books, 1976), 380.
22. Russell, 185.
23. Proverbs 16:18, translation mine.
24. See Chopra, *Ageless Body*, 71.
25. Csikszentmihalyi, *Flow*, 64.
26. Talmud, Ethics of the Fathers 4:4, translation mine.
27. See e.g., Solomon Ibn Gabirol, *The Improvement of the Moral Qualities*, trans. Stephen S. Wise (New York: Columbia University Press, 1901), 79, and Jacob Anatoli, *Malmed ha-Talmidim* (Lyck, Poland: n.p., 1866), 152b.
28. Russell, 72.
29. Csikszentmihalyi, *Flow*, 194.
30. On the limits of creativity, see e.g., Rollo May, *The Courage to Create* (New York: Bantam, 1976), 133–48.

31. Quoted from Wilbur's poem "The Genie in the Bottle," in Singer, 59.
32. On the dangers of trying to be perfect, see Kushner, *How Good Do We Have To Be?*
33. Quoted in Csikszentmihalyi, *Flow,* 191.
34. Thomas H. Johnson, ed., *The Complete Poems of Emily Dickinson* (Boston: Little Brown and Co., 1960), 433.
35. Jung, 66.
36. Quoted in Chopra, *Ageless Body,* 34.
37. Cited in Sheehy, *Pathfinders,* 451.
38. Quoted in Frankl, *The Doctor and the Soul,* 32.
39. Csikszentmihalyi, *The Evolving Self,* 207–49.
40. John Stuart Mill, *Utilitarianism* (Indianapolis, Ind.: Bobbs-Merrill 1957), 14.
41. Bellah, 295.
42. See Csikszentmihalyi, *Flow,* 168.
43. See Csikszentmihalyi, *Finding Flow* (New York: Basic Books, 1997), 12.
44. Hermann Hesse, *Siddhartha,* trans. Hilda Rosner (New York: Bantam Books, 1971), 71–72.
45. Quoted in Huffington, 61.
46. Quoted in May, *Man's Search for Himself,* 117.
47. Quoted in ibid., 118.
48. Russell, 239.
49. See May, *Man's Search for Himself,* 28.
50. Quoted in Bellah, 253–54.
51. Quoted in Seldes, 946, from Mumford's 1940 book *Faith for Living.*

Chapter Nine
1. Irving Singer, *The Pursuit of Love* (Baltimore: The Johns Hopkins University Press, 1994), 2. See Singer's study of understandings of the nature of love in the history of Western civilization: Irving Singer, *The Nature of Love* 2d ed., 2 vols. (Chicago: University of Chicago Press, 1987).
2. Quoted in Russell, 38.
3. Singer, *The Pursuit of Love,* 13.
4. Quoted in May, *Love and Will,* 28.
5. Ibid., 47.

6. In this regard, see Sam Keen's idea of "destructive fidelity," in his *To Love and Be Loved* (New York: Bantam Books, 1997), 194.
7. Erich Fromm, *The Art of Loving*, 37.
8. Ibid., 107.
9. On love as a catalyst for healing and well-being, see e.g., Dossey, 109–117.
10. Talmud, Pesahim 112a.
11. Fromm, *The Art of Loving*, 24–35.
12. Frankl, *The Doctor and the Soul*, 108.
13. See William Frost, ed., *Selected Works of John Dryden* (New York: Holt, Rinehart and Winston, 1953), "Chaucer," 313.
14. Quoted in Frankl, *The Doctor and the Soul*, 132.
15. See Robert Sternberg, "Triangulating Love," in Robert Sternberg and Michael L. Barnes, eds., *The Psychology of Love* (New Haven, Ct.: Yale University Press, 1988), 119–39.
16. Leone Ebreo, *The Philosophy of Love*, trans. F. Friedberg-Seeley and Jean H. Barnes (London: Soncino, 1937).
17. Aristotle, *Nicomachean Ethics* (Indianapolis, Ind.: Bobbs-Merril, 1962), book VIII, beginning, 1155a.
18. Hammarskjold, 4.
19. Blake, "Proverbs from Hell," in *William Blake*, 97.
20. Talmud, Ta'anit 23a.
21. From a letter of William James to his wife, quoted in Erik H. Erikson, *Identity: Youth and Crisis* (New York: W. W. Norton, 1968), 19.
22. Quoted in Peter McWilliams, *Do It!* (Los Angeles: Prelude Press, 1994), 199.
23. Tolstoy, "A Confession," 683.

Chapter Ten

1. See Alexander Heidel, *The Gilgamesh Epic and Old Testament Parallels* (Chicago: University of Chicago Press, 1967). I originally used another translation that I can no longer locate.
2. Quoted in Csikszentmihalyi, *Creativity*, 225.
3. John Keats, *Selected Poetry and Letters* (New York: Holt, Rinehart and Winston, 1951), 329. In a letter to his brother and sister-in-law, George and Georgiana Keats, John Keats rejects the age-old view of life as a "vale of tears" in favor of the view that life is a "vale of Soul-making."

4. Quoted on the epigraph page in Chopra, *Ageless Body.*
5. Talmud, Berakhot 57b, translation mine.
6. See Louis Untermeyer, ed., *A Concise Treasury of Great Poems* (New York: Simon and Schuster, 1960), 326.

Chapter Eleven

1. I heard this from my mentor, the late Rabbi Abraham Joshua Heschel. This saying is attributed to Israel of Rhyzen and also to Mendel of Kotzk, and perhaps to other Hasidic masters as well.
2. Susan Howatch, *Mystical Paths* (New York: Alfred A. Knopf, 1992), 216.
3. Mitchell, 137, emphasis mine.
4. On sin and repentance in Jewish theology, see e.g., Byron L. Sherwin, *In Partnership with God: Contemporary Jewish Law and Ethics* (Syracuse, NY: Syracuse University Press, 1990), 119–30, and Byron L. Sherwin and Seymour J. Cohen, *How To Be a Jew* (Northvale, NJ: Jason Aronson, 1992), 59–78.
5. Bahya ben Asher, *Kad ha-Kemah* (Lwow, Ukraine: n.p., 1892), 66a, translation mine.
6. Talmud, Ketubot 5b.
7. Talmud, Arakhin 15b.
8. See the discussion in Sherwin and Cohen, xii, 61.

Bibliography

Appleyard, Bryan. *Understanding the Present: Science and the Soul of Modern Man.* New York: Doubleday, 1992.

Arieti, Silvano. *Creativity.* New York: Basic Books, 1976.

Barrett, William. *Death of the Soul.* Garden City, NY: Doubleday, 1986.

———. *The Illusion of Technique: A Search for Meaning in a Technological Civilization.* Garden City, NY: Doubleday, 1978.

———. *Irrational Man: A Study in Existential Philosophy.* Garden City, NY: Doubleday, 1958.

———. *Time of Need.* New York: Harper and Row, 1972.

Bellah, Robert N., et al. *Habits of the Heart.* Berkeley: University of California Press, 1985.

Boorstin, Daniel. *The Image: A Guide to Pseudo-Events in America.* New York: Harper and Row, 1964.

Bronowski, J. *The Ascent of Man.* Boston: Little, Brown, 1973.

———. *The Identity of Man.* Garden City, NY: The Natural History Press, 1966.

Camus, Albert. *The Myth of Sisyphus and Other Essays.* Translated by Justin O'Brien. New York: Alfred A. Knopf, 1955.

———. *The Stranger.* Translated by Matthew Ward. New York: Vintage Books, 1989.

Connelly, Marc. *The Green Pastures.* New York: Holt, Rinehart and Winston, 1967.

Csikszentmihalyi, Mihaly. *Creativity.* New York: HarperCollins, 1996.

———. *The Evolving Self.* New York: HarperCollins, 1993.

———. *Finding Flow.* New York: Basic Books, 1997.

————. *Flow: The Psychology of Optimal Experience.* New York: HarperCollins, Inc., 1990.

Cumming, Robert D., ed. *The Philosophy of Jean-Paul Sartre.* New York: Random House, 1965.

Dante. *The Divine Comedy.* Translated by C. H. Sisson. New York: Oxford University Press, 1993.

Descartes, René. *Discourse on Method.* Translated by Donald A. Cress. Indianapolis, IN: Hackett Publishing Co., 1980.

Dudley, Kathryn. *End of the Line.* Chicago: University of Chicago Press, 1993.

Durant, Will. *On the Meaning of Life.* New York: Ray Long and Richard R. Smith, 1932.

Edwards, Paul. "Meaning and Value of Life." *The Encyclopedia of Philosophy.* New York: Macmillan, 1972.

Erikson, Erik H. *Identity: Youth and Crisis.* New York: W. W. Norton, 1968.

Fox, Matthew. *The Reinvention of Work.* New York: HarperCollins, 1994.

Frankl, Viktor E. *The Doctor and the Soul.* Translated by Richard and Clara Winston. New York: Alfred A. Knopf, 1955.

————. *Man's Search for Meaning.* Translated by Ilse Lasch. New York: Washington Square Press, 1963.

Fromm, Erich. *Escape from Freedom.* New York: Avon Books, 1965.

————. *The Sane Society.* New York: Holt, Rinehart and Winston, 1955.

Gergen, Kenneth J. *The Saturated Self.* New York: Basic Books, 1991.

Glass, James M. *Shattered Selves: Multiple Personality in a Postmodern World.* Ithaca, NY: Cornell University Press, 1993.

Goleman, Daniel. *Emotional Intelligence.* New York: Bantam Books, 1997.

Gross, Martin. *The Psychological Society.* New York: Random House, 1987.

Hart, Jeffrey. *When the Going Was Good: American Life in the Fifties.* New York: Crown Publishers, 1982.

Harrison, Bennett and Barry Bluestone. *The Great U-Turn: Corporate Restructuring and the Polarizing of America.* New York: Basic Books, 1988.

Heschel, Abraham Joshua. *God in Search of Man.* New York: Harper and Row, 1955.

————. *A Passion for Truth.* New York: Farrar, Straus and Giroux, 1983.

————. *Who Is Man?* Stanford: Stanford University Press, 1965.

Horney, Karen. *The Neurotic Personality of Our Time.* New York: W. W. Norton, 1937.

Howatch, Susan. *Mystical Paths.* New York: Alfred A. Knopf, 1992.

Huffington, Arianna. *The Fourth Instinct: The Call of the Soul.* New York: Simon and Schuster, 1994.

Ibn Falaquera, Shem Tov ben Joseph. *The Book of the Seeker.* Translated by M. H. Levine. New York: Yeshiva University Press, 1976.

Ibn Gabirol, Solomon. *The Improvement of the Moral Qualities.* Translated by Stephen S. Wise. New York: Columbia University Press, 1901.

Ibn Pakuda, Bahya. *The Book of Direction to the Duties of the Heart.* Translated by Menahem Mansoor. London: Routledge and Kegan Paul, 1973.

Jung, Carl Gustav. *Modern Man in Search of a Soul.* Translated by W. S. Dell and Cary F. Baynes. New York: Harcourt, Brace, 1933.

Keen, Sam. *Apology for Wonder.* New York: Harper and Row, 1969.

———. *Hymns To an Unknown God.* New York: Bantam Books, 1994.

———. *To a Dancing God.* New York: Harper and Row, 1970.

———. *To Love and Be Loved.* New York: Bantam Books, 1997.

Kierkegaard, Soren. *Either/Or.* 2 vols. Translated by Walter Lowrie. Garden City, NY: Doubleday, 1959.

———. *The Present Age.* Translated by Alexander Dru. New York: Harper and Row, 1962.

Kosinski, Jerzy. *Blind Date.* Boston: Houghton Mifflin, 1977.

———. (pseud. Joseph Novak). *The Future Is Ours, Comrade.* Garden City, NY: Doubleday, 1960.

———. "A Nation of Videots." *Media and Methods.* 11:8 (April 1975).

Kushner, Harold. *How Good Do We Have To Be?* Boston: Little, Brown and Co., 1996.

———. *When All You've Ever Wanted Isn't Enough: The Search for a Life That Matters.* New York: Pocket Books, 1986.

La Mettrie, Julien Offray de. *Man, A Machine.* Chicago: Open Court, 1961.

Lasch, Christopher. *The Culture of Narcissism.* New York: Warner Books, 1979.

Lovejoy, Arthur O. *The Great Chain of Being.* Cambridge: Harvard University Press, 1936.

MacIntyre, Alasdair. *After Virtue.* South Bend, Ind.: University of Notre Dame Press, 1984.

Maslow, Abraham H. *The Further Reaches of Human Nature.* New York: Penguin, 1971.

May, Rollo. *The Courage to Create.* New York: Bantam, 1976.

————. *The Cry for Myth.* New York: Dell, 1991.

————. *Love and Will.* New York: W. W. Norton, 1969.

————. *Man's Search for Himself.* New York: W. W. Norton, 1953.

————. *Psychology and the Human Dilemma.* New York: W. W. Norton, 1967.

McWilliams, Peter. *Do It!* Los Angeles: Prelude Pres, 1994.

Mill, John Stuart. *Utilitarianism.* Indianapolis, Ind.: Bobbs-Merrill, 1957.

Mitchell, Stephen. *Hope and Dread in Psychoanalysis.* New York: Basic Books, 1993.

The National Commission on Excellence in Education. *A Nation at Risk: The Full Account.* Cambridge: USA Research, 1984.

Newman, Katherine S. *Declining Fortunes: The Withering of the American Dream.* New York: Basic Books, 1993.

Ornstein, Robert, and David Sobel. *Healthy Pleasures.* Reading, Mass.: Addison-Wesley, 1989.

Ortega y Gasset, José. *The Revolt of the Masses.* New York: W. W. Norton, 1957.

Peck, M. Scott. *The Road Less Traveled.* New York: Touchstone, 1978.

Rieff, Phillip. *The Triumph of the Therapeutic.* New York: Harper and Row, 1966.

Roof, Wade Clark. *A Generation of Seekers: The Spiritual Journeys of the Baby Boom Generation.* San Francisco: HarperSanFrancisco, 1993.

Russell, Bertrand. *The Conquest of Happiness.* New York: Book League of America, 1930.

Saint-Exupéry, Antoine de. *Wind, Sand and Stars.* Translated by Lewis Galantiere. New York: Harcourt, Brace and World, 1967.

Sartre, Jean-Paul. *Being and Nothingness.* Translated by Hazel E. Barnes. New York: Philosophical Library, 1956.

————. *The Condemned of Altona.* Translated by Sylvia and George Leeson. New York: Vintage Books, 1961.

Sheehy, Gail. *Passages.* New York: Bantam Books, 1976.

————. *Pathfinders.* New York: Bantam Books, 1982.

Singer, Irving. *Meaning in Life.* New York: Free Press, 1992.

Skinner, B. F. *Beyond Freedom and Dignity.* New York: Bantam, 1984.

Slater, Philip. *The Pursuit of Loneliness.* Boston: Beacon Press, 1976.

Sternberg, Robert J. *The Nature of Creativity.* New York: Cambridge University Press, 1988.

————. *Wisdom: Its Nature, Origins, and Development.* New York: Cambridge University Press, 1990.

Sykes, Charles J. *A Nation of Victims: The Decay of the American Character.* New York: St. Martin's Press, 1992.

Tawney, R. H. *The Acquisitive Society.* New York, 1920.

Taylor, Charles. *The Ethics of Authenticity.* Cambridge: Harvard University Press, 1991.

Tocqueville, Alexis de. *Democracy in America.* Translated by George Lawrence. New York: Doubleday, 1969.

Tolstoy, Leo. "A Confession." In *The Portable Tolstoy,* edited by John Bayley, New York: Penguin Books, 1978.

————. *The Death of Ivan Ilych and Other Stories.* Translated by Aylmer Maude. New York: New American Library, 1960.

Underhill, Evelyn. *The Spiritual Life.* London: Hodder and Stoughton, 1937.

Watts, Alan W. *The Way of Zen.* New York: Pantheon, 1957.

————. *The Wisdom of Insecurity.* New York: Vintage Books, 1951.

Whyte, William H. *The Organization Man.* New York: Simon and Schuster, 1956.

Wiesel, Elie. *Souls on Fire.* New York: Random House, 1972.

Wilson, Bryan, ed. *Rationality.* New York: Harper and Row, 1971.

Yankelovich, Daniel. *New Rules.* New York: Random House, 1981.

The Spiritual Art of Dialogue
Mastering Communication for Personal Growth,
Relationships, and the Workplace
Robert Apatow, Ph.D. • 0-89281-674-0
$22.00 cloth • 208 pages, 6 x 9

The concept of dialogue, developed by Socrates and Plato, is at the core of the Western intellectual tradition. It is also an accessible technique for anyone seeking to reach a higher level of consciousness. *The Spiritual Art of Dialogue* will show you, with clear and detailed lessons, how to use personal dialogue to work through the difficulties that hinder achievement of goals and satisfying relationships. This ancient philosophical method can be used by anyone seeking to deepen self-understanding.

Available at bookstores
or order from
Inner Traditions
P.O. Box 388,
Rochester, VT 05767
•
For shipping please add $3.50 for first book,
$1.00 for each additional book
•
1-800-246-8648
www.InnerTraditions.com

Creative Visualization

Using Imagery and Imagination
for Self-Transformation
Ronald Shone • ISBN 0-89281-707-0
$12.95 pb • 176 pages, 5 ³/₈ x 8 ¹/₄

All the great cultures of the world have recognized that
human beings can transform the circumstances and conditions
of their lives by visualizing powerful images. *Creative Visual-*
ization is a guide to recovering and improving your powers
of imagination and using them for positive change in your
life. By means of deep relaxation and visualization techniques,
Ronald Shone shows you how to succeed in business, excel
in sports, improve your memory, achieve goals, raise
energy levels, overcome shyness, relieve pain, and improve
your health.

Centering

A Guide to Inner Growth
Sanders G. Laurie and Melvin J. Tucker
ISBN 0-89281-420-9 • $9.95 pb
224 pages, 5 ³/₈ x 8 ¹/₄

"Centering has all the right stuff. If you were going on a trek and
were going to take only one book, this one might be a good choice."
Transformation Times
For the attainment of a successful life—including better
health and relationships, relief from stress, career satisfaction,
and finacial security—*Centering* offers a unique system of
meditation techniques to help you take charge of your destiny
and realize your full potential.

Creating the Work You Love
Courage, Commitment, and Career
Rick Jarow • ISBN 0-89281-542-6
$14.95 • 216 pages, 6 x 9

Traditional career guides inventory the individual skills,
talents and abilities that correlate to specific existing jobs.
This book presents an alternative approach, using self-
reflective exercises based on the seven chakras, to help
you determine the elements you need to create a life filled
with meaning and purpose. Concentrating on the attributes
associated with each chakra, the author guides you in
bridging personal priorities and the external activities of
the work world.

Lucid Waking
Mindfulness and the Spiritual Potential of Humanity
Georg Feuerstein • ISBN 0-89281-613-9
$22.95 cloth • 256 pages, 5 $^3/_8$ x 8 $^1/_4$

Lucid waking means bringing an intense awareness to the
business of living by meeting the challenges of existence
sanely, creatively, and philosophically. It is the goal of all the
great spiritual traditions of the world. Rich with philosophy
and insight from one of our most gifted chroniclers of inner
experience, *Lucid Waking* is a statement of unshakable faith in
the great potential of humanity.

*"From one of our culture's wisest scholars comes a book that is
as clear and compelling as anything recently written about spiritual
understanding. Reading Lucid Waking is a spiritual experience." —*
**Larry Dossey, M.D., author of *Prayer Is
Good Medicine* and *Healing Words***

Less is More

Ancient and Modern Voices
Raised in Praise of Simplicity
Edited by Goldian VandenBroeck
ISBN 0-89281-554-X • $14.95
334 pages, 6 x 9

This thought-provoking anthology brings together diverse maxims on the art of creative living, inspired by the natural laws of economy and conservation. This book draws us into the company of men and women of genius whose writings stress the importance of living simply— a message of profound urgency to our throwaway society. Those who aspire to simplicity will meet here the thoughts of others who found, in voluntary poverty, true satisfaction in their lives.